Intercultural Parenting and Relationships

"Dr. Bhugun has provided a compelling and important contribution to this otherwise under-researched area of intercultural family relationships in the 21st century. This book is grounded in empirical research and reflects Bhugun's obvious passion for the most contemporary intercultural family social science inquiry. The chapters, herein, move all of us beyond deficit stereotypes towards a more nuanced representation of both challenges and benefits in psychotherapy, particularly in the field of couples/marital/family counseling. This enlightening and practical book offers innovations in theory and clinical practice; a highly recommended read for students and seasoned clinicians across all disciplines."

—Shari Munch, *Ph.D., LCSW, Associate Professor, School of Social Work, Rutgers, The State University of New Jersey, USA*

"In this book, Dr Dharam Bhugun reflects on his longstanding clinical work and research with intercultural couples and families, and his own personal experience of the phenomenon, to provide valuable information and insights to current and future intercultural families, academics, and clinicians in the field of psychotherapy and counselling. This book could not have come at a better time where globalisation has broken barriers between human beings, and highlights the reality of intercultural relationships and parenting, including challenges, benefits and opportunities, and great strategies and advice for successful management of family discourses. The intimate testimonies, drawn from the lived experiences of intercultural couples, are the highlight of this book."

—Rajen Vurdien, *Ph.D., M.Ed., M.A., B.A., Superintendent-President of Pasadena College, Pasadena, CA, USA*

Dharam Bhugun

Intercultural Parenting and Relationships

Challenges and Rewards

palgrave
macmillan

Dharam Bhugun
Southern Cross University
Gold Coast, QLD, Australia

ISBN 978-3-030-14059-5 ISBN 978-3-030-14060-1 (eBook)
https://doi.org/10.1007/978-3-030-14060-1

Library of Congress Control Number: 2019933868

Cover illustration: Maram_shutterstock.com

This Palgrave Macmillan imprint is published by the registered company Springer Nature Switzerland AG
The registered company address is: Gewerbestrasse 11, 6330 Cham, Switzerland

I dedicate this book to my late mother and father who believed in my human capital and taught me the values of education, responsibility and respect; my sister Chandranee whose educational pathways were disrupted to care for me; my beautiful children Ireena, Vick, Yasmin, Georgia, Madeline and grandchildren Jasmine, Evelyn, Dylan, Darcy and Tyson for inspiring me in this academic journey; and my most beautiful wife Helen, for believing in me and supporting me unconditionally.

Foreword

How do parents in relationships that cross racial, ethnic and faith lines bring up their children? What goals do they have, what benefits do they see, what support do they seek, what challenges do they face, and what strategies do they use in negotiating issues of difference and belonging in their daily lives? The asking of such questions is taking on increasing significance as patterns of globalisation, migration and integration continue to bring people together in ways that are often in sharp contrast with what has come before. Of course, intercultural families are not a new phenomenon. In every corner of the world, racial and ethnic mixing has a longstanding and complex history, though of course many interracial and interethnic intimacies have been far from equal; indeed, violence and coercion are at the heart of so many of these histories. Moreover, even when willingly entered into, social if not often legislative barriers have persistently been in place to thwart those relationships that crossed racial and ethnic lines, from the Tang Dynasty edict of 836 prohibiting Chinese people marrying "dark peoples", to legislation in the USA as late as 1967 against "miscegenation". Yet racial and ethnic mixing has continued around the world nonetheless and, increasingly, by choice. As the twenty-first century unrolls, such intimacies are striking not only in their increasing and willing global occurrence but also in the ways that long-held traditional attitudes towards them are being questioned, re-examined and reordered.

At the vanguard of this re-examination process is an international body of scholarly work that is exploring what it means, for self and for society, when racial, ethnic and faith lines—in many cases simultaneously so—are crossed. While certain sites in the late twentieth century have long dominated academic introspection—namely, Brazil, South Africa and, most particularly, the USA—other locales are increasingly attracting scholarly attention: in recent years, for example, as well as the now well-established literature on contemporary racial and ethnic mixing and mixedness in the UK (see, among others, the works of Ann Phoenix, Jayne Ifekwunigwe, Miri Song & Peter Aspinall, France Winddance Twine, and Chamion Caballero & Rosalind Edwards) there is also a burgeoning and fascinating body of work focusing on South East Asia and Australasia (see, among others, the works of Jian Zhixiang, Zarine Rocha & Farida Fozdar, and Maki Meyer).

Excitingly, such work is also developing new and innovative frameworks and lenses through which to examine racial and ethnic mixing and mixedness. Recent scholarship in these expanding sites of interest has noted that while there may be some resonance across geographical sites, it is not always useful or insightful to transpose or apply directly understandings and conceptualisations developed elsewhere, including those frameworks that have developed from the US literature which has so greatly shaped the scholarly discourse on what has come to be known as "Critical Mixed Race Studies". Similarly, the traditional focus of mixedness—the identity of the mixed-racial or ethnic individual—is expanding to include other points of enquiry: couple relationships, family and friend dynamics, the role of class, sexuality and gender, as well as the wider impact and influence of socio-historical, political and geographical contexts. For the most part, this body of work is led by those with personal experiences of crossing racial, ethnic and faith backgrounds themselves and, as is common with "insider-led" studies, consequently provides a firm challenge to those traditional negative perspectives of interracial and interethnic intimacies that were so frequently formed by "outsider" approaches, where psychological and social dysfunction and ostracism were so often assumed to be the dominant forces and experiences in the lives of mixed-racial and ethnic people and their families.

Into this field, Dharam Bhugun's book *Intercultural Parenting and Relationships* is a much-welcomed addition. Surprisingly, despite the increasing racial, ethnic and cultural mixing that has been occurring in Australia as a result of modern migration, there is little contemporary work that addresses the experiences, challenges and advantages faced by such mixed-Australian families since Carmen Allen and Luke Allen's excellent work in the late 1990s. With the publication of *Intercultural Parenting*, however, we are now thankfully provided with a highly insightful and original contribution to understandings of such Australian families in the twenty-first century. A highly qualified practitioner who is grounded in rigorous academic scholarship, Dharum Bhugun not only contributes new data on Australian families of mixed-Anglo-Australian and recent migrant descent but also provides practitioners with advice and insights on how to enhance their cultural competence, awareness and sensitivity when working with intercultural families. Honest but sensitive, Bhugun's writing allows the complexity and diversity of intercultural parenting to be brought to the fore, highlighting the ways in which intercultural parenting can be both as ordinary and untypical as "monocultural" parenting, alongside insights into how parents in intercultural families strive to make the experience of growing up "mixed" a rich and positive one for their children. At the same time, Bhugun does not shy away from addressing how the challenges common to all parents can be exacerbated in mixed families or how they can be unique as a result of cultural difference. Furthermore, he locates all these experiences in a wider framework which recognises how the lives of those mixing and of mixed race and ethnicity are intricately influenced by other contextual and often external factors such as environment, gender, socio-economic status, extended family, friends, diasporic communities, religion and individual/personality characteristics.

Such a reflexive and nuanced approach thus sheds light not only on the experiences of mixed-racial ethnic and families not only in Australia but globally. As such, in reading *Intercultural Parenting*, scholars, practitioners as well as parents will benefit from both valuable new insights into the challenges and benefits of intercultural parenting in Australia in particular, alongside direct and practical information to help better understand the benefits as well as the challenges that are commonly faced by so many parents who are raising their children in racially and ethnically mixed homes across the world.

London, England

Dr. Chamion Caballero
Co-author of *Mixed Race Britain in the Twentieth Century* (Palgrave Macmillan, 2018)

Senior Visiting Research Fellow
Goldsmiths, University of London
London School of Economics

Acknowledgements

This book is the product of not only my curiosity into the emerging globalised phenomena of intercultural parenting, but more so the contributions of the lovely intercultural parents who gave up their precious time to share their experiences. Their stories were inspiring and hopefully very useful as a great educational tool for current and future intercultural parents. I hope that you have gained something from this experience as I have gained from your experience. Thank you for talking to me.

My special thanks go to Professor Mark Hughes, Dr. Elaine Nuske and Dr. Liz Reimer (Southern Cross University) for their unwavering academic insights, guidance and encouragement through my research journey. I would also like to thank Professor Robert Bland and Dr. Debby Lynch (University of Queensland) who have been instrumental in the early part of my research. To all my academic colleagues and friends, thank you for your unconditional support and help regarding technological insights.

Finally, my heartfelt gratitude goes to my angel wife Helen for the encouragement, tireless support and sacrifices she made to help me achieve my dream. You have been my strength all along and one of the most loving, kind and giving person I have ever come across.

I owe all I am to all of you.

Dharam Bhugun

Contents

List of Figures

List of Tables

1
Introduction

This book describes the experiences of parenting in intercultural relationships. It includes mostly an exploratory study (Bhugun, 2016) which addresses the dynamics of parenting among intercultural couples, in which one parent is Anglo-Australian and their opposite-sex partner is a non-Anglo-Australian person who has migrated to and lives in Australia. The focus on culture and the term intercultural encompasses the different notions of ethnic, interethnic, racial, interracial, religious, interfaith and country of birth.

The growth of immigration and social diversity, changes in social and political ideologies and advances in global technology have contributed to increased cultural exchange in human relationships and an increase in intercultural marriages and relationships in Australia and worldwide. Consequently, the intercultural parenting experience is emerging as an important phenomenon within society. Intercultural parenting remains an understudied phenomenon in Australia and globally. Parenting experiences can be both challenging and rewarding for intercultural couples and their children. Much of the Australian research has focussed on parenting styles among different cultural groups. The focus of discussion in intercultural relationships tends to be on the children of couples from

D. Bhugun, *Intercultural Parenting and Relationships*,
https://doi.org/10.1007/978-3-030-14060-1_1

mixed cultures and races, rather than on the experience of the parents themselves. This book seeks to address the gap. In this book, relationship refers to the couple's dyad, that is between the mother and father as the focus is on the couple's lived experiences of parenting and their relational dynamics. Intercultural couple refers to participants comprising an Anglo-Australian-born with a partner who migrated to Australia from another country.

This book aims to explore the experiences of intercultural parents raising their children together. It seeks to explore the tools parents use to negotiate cultural differences in their child rearing practices, and explore the challenges, as well as the benefits and opportunities of intercultural couples in their parental practices. To achieve this, key questions that guided the interview included: What are the experiences of intercultural couples in parenting their children? What are the challenges and conflicts of intercultural parenting? What are the positive experiences of intercultural parenting? How do intercultural parents negotiate cultural differences and integrate cultural values in their parenting styles? How can the findings inform intercultural parents and helping professionals?

The focus is on the experiences of intercultural parents who do not seek professional help. This book reflects on findings that may assist current and future intercultural parents, add to the family systems theory respecting intercultural parenting, and suggest possible organisational policy and clinical implications for therapists and counsellors.

Key Terms

The literature uses many terms interchangeably to describe different aspects of cross-cultural dynamics and the use of those different terms can sometimes cause confusion. It is therefore important to outline the definition of the terms in order to provide the reader with a clearer picture regarding how the terms were used in this study.

Culture was defined as a unique set of customs, languages, religious beliefs, attitudes and behaviours shared by a group of people and passed on from generation to generation (Sodowsky, Lai, & Plake, 1991; Sue & Sue, 1990). These collective beliefs, values and behaviours provide members with a shared sense of identity (Triandis, 1994). Culture is seen as the factor influencing variations in intercultural parenting practices (Forehand & Kotchick, 1996), and as the driving force for parental behaviour (Ogbu, 1981). It is important to understand the broader definition of culture and that intercultural parents and couples may identify with more than one culture or subculture. In this study, the perception of the participants themselves regarding their cultural differences was emphasised, rather than the author's perception.

Intercultural is the interactions between members of different cultures (Ting-Toomey, 1999). In this study, the term intercultural encompasses the different notions of ethnic, interethnic, racial, interracial, religious, interfaith and country of birth.

Intercultural couples are adults in a relationship who come from different cultural backgrounds (Perel, 2000; Ting-Toomey, 1999).

Parenting is the process of promoting and supporting the physical, emotional, social and intellectual development of a child from infancy to adulthood (Belsky, 1984).

Intercultural parents in this study are intercultural couples who are in a married or de facto relationship and raising biological children together in a single house (Crippen, 2008).

Intercultural parenting results from intercultural couples who are raising children conjointly.

Transcultural is the new family culture that is created when the cultures of two people from different backgrounds intersect (Crippen, 2008)

Acculturation is the cultural exchange that occurs when two or more cultures intersect, resulting in changes to the dynamics of both the migrating and host cultures (Berry, 1990).

Reverse acculturation is the process where an acculturated individual practices his/her heritage culture in the host culture (Kim & Park, 2009).

Current Knowledge About Intercultural Parenting and Relationship

Since the rise of globalisation and multiculturalism, scholars from around the world have recognised the need to explore cultural issues relating to mixed marriage and intercultural families (Bornstein, 1991; Bystydzienski, 2011; Nakazawa, 2003; Qian & Lichter, 2007; Romano, 2001; Rubalcava & Waldman, 2004; Singla, 2015; Sullivan & Cottone, 2006). Culture is a subjective and fluid concept and has therefore been defined widely and diversely by academics. Ogbu (1999) defined culture as “a people's adaptive way of life” (p. 74) which comprises of the customary ways of people's behaving, the assumptions, expectations and emotions underlying those behaviours, the artefacts that are meaningful to the people, political and social institutions, and cultural patterns of talking, feeling and thinking. Intercultural couples, with differences in cultural values, and previous exposure to different cultural practices with respect to such things as rules, norms of behaviour and cultural expectations, can experience internal conflicts and stress during the relationship, especially when they have children (Bustamante, Nelson, Henriksen, & Monakes, 2011; Negy and Snyder, 2000; Romano, 2001).

Falicov's (1995) studies of cross-cultural families concluded that continuous interaction with a spouse from a different culture can be compared to the experience of a migrant in a new culture. Like immigrants, intercultural couples are reported to experience multiple and often conflicting cultural realities, for example, African or Asian versus European Australian culture. As such, intercultural couples can experience different levels of acculturation which can have significant impact and influence on family relations and parenting styles. It is possible to identify paucity in research on acculturation processes experienced by intercultural couples and parents, especially for non-clinical intercultural couples and parents. However, Crippen and Brew (2013) developed a model of five strategies of cultural adaptation, based on process of acculturation, in intercultural parenting: assimilation, cultural tourism, cultural transition, cultural amalgamation and dual biculturalism.

Different cultures across the globe value different parenting styles. Parents' beliefs such as values, goals and attitudes, and parenting practices are widely emphasised in the study of parenting as shaping parenting behaviours. Parenting is mostly influenced by factors such as cultural, social and political context, socio-economic status, gender, environment and the family system (Harkness & Super, 1995; Jamrozik & Sweeney, 1996). However, parenting concepts have evolved globally over the years. "Generational, social and media images -culture- of caregiving and childhood play formative roles in generating and guiding parental cognitions" (Bornstein, 2012, p. 213). Changes in social structures, migration, social and economic development, present parents with different challenges and socialisation processes that needed to be addressed further.

While parenting goals and objectives may be considered universal, the methods of achieving these goals are not universal and are specific to the context of the family existence. LeVine (1988) emphasised that "each culture, drawing on its own symbolic traditions, supplies models for parental behaviour that, when implemented under local traditions, become culture-specific styles of parental commitment" (p. 8). According to Crohn (1995) and Romano (2001) conflict arises in intercultural parenthood because the latter uncovers the underlying cultural differences and discrepancies in the real core values of the intercultural partners which were not of much concern previous to parenthood. In a study of new mothers from Australia and Lebanon living in Australia (Goodnow, Cashmore, Cotton, & Knight, 1984), expectations of timetables for child development and milestones were different and shaped by culture.

Parents usually create their own parenting style based on several evolving factors such as one's own parents and cultural influences, which they either adopt or reject (Santrock, 2007). There are many influential theories on parenting styles. One of the most cited theories is that of developmental psychologist Baumrind (1971). Her research highlighted four basic elements that divide normative parenting styles in an effort to inform successful parenting: responsiveness versus unresponsiveness and demanding versus undemanding from which she identified three main parenting styles: authoritarian, authoritative and permissive. A fourth parenting style termed "neglectful" was later introduced by Maccoby and Martin (1983). However, Baumrind's (1971, 1989) and Maccoby and Martin's (1983) typologies in regard to universal applications have been criticised as being biased because they are influenced by western cultural constructs and based on the findings of western white North American middle-class families. They do not relate to culture-specific ways of parenting. Studies of African and Arabic migrant families settling in Australia found that African and Arabic migrant families come from collectivist cultures that embrace authoritarian parenting style, and value interdependence, respect for authority and elders, and corporal punishment (Ebbeck & Cerna, 2007; Renzaho, McCabe, & Sainsbury, 2011; Sims & Omaji, 1999). According to these authors, migrant families found it challenging to reconcile the parenting style of their home country with state-legislated parenting policies in Australia. In Australia, Anglo-Australian parents use a mostly authoritative style of parenting which would imply that Anglo-Australian parents use inductive approaches when disciplining their children (Kolar & Soriano, 2000).

Intercultural couples often have the task of navigating through and negotiating and resolving their cultural differences to enhance their relationship. According to Bystysdzienski (2011), intercultural couples negotiate differences at two levels: between the partners in the couple relationship, and between the couple and individuals and groups outside the partnership such as extended family members, friends and community members. Although conflicts occur in all relationships, the challenges are exacerbated for intercultural couples because of cultural differences. Common concerns in intercultural relationships are described as: values, gender, religion, childrearing, money, sexuality, social class, language (Frame, 2004) and barriers to communication (Romano, 2001); two separate individuals have crossed over to form a relationship, negotiating divergent cultural values, determining place of residence and making decisions which are also influenced by external forces such as extended family and community members (Adams, 2004);

and lack of similar socialisation processes in facilitating marital agreement compared to mono-cultural couples from the same economic, social and cultural background (Crippen, 2008; Ho, 1990).

Other challenges for intercultural couples are described as social attitudes from encouragement and acceptance to hostility and intolerance (Bhugra & De Silva, 2000); non-acceptance from families and cultural groups, social ostracism and problems of adjustment in communities (Kilian, 2001; McFadden & Moore, 2001; Zebroski, 1999); families of origin influencing the role of grandparents and the hierarchical ranking of members in the extended family system (Hsu, 2001). Factors in the internal and external environment of the couples, including ethnic, social, political and economic conditions, can significantly impact on the relationship status of the intercultural relationship. Rosenblatt, Karis, & Powell (1995) described concerns for intercultural couples in three domains: (1) power dynamics regarding the impact of social class, wealth and language issues; (2) an evolving couple system, which suggests that intercultural couples may not share their understanding of what marriage means; and (3) ecosystems, which addresses issues of race, gender and the involvement of family. The common concerns mentioned above for intercultural couples are the focus of this book.

Cultural differences often trigger conflict from which intercultural couples can experience high levels of stress and tension (Bhugra & De Silva, 2000; Bustamante et al., 2011; Chan & Smith, 1995; Crohn, 1998; Falicov, 1995; McFadden & Moore, 2001; Moffitt, 2012; Negy & Snyder, 2000). Layers of stress included conflicts in cultural code, cultural differences, disapproval from family, friend and institutions, cultural stereotyping, maximising or minimising difference and similarity by couples, unbalanced view of the world causing polarisation and disharmony, cultural transition from one stage and place to another, individual or family life cycle issues, styles of communication and child rearing values. Intercultural couples may be more dysfunctional, and conflicts are more likely to result in marriage dissatisfaction or even divorce than those of mono-cultural couples (Durodoye, 1994; Falicov, 1995; Gaines & Brennan, 2001; Monahan, 1970; Okitikpi, 2009;

Rankin & Maneker, 1987; Rosenblatt et al., 1995; Skowronski et al., 2014).

Intercultural couples may face additional challenges as a result of cultural conflicts over parenting (Berg-Cross, 2001; Hsu, 2001; Keller et al., 2004; Romano, 2001). The birth of a child becomes a stress point for all couples because of the necessary realignment from a marital dyad to a family dyad (Beck, 1988; McDermott & Fukunaga, 1977) because previous cultural negotiations are not totally relevant to the new transcultural family environment, and because of couples who previously ignored or minimised the impact of their cultural differences (Bhugra & De Silva, 2000; Crohn, 1995; Romano, 2001). According to Ho (1990), the birth of a child may reignite the couple's childhood experiences and beliefs about parenting. Examples of the variations in child rearing practices would be differences in fundamental values such as interdependence, autonomy, conformity and obligation (Mann & Waldron, 1977); contradictory goals and conflicts over discipline and parenting styles, racial and cultural identification, appropriate age of individuation and separation from the family of origin; expectation of child behaviour; levels of emotional involvement with the child such as distal versus proximal styles (Hsu, 2001; Keller et al., 2004); and reduced marital satisfaction (Durodoye, 1994; Fu, Tora, & Kendall, 2001).

Other sources of conflict over parenting include the other's norms, values, religious beliefs, meanings and rituals (Perel, 2000; Romano, 2001); gender roles and ethnicity (Mackey & O'Brien, 1989; Tseng, 1977); educational goals, forms of parent-child relationships, conflicting styles of parenting between the spouses (Berg-Cross, 2001); discrepant child rearing expectations (Imamura, 1990); roles and expectations of the extended family (Bhugun, 2016; Gupta, 2008; Joshi & Krishna, 1998); and communication patterns between parents and children (McDermott & Fukunaga, 1977).

Generally, intercultural couples are keen to negotiate and resolve their cultural differences. Romano (2001) described that couples negotiate their differences in one of four ways: (1) one partner solely embraces the cultural practices of their partner; (2) couples may seek compromise whereupon both relinquish aspects of their own culture and reach for equal cultural practices; (3) the couple ignores their differences, including traditions and norms and search for neutral grounds; or (4) the couple comes to a consensus whereupon each partner retains aspects of culture that are of important significance to them. In his later revised study (2008), Romano pointed out that successful intermarried couples share similar desires and expectations regarding commitment to their relationship and views about each other's roles as husband and wife. According to this author, the key factors for positive marital adjustment in intercultural relationship include cultural appreciation, commitment, sensitivity, flexibility, common goals, sense of humour, love, sense of adventure and positive self-image.

In their study on parenting "mixed" children, Caballero, Edwards, & Puthussery (2008) found that the parents dealt with ongoing challenges about their own and children's differences and sense of identity and belonging by refraining from regarding the problem as embedded in ascribed and cultural differences but rather "they could shift to seeing it as a difference that stemmed from personal preferences which was then more amenable to negotiation and accommodation" (p. 54). They identified three approaches in the parents' description of raising their children: an individual approach, a mix approach and a single approach. Singla (2015) came up with similar findings.

Crippen and Brew (2013) developed a typology of parenting strategies used by intercultural parents, with an underlying model to explain why parents used those strategies. The underlying model included "constructions of difference and degree of mutual acculturation" (2013, p. 266). The strategies used by the intercultural couples were influenced "by and an intersection of the country of residence and level of acculturation; gender and/or primary caregiver influence; desire to transmit culture of origin; and opportunities for cultural immersion experiences" (2013, p. 269). This study sought to further understand why intercultural couples select these different strategies for conflict resolution over parenting.

While acknowledging the fact that intercultural couples face some challenges and negative stereotypes, theoretical influences on intercultural relationships and parenting are slowly evolving from a deficit to a strength-based perspective, highlighting the benefits and opportunities of intercultural relationships and parenting, and the processes for their success (Bhugun, 2016, 2017a, 2017b; Bratawidjaja, 2007; Bustamante et al., 2011; Crippen, 2008, 2011; Irastorza & Devoretz, 2009; Ruebelt, Singaravelu, Daneshpour, & Brown, 2015; Seshadri & Knudson-Martin, 2013; Yancey & Lewis, 2009; Yodanis, Lauer, & Ota, 2012). According to Bustamante et al. (2011), despite culture-related stressors experienced by intercultural couples, other studies of intercultural relationships and parenting have "viewed intercultural relationships as an additive or enriching interaction in which individuals either learn from each other and blend or move beyond cultural differences through appreciation and humour" (p. 155).

Comprehensive studies of cross-cultural marriages (Bhugun, 2016; Bystydzienski, 2011; Crippen, 2011; Falicov, 1995, 2014; Moffitt, 2012; Molina, Estrada, & Burnett, 2004; Romano, 2001), identified the rewards of their relationships, including: developing a deeper understanding of self; cultivating an international identity; providing their offspring a richer world; a sense of belonging to the evolving multicultural world; cultural competency; and "broader, stronger social and cognitive skills sets, as well as personal strength such as cultural adaptation, intercultural effectiveness, greater interpersonal flexibility, and less ethnocentric attitudes" (Crippen & Brew, 2007, p. 112; Crippen, 2011). According to Bystydzienski (2011), despite external negative attitude and stereotypes, intercultural unions are a source of satisfaction for the partners, bridge divisions and reduce inequalities between persons of culturally diverse backgrounds.

Ruebelt et al. (2015) identified several strengths characteristics in intercultural couples such as cross-cultural adaptation and awareness, creation of unity and shared reality, establishment of strong interpersonal foundation, two-way acculturation, tarof and transculturation. Some studies have focussed on the processes that shape successful intercultural relationships (Falicov, 1995; Gaines & Agnew, 2003; Molina et al., 2004; Yancey & Lewis, 2009). Falicov (1995) identified a stage of cultural transition for intercultural couples that can lead to enrichment for each partner in the relationship, and that mutual adaptation and accommodation can lead to increased cultural sensitivity, understanding and tolerance of diversity, personal transformation and mutual acculturation.

The same can be said for children of those relationships. It exposes intercultural couples to different forms of parenthood from which they can negotiate entrenched cultural norms and values. Crippen (2011) identified several transformative opportunities for intercultural couples and children. Transformative opportunities for couples included the enhancement of cultural competency through "the development of a broader frame of reference, increased cultural sensitivity and tolerance for diversity; access to other models of parenting and the opportunity to confront and negotiate imprinted cultural values; and parenting in another language provides an opportunity to learn or create a different style of parenthood than that which was modelled in childhood" (p. 7). Intercultural couples tend to bring up bicultural children who have a broader worldview (Bhugun, 2016), are aware of the complexities of different cultures (Romano, 2001), and gain a sense of "cultural belonging, increased cultural literacy, [cultural] adaptability, and heightened empathy" (Crippen, 2011, p. 8). My aim in this book is to explore the experiences of intercultural couples and parents from the strength-based perspectives.

Research with a particular focus on the experiences of intercultural parents is limited, and needs to be extended beyond black-white and Asian-white couples in the global context. Due to the global increasing rate of intercultural relationships, intercultural couples include a broader spectrum of cultures other than black-white, Asian-white and Hispanic-white unions, such as Indian, Asian, African, Islamic/Arabic, Hispanic, Islander and Caucasian relationships. This book includes a greater diversity of the cultural communities in Australia (Fig. 1.1), and expands on current understanding and knowledge of the strength and transformative opportunities for couples and children in intercultural marriages and relationships.

No	Names	Gender	Age	Years in relationship	Country of origin	Religion	Education	Children and Age
1	Azumi Bill	F M	46 67	12	Japanese Australia	Budhist Christian	Graduate High School	2: 7 & 11 yrs
2	Carol Jay	F M	48 45	25	Australia Indian	Christian Hindu	Graduate Graduate	2: 14 & 17 yrs
3	Anya Rajack	F M	31 36	17	Australian Indonesian	Islam Islam	High School Tertiary	4: 1, 5, 11 & 13 yrs
4	Tammy Manuel	F M	33 34	12	Australian African	Christian Christian	Diploma Diploma	2: 1 & 10 yrs
5	Simla Daniel	F M	34 50	8	African Australian	Christian Christian	P-graduate High School	1: 4 yrs
6	Murielle Jeehan	F M	35 43	14	Australian Turkish	Islam Islam	Graduate Diploma	3: 5, 9 & 10 yrs
7	Kylie Malai	F M	43 39	19	Australia Thailand	Christian Budhist	P-graduate High School	2: 10 & 14 yrs
8	Cathy Will	F M	41 54	16	Australian N-Zealand	Christian Christian	Graduate High School	2: 11 & 13 yrs
9	Rula John	F M	28 33	6	Tongan Australian	Christian Christian	Diploma Graduate	2: 2 & 5 yrs
10	Ng Josh	F M	34 33	5	Vietnamese Australian	Budhist Christian	Diploma Graduate	1: 21 months
11	Michelle Jim	F M	56 53	27	Filipino Australian	Christian Christian	Graduate High School	Twins: 18 yrs
12	Naomi Pravin	F M	33 37	14	Australian Indian	Christian Sikh	Graduate Graduate	1: 4 yrs
13	Yan Gary	F M	37 55	4	Chinese Australian	Christian Christian	Graduate P-Graduate	2: 3 yrs & 1 month
14	Sarah Samuel	F M	44 48	19	Hong Kong Australian	Catholic Catholic	Graduate High School	2: 11 & 14 yrs

Fig. 1.1 Research participants demographic developed for this study

My Role as the Researcher

The quality of information or data obtained is dependent on the interviewer and the nature of the relationship and interaction between the participant and the researcher (Burgess, 1984; Minichiello, Sullivan, Greenwood, & Axford, 2004; Patton, 2002). Based on the purpose of the study and the population and phenomenon under study, it was useful for me to describe important aspects of myself, including linguistic and cultural knowledge, assumptions and biases and experiences to qualify my ability to conduct the research (Greenbank, 2003).

This research stemmed from my lengthy work experience as a psychosocial therapist/counsellor in the government and private practice, and my own personal experience and relationships with other parents and friends who are in intercultural marriages. The parents I work and socialise with often seek guidance regarding frequent challenges in raising their children within different cultural and family values. From a clinical perspective, the cultural differences seem to cause family conflict, social and psychological disturbance in couples and children, domestic violence and sometimes relationship breakdowns.

In both these roles, I have witnessed the multiple realities of intercultural parenting. I have had the feeling that the participants, being aware of my intercultural family background, were receptive to my questions and forthcoming about their context. The absence of published literature and knowledge in Australia, on this very important and growing phenomenon, motivated me to undertake this study. I was interested in understanding the particular conflicts and constraints, the benefits and opportunities of intercultural couples in their everyday parental role, and the strategies parents apply in negotiating cultural differences in their child rearing approach.

In designing this study, I was aware of the challenge I raised by having an "insider" perception and preconception of the phenomenon from my role as an intercultural parent and professional counsellor. Given that the quality of qualitative data is influenced by the nature of the relationship between the participants and researcher (Minichiello et al., 2004), a limited personal disclosure was employed to gain what Rubin & Rubin (1995) described as "insider status" which facilitated rapport and access to participants. As Rubin & Rubin (1995) also noted, in order to learn about culture, one must be allowed to cross boundaries and be accepted. Given my insider experiences and assumptions about intercultural relationships and parenting, it was important to focus on what I am trying to discover and to acknowledge my bias. Potential biases were minimised by seeking a wide range of participants' perspectives, and elucidating narratives of their lived experiences. I also carried out "member checking" (Lincoln & Guba, 1985) by checking with the participants that their experiences were properly reflected in the transcript of their interviews to ensure credibility and reliability.

Research Design and Methods

Theoretical Framework

The methodology of this exploratory study considers our knowledge and social construction of the phenomenon under study. Several scholars proposed that social reality and meaning are co-constructed, thus reflecting a social constructionism epistemological approach that considers knowledge of the world as being socially and culturally constructed. Knowledge of phenomena is determined by issues such as sociocultural factors, shared understanding of meaning, traditions, artefacts, language and practices (Gergen, 1985), and how people construct their perceived reality (Berger & Luckmann, 1996). Another basic tenet of the social constructionism paradigm is that the social construction of reality reflects on the subjective experience of everyday life (Berger & Luckmann, 1996) and by those engaged in the research process. This paradigm is guided by two important elements: (1) it assumes that human beings create a model of the social world and its function to rationalise their experience and, (2) that people construct reality through the use of language as forms of communication (Leeds-Hurwitz, 2009).

In his earlier writings, Gergen (1985) argued that social constructionism is an interpretation of social phenomena based on social interactions and experiences over time, instead of just individual experience. This approach appears very applicable to understanding the situations of Intercultural couples given that the realities of their lived experiences are co-constructed over time through their interactive relationship and ecological environment. According to Young & Colin (2004), "as an epistemology, social constructionism asserts that knowledge is historically and culturally specific; that language constitutes rather than reflects reality, and is both a pre-condition for thought and a form of social action; that the focus of enquiry should be on interaction, processes, and social practices" (p. 377). When parents from two different cultural backgrounds raise children together, they co-construct meaning about their parenting experiences and social reality, based on their historical, cultural and contextual experience of the phenomenon.

According to Schwandt (2003), "we do not construct our interpretations in isolation, but against a backdrop of shared understanding, practices, and languages" (p. 197). In line with Schwandt (2003), it is possible that there is a shared understanding that can be used to communicate and co-construct a mutual discourse of intercultural parenting. With intercultural parenting, it is assumed that those who come from different cultural communities can mediate their contextual differences through intersubjective communication. Therefore, this study attempted to understand the realities constructed by intercultural parents in their social and contextual environment (Creswell, 2003).

The social constructionism paradigm enabled me to explore subjective interpretations of intercultural parenting and challenge permanent knowledge bases for truth claims. This view is very important when discussing parenting issues, which has historically been dictated by prescribed ways of knowing. Discussions about parenting in the wider society often focus on the universal, mainstream, majority or western views of parenting and pay less attention to other non-western and cultural approaches to parenting (Lamb & Lewis, 2010; Patcher & Dumont-Mathieu, 2004; Romano, 2001; Suizzo, 2007). The taken-for-granted styles and practices of parenting is different in the context of intercultural parenting, in that meaning is co-constructed in the current social and contextual environment of intercultural parents. According to Romano (2001), intercultural couples have a unique parenting experience, which is different from other homogenous couples (Romano, 2001).

Social constructionism is a widely applied and accessible theoretical framework for investigating family studies. It has been used in studies of parenting and intercultural relationship (Arendell, 1997; Biever, Bobele, & North, 1998; Crippen, 2008; Leeds-Hurwitz, 2002; Seshadri & Knudson-Martin, 2013) but only in a few studies of intercultural parenting (Crippen, 2008; Hubber, 1998; Moffitt, 2012). Given that the meaning of parenting experiences is co-constructed in the social and contextual environment of intercultural parents when dealing with differences and belongingness, the social constructionist framework was therefore deemed necessary and appropriate to an exploration of the experiences of intercultural parents in this current study.

Since intercultural parenting is a complex phenomenon, the study required a qualitative research approach, because of its flexibility and ability to capture detailed textual descriptions of the participants' experiences (Creswell, 2003). Qualitative research is suitable for research in the social sciences because it embraces subjectivity and a holistic world view (Lincoln & Guba, 1985). It focusses on the social construction of reality (Denzin & Lincoln, 2000). Goldstein, Safarik, Reibolt, Albright, & Kellett (1996, p. 299) also argued that qualitative methodology is "responsive to the unique characteristics of culturally diverse groups" as it adequately responds to the complexities in studying culture and other variables that are impacted by it such as gender, ethnicity and socio-economic status. This approach is also "consonant with a theoretical commitment to the importance of language as a fundamental property of human communication, interpretation and understanding" (Smith & Dunworth, 2003, p. 603).

The flexibility of the qualitative methodology used in this study enabled the research to be culturally contextualised and thus appropriate to all the cultures involved in the study. As such, the study used a qualitative research method as the method of enquiry, as it sought to provide a rich description and meanings participants gave to their inner experiences of intercultural parenting.

Data Collection and Analysis

All the volunteer participants in this research were from the State of Queensland in Australia. In Queensland people speak more than 220 languages, practice more than 100 religious beliefs and originate from more than 220 countries (Australian Bureau of Statistics, 2014). The representation of the broad multicultural communities increased the chances of reaching the target population for this study. Twenty-eight participants (14 couples) were recruited and interviewed conjointly. Participants were recruited from responses following two media interviews of the author and from a list of contacts I obtained during community workshops I facilitated on family matters, and immigrant and refugee settlement programmes Queensland.

A purposive sampling strategy, including criterion and snowball methods (Patton, 2002) was employed to recruit the volunteer participants for this study. Snowball sampling is a purposive sampling recruitment strategy to locate participants who fit the inclusion criteria. The snowball method is a word-of-mouth approach whereby selected participants were asked to identify as well as refer other potential participants for the study. Patton (2002) suggested that purposive sampling strengthens qualitative research because it enables the researcher to have a deeper insight of the phenomenon under study. Given the qualitative nature of this study, I selected a small information-rich sample which allowed me to explore participants' experiences "in great depth" (Patton, 2002, p. 227).

In this study, intercultural couples were the unit of analysis and the following inclusion criteria were required: (1) One person was Anglo-Australian and their opposite-sex partner was a non-Anglo-Australian person who had migrated to and lived in Australia for at least 2 years. The criteria for participants who immigrated to Australia from another country of origin were intended to enable insights into the primary socialisation process of the participant in the country they were born and raised. Likewise, the period of time the immigrant intercultural parent lived in Australia was an important criterion to include because the number of years immigrants settle in the host country impacts on factors such as integration, adaptation, assimilation and acculturation that in turn impacts on parental behaviours (Berry, 1990; Papps, Walker, Trimboli, & Trimboli, 1995; Sims & Omaji, 1999). Also, Immigrant's cognitions and behaviour change over time from continuous exposure to other cultures (Bornstein & Cote, 2003); (2) participants from the broad Australian community, including diverse cultures and backgrounds such as different countries of origin, religions, ethnic heritages and racial identities in an effort to maximise cultural diversity. This is well reflected as shown in Fig. 1.1 regarding participants' demographics. Participants in this study were from white Anglo-Australian, Asian, Indian, African, Arabic, Islamic and Pacific Islander backgrounds. There are other cultures in Australia whose experiences of intercultural parenting could have enriched this study, but did not participate in this study; (3) the participants were literate and spoke English, as there was an expectation that they would understand the questions and be able to express their experiences; (4) Married or de facto heterosexual intercultural couples, who were the biological parents of their children, and living together in order to extract rich data to adequately reflect on their relationship patterns and the process of parenting their mixed-heritage children. This criteria was used in other overseas studies of intercultural relationship and parenting (Bratawidjaja, 2007; Crippen, 2008); (5) the intercultural couples were together raising children aged 0–23 and living at home. This age bracket for the children was purposefully selected to reflect on the parenting styles and practices of the parents during the developmental stages of the children because parenting style, discipline and racial and cultural identification of the child could be sources of conflict during the developmental stages (Tseng & Hsu, 1991); and (6) selection was restricted to participants who were prepared to be interviewed together. The conjoint interviews provided opportunities for the researcher to compare the perspective of each participant and to understand how the participants construct and co-construct meaning and knowledge about similarities and differences in their relational and parenting experiences.

From a social constructionist perspective, the conjoint interviews pointed to the ways in which couples/parents co-construct their roles and identities as parents together (Gergen, 2009). According to McNeil et al. (2014), trying to understand the perceptions of one parent without simultaneously understanding the partner's role and their relationship together is an incomplete exercise, because ultimately, parents develop their roles from being part of the family and the larger social environment and structure in which they are immersed. Most previous research relating to couples and intercultural couples used conjoint interviews (Bratawidjaja, 2007; Bustamante et al., 2011; Crippen, 2008; Horowitz, 1999; Hubber, 1998; Luke & Luke, 1998; McNeil et al., 2014).

Participants who were separated, divorced and could not do a joint interview were excluded because the focus of the study is on the processes couple living together engage to perceive, communicate and negotiate cultural differences.

This qualitative exploratory study required a data-gathering method consistent with the framework of social constructionism. The semi-structured interview is one such method and was used in this study to interview participants conducted between August 2011 and September 2014. Semi-structured interviews have been widely used in studies of couple relationships and parenting (Bratawidjaja, 2007; Hubber, 1998; McNeil et al., 2014). Interviews are important when one cannot observe or know how participants experience their world. In this study, a face-to-face semi-structured, audio-taped interview provided the opportunity to explore the meanings intercultural parents attach to their experiences.

Fourteen in-depth semi-structured interviews with 14 intercultural couples (28 participants) were conducted to elicit the perceptions of intercultural couples who have experienced the phenomenon. According to some qualitative methodologists (Creswell, 1998), "one round of long interviews with at least 10 participants could be enough to reach saturation" (cited in Bustamante et al., 2011, p. 157). The length of the interviews, using open-ended questions, ranged between one to one and half hours. The audio-taped interviews were then transcribed verbatim concurrently for analysis. All the participants' names and other identifiable information were modified and special codes were allocated to their transcripts to ensure confidentiality.

This study required a social constructionist analytical method that could transform data regarding participants' meaning and perceived realities of the phenomenon under study into emergent themes and findings. One such method is thematic analysis which is a popular qualitative analytic method "for identifying, analysing and reporting patterns (themes) within data" (Braun & Clarke, 2006, p. 79). According to Braun and Clarke (2006) "thematic analysis conducted within a social constructionist framework cannot and does not focus on motivation or individual psychologies, but instead seeks to theorise the socio-cultural contexts and structural conditions that enable the individual accounts that are provided" (p. 85). It was therefore a suitable method to examine the realities and meaning-making of intercultural parent in raising their mixed culture children. I used the general data analysis strategy outlined by Braun and Clarke (2006) to code and understand meaning in complex data on the experiences of the intercultural parents.

The analysis started with the process of coding each participant's transcripts. An inductive analysis process was used to discover important patterns and themes in data. Direct quotes from participants that matched the relevant themes and sub-themes were then used to support the analytical findings. Four major themes emerged from the results and interpretation of the empirical data on the experiences of intercultural parenting. The themes are discussed against other relevant global studies regarding intercultural parenting and relationship.

1. Cultures coming together
2. Power relations
3. Reverse acculturation/enculturation
4. Strategies for making intercultural parenting work.

It is noteworthy that although the themes are distinct and presented separately, there is some overlap between them. For example, parental goals and values are represented across other themes. Also, because the experience of parenting is related to the experience of being a couple, especially in the intercultural situation, these themes are reflected in both contexts.

Participants Demography and Background

The participants reflected a diverse national and cultural background, socio-economic status (level of education, profession), religious affiliation, level of acculturation, length of the relationship and number of children (Fig. 1.1), which helped to generate a rich perception of intercultural parenting experiences. Intercultural couples/parents encompassed racial, ethnic, religious/faith and nationality dynamics. As Sullivan & Cottone (2006) described, race, ethnicity, religion and national origin are the most important factors that characterise differences between intercultural couples. In a social constructionist perspective, race is a social construct rather than a category that has meaning in view of its ancestral origin.

Although this book is written in the Australian context, much of its background contents are based on international scholarships and literature reviews, thus reflecting the international context. The findings of this study cannot be generalised because of its qualitative nature. However, they may be transferrable to other international context, settings and groups that share similar characteristics (Lincoln & Guba, 1985; Streubert & Carpenter, 1999). This study generated rich thick data of the experiences of intercultural parenting, presented in the findings Chapters 3–5, and can be used to determine transferability to other settings in Australia, and globally. The trend in intercultural relationships and parenting dynamics from immigration in Australia, with resultant challenges and benefits, is well reflected from immigration in other developed and developing countries such as USA, UK, Canada, Germany and Denmark. Therefore the results and findings of the Australian study may be transferrable to the global context.

Some of the findings in the study concurred with findings in previous studies. However, the current study revealed some important new findings within the Australian context, which can also be transferable to the global context: (a) reverse acculturation, (b) reciprocal acculturation, (c) shift towards authoritative parenting styles, (d) selfless parenting style (e) power relations in parenting practices, (f) disparity regarding the level of support and involvement between ethnic and white Australian extended families, (g) friends perceived as family members, (h) intercultural couples/parents also experienced significant benefits and opportunities, besides challenges and constraints. Counsellors and therapists would benefit from exploring and focussing on the positive experiences as sources of strength for their clients and show cultural sensitivity and respect when dealing with intercultural couples and families.

A number of organisational policies, clinical implications for therapists and recommendations for future research are suggested in Chapter 6. Important organisational policy recommendations include: (1) universities and subsidiary educational institutions that provide marriage and relationship counselling courses need to introduce special modules regarding cultural literacy that focus on intercultural relationships and families, (2) professional helping organisations need to provide information and support services that are exclusive and appropriate to the needs of intercultural families, (3) implementation of cultural awareness and sensitivity, besides cultural competency in counselling agencies and practices, (4) the addition of the "Mixed" category in the Australian Census question regarding ethnic to help policy-makers and researchers seeking data based on Census categories.

Recommendations for therapist/counsellors include: (1) exploring both the challenges and benefits that intercultural couples experience, (2) exploring the internal and external contexts of intercultural dynamics, (3) understanding that some of the concerns by intercultural couples and parents are common to those of non-intercultural couples and parents. Therefore the provision of services and interventions needs to be balanced between cultural needs versus individual and contextual needs as opposed to the 'intercultural' aspect only and (4) some of the popular therapeutic approaches that can be used in intercultural and mixed family domains are: Cognitive Behavioural Therapy; Narrative Therapy; Strength-Based Therapy; Solution-Focused Therapy; and Emotional Focused Therapy.

Outline of the Book

This book is organised into five chapters which provides in-depth analysis and meaning to the phenomenon of intercultural parenting. It is my hope that the inner experiences of intercultural parents from the empirical study will inform current and future intercultural couples and families, researchers and academics and allied health clinicians.

Chapter 2 presents an overview of intercultural relationship and parenting in the Australian context. The growth of immigration and social diversity, changes in social and political ideologies and advances in global technology have prompted a trend towards an increase in intercultural relationships in Australia. According to the Australian Bureau of Statistics (ABS, 2017), about 31.9% of married couples were in a relationship between Australian-born and overseas-born partners. Given the changes in the cultural landscape of Australia, they are likely to impact on family structures as well as parenting behaviours and practices that may not occur in mono-cultural families. Consequently, intercultural parenting is emerging as an important family dynamic in Australian society.

Chapter 3 presents the major analytical theme "cultures coming together", and includes several sub-themes about experiences relating to cultural identity, culture shock, racism and rejection, marriage disapproval, values and customs, gender roles and beliefs, language and communication, parenting practices, contextual influences and benefits and opportunities of intercultural parenting.

Chapter 4 presents two important issues regarding power relations and reverse acculturation/enculturation. Power issues are related to parenting, language and communication, gender and insider/outsider status. Reverse acculturation/enculturation is related to valuing ethnic heritage and host culture, reciprocal acculturation, global culture and shift in parenting styles and practices.

Chapter 5 describes strategies for making intercultural parenting work such as problem solving tools and survival techniques.

Chapter 6 provides implications for theory, policy, educators and professional practice, addresses strengths and limitations of the study, and examines areas for possible future research.

References

Adams, J. (2004). "This is not where I belong": The emotional, ongoing, and collective aspects of couples' decision making about where to live. *Journal of Comparative Family Studies, 35*(3), 459–485.

Arendell, T. (1997). A social constructionist approach to parenting. In T. Arendell (Ed.), *Contemporary parenting: Challenges and issues* (pp. 1–44). Thousand Oaks, CA: Sage.

Australian Bureau of Statistics. (2014). *Australian social trends 2014: ABS 4102.0*. Canberra: Australian Bureau of Statistics.

Australian Bureau of Statistics. (2017, March). *Australian Demographics Statistics*. Canberra: Australian Bureau of Statistics.

Baumrind, D. (1971). Current patterns of parental authority. *Developmental Psychology Monograph, 4*(1, Pt. 2), 1–103. https://doi.org/10.1037/h0030372.

Baumrind, D. (1989). Rearing competent children. In W. Damon (Ed.), *Child development today and tomorrow* (pp. 349–378). San Francisco: Jossey-Bass.
Beck, A. T. (1988). *Love is never enough: How can couples overcome misunderstandings, resolve conflicts, and solve relationship problems through cognitive therapy*. New York: HarperCollins.
Belsky, J. (1984). The determinants of parenting: A process model. *Child Development, 55*(1), 83–96. https://doi.org/10.2307/1129836.
Berg-Cross, L. (2001). *Couples therapy* (2nd ed.). New York: Hawthorne.
Berger, P., & Luckmann, T. (1996). *The social construction of reality: A treatise in the sociology of knowledge*. Garden City: Anchor.
Berry, J. W. (1990). Psychology of acculturation: Understanding individuals moving between cultures. In R. W. Brislin (Ed.). *Applied cross-cultural psychology* (pp. 232–253). Thousand Oaks, CA: Sage.
Bhugra, D., & De Silva, P. (2000). Couple therapy across culture. *Sexual and relationship therapy, 15*(2), 184–192.
Bhugun, C. D. (2016). *The experiences of intercultural parenting in Australia* (PhD thesis). Southern Cross University, Australia.
Bhugun, D. (2017a). Intercultural parenting in Australia: Managing cultural differences. *The Family Journal: Counselling and Therapy for Couples and Families, 25*(2), 187–195.
Bhugun, D. (2017b). Parenting advice for intercultural couples: A systemic perspective. *Journal of Family Therapy, 33*(3), 454–477.
Biever, J. L., Bobele, M., & North, M. W. (1998). Therapy with intercultural couples: A post-modern approach. *Counselling Psychology Quarterly, 11*(2), 181–188. https://doi.org/10.1080/09515079808254053.
Bornstein, M. H. (Ed.). (1991). *Cultural approaches in parenting*. Hillsdale, NJ: Lawrence Erlbaum.
Bornstein, M. H. (2012). Cultural approaches to parenting. *Parenting Science Practice, 12*(2/3), 212–221.
Bornstein, M. H., & Cote, L. R. (2003). Cultural and parenting cognitions in acculturating cultures. *Journal of Cross-Cultural Psychology, 34*(3), 323–340. https://doi.org/10.1177/0022022103034003007.
Bratawidjaja, A. (2007). *The experience of being parents of mixed-heritage children: Phenomenological analysis* (Unpublished doctoral dissertation). Kansas State University, Kansas.
Braun, V., & Clarke, V. (2006). Using thematic analysis in psychology. *Qualitative Research in Psychology, 3*(2), 77–101.

Burgess, R. G. (1984). *In the field: An introduction to field research.* London: Routledge.
Bustamante, R. M., Nelson, J. A., Henriksen, R. C., Jr., & Monakes, S. (2011). Intercultural couples: Coping with culture-related stressors. *The Family Journal: Counselling and Therapy for Couples and Families, 19*(2), 154–164. https://doi.org/10.1177/1066480711399723.
Bystydzienski, J. (2011). *Intercultural couples: Crossing boundaries, negotiating differences.* New York and London: New York University Press.
Caballero, C., Edwards, R., & Puthussery, S. (2008). Parenting 'mixed' children: Negotiating difference and belonging in mixed race, ethnicity and faith families. *Joseph Rowntree Foundation.* Retrieved August 15, 2011, from https://www.researchgate.net/profile/Chamion_Caballero/publication/265537866_Parenting_'Mixed'_Children_Difference_and_Belonging_in_Mixed_Race_and_Faith_Families/links/54b911660cf28faced626ac3.pdf.
Chan, A. Y., & Smith. K. R. (1995). Perceptions of marital stability in black-white marriages. In C. K. Jacobson (Ed.), *American families: Issues in race and ethnicity* (pp. 369–386). New York: Guildford.
Creswell, J. W. (1998). *Qualitative inquiry and research design: Choosing among five traditions.* Thousand Oaks, CA: Sage.
Creswell, J. W. (2003). *Research design: Qualitative, quantitative and mixed-methods approaches* (2nd ed.). Thousand Oaks, CA: Sage.
Crippen, C. (2008). *Cross-cultural parenting: Experiences of intercultural parents and constructions of culturally diverse families* (Unpublished doctoral dissertation). University of New England, Australia.
Crippen, C. (2011). *Working with intercultural couples and families: Exploring cultural dissonance to identify transformative opportunities.* Retrieved June 20, 2012, from https://www.counseling.org/resources/library/vistas/2011-V-Online/Article_21.pdf.
Crippen, C., & Brew, L. (2007). Intercultural parenting and transcultural family: A literature review. *The Family Journal: Counselling and Therapy for Couples and Families, 15*(2), 107–115. https://doi.org/10.1177/1066480706297783document.
Crippen, C., & Brew, L. (2013). Strategies of cultural adaptation in intercultural parenting. *The Family Journal: Counselling and Therapy for Couples and Families, 21*(3), 271–263.
Crohn, J. (1995). *Mixed matches: How to create successful interracial, interethnic, and interfaith relationships.* New York: Random House.

Crohn, J. (1998). Intercultural couples. In M. McGoldrick (Ed.), *Revisioning family therapy: Race, culture, and gender in clinical practice* (pp. 295–308). New York: Guildford.

Denzin, N. K., & Lincoln, Y. S. (2000). *The Sage handbook of qualitative research.* Thousand Oaks, London, and New Delhi: Sage.

Durodoye, B. (1994). Intermarriage and marital satisfaction. *Texas Counseling Association Journal, 22*(1), 3–9.

Ebbeck, M. A., & Cerna, C. H. D. (2007). A study of child rearing practices among selected Sudanese families in South Australia: Implications for child care service selection. *Early Childhood Education Journal, 34*(5), 307–314. https://doi.org/10.1007/s10643-006-0129-4.

Falicov, C. J. (1995). Cross-cultural marriages. In N. S. Jacobson & A. S. Gurman (Eds.), *Clinical handbook of couple therapy* (pp. 231–246). New York: Guildford.

Falicov, C. J. (2014). *Latino families in therapy* (2nd ed). New York: The Guilford Press.

Forehand, R., & Kotchick, B. A. (1996). Cultural diversity: A wake-up call for parent training. *Behavior Therapy, 27*, 187–206.

Frame, M. W. (2004). The challenges of intercultural marriage: Strategies for pastoral care. *Pastoral Psychology*, *52*(3), 219–232.

Fu, X., Tora, J., & Kendall, H. (2001). Marital happiness and inter-racial marriage: A study in a multi-ethnic community in Hawaii. *Journal of Comparative Studies, 32*(1), 47–64.

Gaines, S. O., Jr., & Agnew, C. R. (2003). Relationship maintenance in intercultural couples: An interdependence analysis. In D. J. Canary & M. Dainton (Eds.), *Maintaining relationships through communication: Rational, contextual, and cultural variations* (pp. 231–253). Mahwah, NJ: Lawrence Erlbaum.

Gaines, S. O., & Brennan, K. A. (2001). Establishing and maintaining satisfaction in multicultural relationships. In J. Harvey & A. Wenzel (Eds.), *Close romantic relationships: Maintenance and enhancement* (pp. 237–253). Mahwah, NJ: Lawrence Erlbaum.

Gergen, K. J. (1985). The social constructionist movement in modern psychology. *American Psychologist, 40*(3), 266–275.

Gergen, K. J. (2009). *Relational being: Beyond self & community*. New York: Oxford University Press.

Goldstein, A. E., Safarik, L., Reibolt, W., Albright, L., & Kellett, C. (1996). An ethnographic approach to understanding service use among ethnically

diverse low income families. *Marriage and Family Review, 24*(3–4), 297–321. https://doi.org/10.1300/J002v24n03_04.
Goodnow, J. J., Cashmore, L., Cotton, S., & Knight, R. (1984). Mother's developmental time tables in two cultural groups. *International Journal of Psychology, 19*(1–4), 193–205.
Greenbank, P. (2003). The role of values in educational research: The case for reflexivity. *British Educational Research Journal, 29*(6), 791–801.
Gupta, L. (2008). A comparison of parenting behaviour between European American and Asian Indian parents. In *ProQuest Dissertations and Theses*. Fayetteville: University of Arkansas.
Harkness, S., & Super, C. M. (1995). Culture and parenting. In M. H. Bornstein (Ed.), *Handbook of parenting: Biology and ecology of parenting* (Vol. 2, pp. 211–234). Mahwah, NJ: Lawrence Erlbaum Associates.
Ho, M. K. (1990). *Intermarried couples in therapy*. Springfield, IL: Charles Thomas.
Horowitz, J. A. (1999). Negotiating couplehood: The process of resolving the December dilemma among interfaith couples. *Family Process, 39*(3), 303–323. https://doi.org/10.1111/j.1545-5300.1999.00303.x.
Hsu, J. (2001). Marital therapy for intercultural couples. In W. S. Tseng & J. Streltzer (Eds.), *Culture and psychology: A guide to clinical practice* (pp. 225–242). Washington, DC: American Psychiatric Publishing.
Hubber, T. (1998). *An exploration of intercultural parenting: The experience of Samoan & New Zealand-European couples* (Unpublished dissertation). University of Auckland, New Zealand.
Imamura, A. E. (1990). Strangers in a strange land: Coping with marginality in international marriage. *Journal of Comparative Family Studies, 21*(2), 171–191.
Irastorza, N., & Devoretz, D. (2009). *Factors affecting international marriage survival: A theoretical approach*. Retrieved January 15, 2016, from http://www.sfu.ca/-devoretz/lecturenotes/sem9.pdf.
Jamrozik, A., & Sweeney, T. (1996). *Children and society: The family, the state and social parenthood*. South Melbourne: Macmillan Education Australia.
Joshi, M. S., & Krishna, M. (1998). English and North American daughters-in-law in the Hindu joint family. In R. Breger & R. Hill (Eds.), *Cross-cultural marriage: Identity and choice* (pp. 171–191). New York: Oxford International.
Keller, H., Lohaus, A., Kuensemueller, P., Abels, M., Yosvi, R., Voelker, S., & Mohite, P. (2004). The bio-culture of parenting: Evidence from five cultural communities. *Parenting: Science and Practice, 4*(1), 25–50.

Killian, K. D. (2001). Reconstituting racial histories and identities. *Journal of Marital and Family Therapy, 27*(1), 27–42. https://doi.org/10.1111/j.1752-0606.2001.tb01137.x.
Kim, Y., & Park, S. (2009). Reverse acculturation: A new cultural phenomenon examined through an emerging wedding practice of Korean Americans in the United States. *Family and Consumer Sciences Research Journal, 37*(3), 359–375. https://doi.org/10.1177/1077727x08330758.
Kolar, V., & Soriano, G. (2000). *Parenting in Australian families: A comparative study of Anglo, Torres Strait Islander, and Vietnamese communities.* Melbourne; Australian Institute of Family Studies.
Lamb, M. E., & Lewis, C. (2010). The development and significance of father-child relationships in two-parent families. In M. E. Lamb (Ed.), *The role of the father in child development* (5th ed., pp. 94–153). Hoboken, NJ: John Wiley & Sons.
Leeds-Hurwitz, W. (2002). *Communicating cultural identities through ritual.* Mahwah, NJ: Lawrence Erlbaum.
Leeds-Hurwitz, W. (2009). Social construction of reality. In S. Littlejohn & K. Foss (Eds.), *Encyclopedia of communication theory* (pp. 892–895). Thousand Oaks, CA: Sage.
LeVine, R. A. (1988). Human parental care: Universal goals, cultural strategies, individual behaviour. In R. A. LeVine, P. M. Miller, & M. Maxwell West (Eds.), *Parental behaviour in diverse societies* (pp. 3–12). San Francisco: Jossey-Bass.
Lincoln, Y., & Guba, E. (1985). *Naturalistic inquiry.* Newbury Park, CA: Sage.
Luke, C., & Luke, A. (1998). Interracial families: Difference within difference. *Ethnic and Racial Studies, 21*(4), 728–753. https://doi.org/10.1080/014198798329847.
Maccoby, E., & Martin, J. A. (1983). Socialization in the context of the family: Parent–child interaction. In P. Mussen and E. M Hetherington (Eds.), *Handbook of child psychology* (Vol. 4, pp. 1–101). New York: Wiley.
Mann, E., & Waldron, J. A. (1977). Intercultural marriage and child rearing. In W. S. Teng, J. F. McDermott, & T. W. Maretzki (Eds.), *Adjustment in intercultural marriage* (pp. 62–80). Honolulu: University of Hawaii Press.
McDermott, J. F., & Fukunaga, C. (1977). Intercultural family interaction patterns. In W. S. Teng, J. F. McDermott, & T. W. Maretzki (Eds.), *Adjustment in intercultural marriage* (pp. 81–92). Honolulu: University of Hawaii Press.

McFadden, J., & Moore, J. L. (2001). Intercultural marriage and intimacy: Beyond the continental divide. *International Journal for the Advancement of Counselling, 23*(4), 261–268. https://doi.org/10.1023/a:1014420107362.

McNeil, T., Nicholas, D., Beaton, J., Montgomery, G., MacCulloch, R., Gearing, R., & Selkirk, E. (2014). The coconstruction of couples' roles in parenting children with a chronic health condition. *Qualitative Health Research, 24*(8), 1114–1125.

Minichiello, V., Sullivan, G., Greenwood, K., & Axford, R. (Eds.). (2004). *Research methods for nursing and health sciences* (2nd ed.). Sydney: Pearson Education Australia.

Moffitt, K. R. (2012). Intercultural parenting in the White House: The transcultural strategies of the Obamas. In A. Gonzalez & T. M. Harris (Eds.), *Mediating cultures: Parenting in intercultural contexts*, (p. 62). Blue Ridge Summit, PA: Lexington Books.

Molina, B., Estrada, D., & Burnett, J. A. (2004). Cultural communities: Challenges and opportunities in the creation of "Happily Ever After" stories of intercultural couplehood. *The Family Journal: Counselling and Therapy for Couples and Families, 12*(2), 139–147.

Monahan, T. (1970). Are intermarriages less stable? *Social Forces, 48*(4), 461–473.

Nakazawa, D. J. (2003). *Does anybody else look like me? A parent's guide to raising multicultural children*. Cambridge, MA: Perseus.

Negy, C., & Snyder, D. K. (2000). Relationship satisfaction of Mexican American and non-Hispanic White American interethnic couples: Issues of acculturation and clinical intervention. *Journal of Marital and Family Therapy, 26*(3), 293–304.

Ogbu, J. U. (1999). Cultural context of children's development. In H. E. Fitzgerald, B. M. Lester, & B. S. Zuckerman (Eds.), *Children of colour: Research, health and policy issues* (pp. 73–92). New York: Garland Press.

Okitikpi, T. (2009). *Understanding interracial relationships*. Dorset, UK: Russell House Publishing.

Papps, F., Walker, M., Trimboli, A., & Trimboli, C. (1995). Parental discipline in Anglo, Greek, Lebanese, and Vietnamese cultures. *Journal of Cross-Cultural Psychology, 26*(1), 49–64.

Patcher, L. M., & Dumont-Mathieu, T. (2004). Parenting in culturally divergent settings. In M. Hoghugi & N. Long (Eds.), *Handbook of parenting: Theory and research for practice* (pp. 88–97). London: Sage.

Patton, M. Q. (2002). *Qualitative research and evaluation methods*. Thousand Oaks, CA: Sage.
Perel, E. (2000). A tourist's view of marriage: Cross-cultural couples-challenges, choices, and implications for therapy. In P. Papp (Ed.), *Couples on the fault line: New directions for therapists* (178–204). New York: Guildford.
Qian, Z., & Lichter, D. T. (2007). Social boundaries and marital assimilation: Interpreting trends in racial and ethnic intermarriage. *American Sociological Review, 72*(1), 68–94. https://doi.org/10.1177/000312240707200104.
Rankin, R., & Maneker, J. (1987). Correlates of marital duration and black-white intermarriage in California. *Journal of Divorce, 11*(2), 51–57. https://doi.org/10.1300/j279v11n02_04.
Renzaho, A. M. N., McCabe, M., & Sainsbury, W. J. (2011). Parenting, role reversals and the preservation of cultural values among Arabic speaking migrant families in Melbourne, Australia. *International Journal of Intercultural Relations, 35*(4), 416–424. https://doi.org/10.1016/j.ijintrel.2010.09.001document.
Romano, D. (2001). *Intercultural marriage: Promises and pitfalls* (3rd ed.). Yarmouth, ME: Intercultural Press.
Romano, D. (2008). *Intercultural marriage: Promises and pitfalls* (3rd ed.). Yarmouth: Intercultural Press.
Rosenblatt, P. C., Karis, T. A., & Powell, R. D. (1995). *Multiracial couples-black & white voices*. Thousand Oaks, CA: Sage.
Rubalcava, L. A., & Waldman, K. M. (2004). Working with intercultural couples: An intersubjective-constructivist perspective. In W. J. Coburn (Ed.), *Transformations in self psychology: Progress in self- psychology* (pp. 127–149). Hillsdale, NJ: Analytic Press.
Rubin, H. J., & Rubin, I. S. (1995). *Qualitative interviewing: The art of hearing data*. Thousand Oaks, CA: Sage.
Ruebelt, S. G., Singaravelu, H., Daneshpour, M. & Brown, C. M. (2015). Exploration of cross-cultural couples' marital adjustment: Iranian American women married to European American man. *Current Psychology, 35*, 437–449.
Santrock, J. W. (2007). *A topical approach to life-span development* (3rd ed.). New York: McGraw-Hill.
Schwandt, T. A. (2003). Three epistomological stances for qualitative inquiry: Interpretivism, hermeneutics, and social constructionism. In N. Denzin & Y. Lincoln (Eds.), *The landscape of qualitative research: Theories and issues* (pp. 292–331). Thousand Oaks, CA: Sage.

Seshadri, G., & Knudson-Martin, C. (2013). How couples manage interracial and intercultural differences: Implications for clinical practice. *Journal of Marital and family Therapy, 30*(1), 43–58. https://doi.org/10.1111/j.1752-0606.2011.00262.x.

Sims, M. R., & Omaji, A. K. (1999). Migration and parenting: A pilot study. *Journal of Family Studies, 5*(1), 84–96.

Singla, R. (2015). *Intermarriage and mixed parenting, promoting mental health and wellbeing: Crossover love.* New York: Palgrave Macmillan.

Skowronski, D., Othman, A. B., Wong, J. Y., Tan, W. S. D., Lum, W. H. G., Waszynska, K. (2014). The outline of selected marital satisfaction factors in intercultural couples based on the Westerner and non-Westerner relationships. *Polish Psychological Bulletin, 45*(3), 345–356.

Smith, J., & Dunworth, F. (2003). Qualitative methodology. In J. Valsiner & J. K. J. Connolly (Eds.), *The handbook of developmental psychology.* London: Sage.

Sodowsky, G. R., Lai, E. W. M., & Plake, B. S. (1991). Moderating effects of sociocultural variables on acculturation variables of Hispanics and Asian Americans. *Journal of Counselling and Development, 70*(1), 194–204.

Streubert, H. J., & Carpenter, D. R. (1999). *Qualitative research in nursing: Advancing the humanistic imperative.* (2nd ed.). Philadelphia, PA: Williams & Wilkins.

Sue, D. W., & Sue, D. (1990). *Counselling the culturally different: Theory and practice* (2nd ed.). New York: Wiley.

Suizzo, M. A. (2007). Parents' goals and values for children: Dimensions of independence and interdependence across four U.S. ethnic groups. *Journal of Cross-Cultural Psychology, 38*(4), 506–530.

Sullivan, C., & Cottone, R. R. (2006). Culture based couple therapy and intercultural relationships: A review of the literature. *The Family Journal, 14*(3), 221–225.

Ting-Toomey, S. (1999). *Communicating across cultures.* New York: Guilford.

Triandis, H. C. (1994). *Culture and social behaviour.* New York: McGraw-Hill.

Tseng, W. S. (1977). Adjustment in intercultural marriage. In W. S. Teng, J. F. McDermott, & T. W. Maretzki (Eds.), *Adjustment in intercultural marriage* (pp. 93–103). Honolulu: University of Hawaii Press.

Tseng, W. S., & Hsu, J. (1991). *Culture and family: Problems and therapy.* New York: Haworth.

Yancey, G., & Lewis, R. (2009). *Interracial families: Current concepts and controversies.* New York: Routledge.

Yodanis, C., Lauer, S., & Ota, R. (2012). Interethnic romantic relationships: Enacting affiliative ethnic identities. *Journal of Marriage and Family, 74*(5), 1021–1037.

Young, R. A., & Colin, A. (2004). Introduction: Constructivism and social constructionism in the career field. *Journal of Vocational Behaviour, 64*(3), 373–388.

Zebroski, S. A. (1999). Black-White intermarriages: The racial and gender dynamics of support and oppositions. *Journal of Black Studies, 30*(1), 123–132.

2

Intercultural Parenting and the Australian Context

> When you go into a relationship, you expect differences or obviously you like differences. So that's why you're together and so when differences come up you know as a couple or parent, you negotiate and you compromise.

As I mentioned in the introduction section, due to increases in intercultural relationships worldwide, including interracial, interfaith and interethnic partnerships (Bratwidjaja, 2007; Bustamante, Nelson, Henriksen, & Monakes, 2011; Caballero, Edwards, & Puthussery, 2008; Crippen, 2008; Gonzalez & Harris, 2012; Luke & Carrington, 2000; Owen, 2002; Singla, 2015) intercultural parenting is also on the rise. This trend is also well reflected in Australia and necessitates a deeper understanding of this emerging phenomenon.

According to the Australian Bureau of Statistics (ABS, 2017), the preliminary estimated resident population of Australia was 24,511,800 people and about 28% of the estimated resident population was born overseas (6.7 million persons). About 31.9% of married couples were in a relationship between Australian-born and overseas-born partners. Importantly, the number of overseas-born spouses from India, Asia, Africa, Middle East and the Pacific Islands also increased significantly.

D. Bhugun, *Intercultural Parenting and Relationships*,
https://doi.org/10.1007/978-3-030-14060-1_2

A similar increase in intercultural marriages has been reported in other countries in the past decades, particularly in the United States (Bikel & Mandarano, 2012; Crippen, 2008; Falicov, 1995; Frame, 2004; Globe Newswire, 2012; Killian, 2013; Qian & Lichter, 2007); U.K. (Caballero et al., 2008; Owen, 2002; Voas, 2008); Canada (Wu, 2011) and Denmark (Singla, 2015). In this context, the term "intercultural" refers to the interactions between members of different cultural groups (Ting-Toomey, 1999). Intercultural couples are adults in a relationship who come from different cultural backgrounds (Perel, 2000).

Given the changes in the cultural landscape of Australia, they are likely to impact on family structures as well as parenting behaviours and practices that may not occur in mono-cultural families. Consequently, intercultural parenting is emerging as an important family dynamic in Australian society. The rise in intercultural parenting presents new dimensions to parenting dynamics which can be challenging as well as rewarding for intercultural couples and children. The above quote from a participant in this study illustrates how intercultural parents manage intercultural parenting influences.

The literature on intercultural parenting and relationships focuses on the psychosocial challenges of intercultural parenting and relationships, such as barriers to communication (Perel, 2000; Waldman & Rubalcava, 2005), conflicts over parenting (Ho, 1990; Romano, 2001) and differences in cultural values (Falicov, 1995; Garcia, 2006; Hsu, 2001; Waldman & Rubalcava, 2005). Past research has also focussed on the nature of relationships between intercultural couples, attitudes towards interracial marriages, issues faced by children in the relationship and cross-cultural comparisons of parenting styles. There is also an assumption that intercultural relationships end up in divorce compared to mono-cultural relationships. However, recent studies have challenged this view and assumptions (Irastorza & DeVoretz, 2009; Kenney & Kenney, 2012). In a review of the literature on intercultural relationships, Sullivan & Cottone (2006) pointed out that "little empirical research has been done with intercultural couples to assist with conceptualisation of problems and useful interventions" (p. 221).

There is limited focus in the literature on the positive experiences of intercultural relationship and parenting dynamics. Falicov (1995) identified that although intercultural couples initially experience some form of conflict with each other's values and beliefs, they can also experience mutual cultural adaptation through increased understanding, tolerance and personal transformations. According to Heller and Wood (2000), intercultural relationships enrich interaction, help negotiating differences and increase intimacy and blending, thus enabling individuals to move beyond the cultural differences.

Parents from racial, ethnic and culturally diverse backgrounds face unique challenges that are under-researched in parenting scholarship. The literature on intercultural relationships suggests that parenthood or childbearing can be a significant source of relationship conflict as a result of divergent perspectives on childhood, parenting styles and practices and the impact of cultural differences among couples (Bhugra & De Silva, 2000; Crippen, 2008; Crohn, 1995; Gaines & Brennan, 2001; Romano, 2001; Singla, 2015). A review of the literature shows no published studies on intercultural parenting in Australia. Only a few Australian studies (Andreoni & Fujimori, 1998; Papps, Walker, Trimboli, & Trimboli, 1995; Sims & Omaji, 1999) have compared parenting between parents from the same cultural background in different ethnic groups, including African, Lebanese and Vietnamese parents.

Most of the literature on intercultural parenting is based on overseas experiences such as in Europe, America and Canada (Bratawidjaja, 2007; Caballero et al., 2008; Crippen, 2008; Keller et al., 2004; Nakazawa, 2003; Wu, 2011) and focused mainly on intercultural parenting between Asian, African American, Hispanic and white Anglo European and American couples. One qualitative study in New Zealand (Hubber, 1998) focussed only on intercultural parenting between New Zealand European and Samoan parents. Another empirical study in Denmark (Singla, 2015) focussed on mixed-parenting between a Danish and South Indian partner. Although Australia has officially endorsed multiculturalism (Beech, 2013) and recorded a quite high degree of intercultural relationships, unfortunately, there have been no published studies in Australia on the lived experiences of intercultural parenting within a single household. Such studies would have helped in understanding the experiences of intercultural parents in this country and how they negotiate their cultural differences in parenting. This book addresses the gap.

As mentioned earlier, Australia is becoming an increasingly multicultural nation and pluralistic society. The recent growth of immigration from Asia, India, Africa, Arab/Islamic countries and the Pacific Islands to Australia has resulted in an increasingly multicultural society and given rise to an increase in intercultural relationships and parenting in Australia. The increase in intercultural relationships and parenting across the broader cultural communities inspired and motivated me to produce this book into the phenomenon of intercultural parenting, which is distinct to the Australian context, rather than relying on overseas data which can be contextually different. However, an important contribution of this book is that the themes are potentially applicable to other similar contexts outside Australia, as it presents real inner experiences and stories of intercultural couples/parents and the voices of migrant parents as outsiders.

Another important contribution and significance of this book is that it seeks to extend the limited literature on the positive experiences and transformations of intercultural relationships and parenting, and generate knowledge of relevance and significance to non-clinical intercultural parents and helping professionals to enable them to understand the salience of cultural differences and experiences of intercultural parenting. It seeks to enable the helping professionals to enhance their cultural competence, awareness and sensitivity and adopt effective therapeutic strategies when dealing with intercultural families. This book can be utilised in various government and private sector organisations such as Universities, schools, child care, hospitals, Centrelink, Family Court, Child Protection Services, Department of Community Services and non-government organisations in their interactions and dealings with intercultural families. It has the potential to provide information to intercultural parents through a range of services such as educational materials in public libraries and community organisations. It will also add to the current theoretical knowledge base of family systems.

In this book, I explore the styles, practices, challenges and strategies parents apply in negotiating cultural differences in their child rearing approach, and the strengths and transformative opportunities of intercultural parenting. Importantly, it reflects on the meaning-making process of everyday interactions of intercultural parents by focusing on the "what is" rather than "what should be" of parents' own experiences of cultural differences.

As outlined in the introduction section, participants have been identified by pseudonyms only to protect their confidentiality. The analysis involved 28 participants (14 couples) from the urban and semi-rural areas of Queensland. The host participants were of Anglo-Celtic background and their immigrant partners were from diverse ethnic backgrounds as shown in Fig. 1.1. All the immigrant partners spoke English as their second language. Two host partners spoke the first language of their partners as their second language. The participants reflected a diverse national and cultural background, socio-economic status (such as level of education and profession), religious affiliation, level of acculturation, length of the relationship and number of children, which helped to generate a rich perception of intercultural parenting experiences. This demographic information about the participants is reflected in Fig. 1.1. A summary of each case study family is presented below to familiarise the reader with the cultural and familial context of their stories.

Case Studies

Couple 1: Kylie and Malai

Kylie is Anglo-Australian and met her Thai husband Malai while she was holidaying on a small island in Thailand called Ko Samui. Malai was working in the tourist industry and called himself a 'jungle boy'. He grew up in a small native village where his parents lived and worked as street food vendors. Malai practices Buddhism and completed high school education. Kylie is a university graduate and works as a teacher. She was brought up in a Christian family on the Gold Coast, with whom she has a great family relationship. Malai migrated to Australia 17 years ago and they had been married for 15 years. They have two children, a girl aged 14 and a boy aged 10. Initially, they lived together at her parents' home and encountered problems with Kylie's father because of his Mai's food culture. They later moved to their own place.

Couple 2: Naomi and Pravin

Naomi is Anglo-Australian and met her Indian husband Pravin in Australia. They were living in the same suburb and catching the bus together to the same University. They got married in India where they lived for 5 years. At the time of the interview, they had been together for 14 years. They have a son aged 5. Naomi is in middle management in the public sector, while Pravin owns two Indian restaurants on the Gold Coast. Pravin is very close to his family in India and travels there quite often. His parents also come to visit his family every year and stay with them for about three months, which according to them is a great source of support and richness for their son. Naomi is Catholic and Pravin, although being Indian does not necessarily practice the Hindu religion to the letter. However, Naomi was shocked when her husband reverted to wearing his toga and grew his hair when they lived in India.

Couple 3: Anya and Rajack

Anja is Anglo-Australian and met her Indonesian Muslim husband Rajack through friends while on holiday in Bali. Rajack was a surfer and came to Australia for a surfing competition where he fell in love with Anja and they got married. Rajack is a house painter and Anja is a school teacher. Anja travelled to Bali to visit Rajack during the holidays until they decided to live in Australia. They have four children, all boys, aged 13, 11, 5 and 9 months. Rajack, being a staunch Muslim was concerned about the children's religion if they were to marry. Anja reported that she voluntarily and happily converted to Islam before they got married. They feel that they are not very welcomed in their neighbourhood in Australia.

Couple 4: Sarah and Samuel

Samuel is Anglo-Australian and met his wife Sarah at his workplace where she also worked. Sarah was originally from the Philippines and migrated with her parents to Hong Kong. Sarah had a previous immersion experience of the Australian culture prior to meeting Samuel as she has been studying and working in Australia. They had been married for 19 years and have two children aged 14 and 11. They have both been brought up in Catholic families and are university graduates.

Samuel is an arts director and Sarah went back to higher studies. Samuel loves Asian food and way of life and their family is more inclined towards Asian culture.

Couple 5: Jim and Michelle

Jim is Anglo-Australian and met his Filipino wife Michelle at her cousin's barbeque party in Sydney where she was living with her father. Michelle's sister taught the Filipino language and was helping Jim as one of her students. Jim travelled to the Philippines regularly before he met Michelle and loved the strong family ties and simple way of living he saw there. This is why he decided to marry someone from the Philippines. Jim did not have a strong family life as his parents divorced when he was fourteen years of age. He reported regretting not having been able to continue his education. Jim is an electrician and his wife Michelle is educated and works in a bank. They have been married for 27 years and have twins aged 18. They are both staunch Catholics and raise their children with strong Catholic religious values.

Couple 6: Manuel and Tammy

Tammy is Anglo-Australian and met her Ugandan husband Manuel through friends in Australia. Manuel came to Australia as an economic migrant and has got very strong extended family ties back in his country home of Uganda as opposed to Tammy who has minimal contact with her extended family. They had been together for 12 years and have two children aged 10 and six months. They are both Catholic and have university degrees. Manuel works in aged care and Tammy is a school teacher. Manuel is very strong-minded about his traditional customs and cultural values such as respect, discipline and work ethics and is in conflict with the Australian ways of parenting.

Couple 7: Daniel and Simla

Daniel is Anglo-Australian and met his wife Simla at a coffee shop in 2005. Simla is from Botswana and had been studying in Australia since 1995. She was just about to finish her Master's degree and was not sure whether to stay in Australia. They have been together for eight years. They have a son aged 4. Simla had been in Australia for 10 years and had exposure and immersion in the Australian culture and, as she said, she knew what she was getting into. Both Daniel and Simla are university graduates. Simla has a very strong extended family network back in Botswana and travels there quite often. Simla misses her cultural background and tries to keep it alive by working in the multicultural sector where she is constantly involved with her African community and cultural activities, traditions and practices. Both Daniel and Simla encourage their son to embrace African culture and multiculturalism.

Couple 8: Bill and Azumi

Bill is Anglo-Australian and his wife Azumi is Japanese. They met in Sydney where they were sharing a rental property together. Azumi had been in Australia only for a short while. Bill then moved to Brisbane and eventually to the Gold Coast for financial reasons. By coincidence, Bill found out that Azumi had moved to the Gold Coast and they became flatmates again and eventually developed a relationship, despite the age difference between the two of them. Bill is 35 years older than Azumi. They had been married for 13 years and have two children aged 11 and 7. Azumi came from a very traditional and conservative Japanese family and her father opposed her marriage to Bill. Eventually, when Azumi's father became sick and needed her to look after him, he agreed for her to marry Bill. Bill and Azumi wanted their children to practice both cultures but were disappointed when the children did not want to learn and speak Japanese and were more inclined to the Australian culture.

Couple 9: Gary and Yan

Gary is Anglo-Australian and his wife Yan is Chinese. They met when Yan was attending English conversation classes run by a local church in Brisbane and where Gary was a volunteer helping with the English lesson classes. They had been married for 5 years and have two children aged 3 years and 3 weeks. Gary was previously married and has two adult sons from his previous marriage but they do not live with him. Both Yan and Gary hold university degrees and Gary was doing some further studies, while Yan was staying at home because of the pregnancy. Her parents were helping her with the pregnancy and looking after their daughter.

Couple 10: Murielle and Jeehan

Murielle is Anglo-Australian and her husband Jeehan is Turkish and a devoted Muslim. They met through friends at the beach on the Gold Coast at the end of the Muslim Ramadan festival and Jeehan and his friends were talking to her about the Muslim religion. Murielle had never heard about Muslims where she grew up. She liked what she heard, because according to her, religion was not much talked about in the Australian culture and in her family. She researched Islam and became Muslim. Then she went on to marry Jeehan. They had been married for 11 years and have three children, aged 10, 9 and 5. They both hold university degrees. Murielle is a part-time University lecturer and Jeehan is continuing with some further studies at the same University. Murielle's parents were initially opposed to the marriage but later accepted Jeehan when they realised that the marriage was working well.

Couple 11: Josh and Ng

Josh is Anglo-Australian and his wife Ng is Vietnamese. They met at the university where they were both studying. Josh is an IT programmer and Ng works in the welfare industry. They had been married for 4 years and have a son aged 20 months. Ng was pregnant at the time of the interview and was expecting her second child in two months. Ng's parents were at her place helping with their son and her pregnancy. Josh is agnostic and his wife is Buddhist. Josh does not have an issue with the child being taught Buddhism and being brought up with Buddhist values because he believes in strong families. He has witnessed firsthand the benefits of strong family values from his wife's side of the extended family, especially since her parents have been around helping and supporting her with their son and her pregnancy.

Couple 12: John and Rula

John is Anglo-Australian and his wife Rula is Tongan who was brought up as an adopted child in New Zealand. Rula described herself as very traditional Tongan but also had some exposure to the "white people's way" as she described it. John travelled to Tonga when his parents were working for the Tongan Government, and was exposed to the Tongan language. John is also quite involved with the Tongan communities and organisations in Australia. They had been married for 7 years and have two children, aged 5 and 2. They are both university graduates Rula was studying at the time of the interview. They are both strong Catholics and quite engaged in church activities.

Couple 13: Cathy and Will

Cathy is Anglo-Australian and her husband Will is Maori New Zealander. She lived in Brisbane and was brought up in an academic environment. She met Will at a party on the Gold Coast. He later moved to Brisbane and they had been married for 13 years and have two children, aged 13 and 11. Cathy is a school teacher. Will was a professional footballer, having retired after a serious injury, and is now a truck driver. Will did not have a healthy and positive upbringing because of serious domestic violence in his family and an authoritarian style of parenting from his father who was in the army. Will had a tendency to follow his father's disciplinary style with the children, which was in conflict with his wife's parenting style. Will admitted to learning a new way of parenting in his new relationship. Cathy was brought up in an upper-class family and was expected to study and marry someone from the same class.

Couple 14: Jay and Carol

Carol is Anglo-Australian and her husband Jay is Fijian Indian. They were both studying at the same university and living in the same area and met at the local pub. They got married only 4 months after they met and had been married for 25 years. They have a daughter aged 17 and a son aged 14. Jay is a financial manager and Carol works in the welfare industry. Both Jay and Carol had a similar upbringing as they grew up in remote country towns on farms, helped their parents on the farm, and lived in similar kind of houses. Carol embraces the Indian culture and Jay has assimilated well in Australia.

The next chapter presents results and discussion pertaining to cultures coming together.

References

Andreoni, H., & Fujimori, K. (1998). Shitsuke: Child-rearing values and practices in a Japanese community in Sydney. *Journal of Intercultural Studies, 19*(1), 69–83.

Australian Bureau of Statistics. (2017, March). *Australian Demographics Statistics*. Canberra: Australian Bureau of Statistics.

Beech, H. (2013, August 19). I am Australian. So Am I. *Time Magazine, 182*(8).

Bhugra, D., & De Silva, P. (2000). Couple therapy across culture. *Sexual and relationship therapy, 15*(2), 184–192.

Bikel & Mandarano LLP. (2012). When intercultural relationships fail: What happens to the children? In Bikel & Mandarano LLP (Ed.), *Offers guidelines for American Judicial System*. New York: Globe Newswire.

Bratawidjaja, A. (2007). *The experience of being parents of mixed-heritage children: Phenomenological analysis* (Unpublished doctoral dissertation). Kansas State University, Kansas.

Bustamante, R. M., Nelson, J. A., Henriksen, R. C., Jr., & Monakes, S. (2011). Intercultural couples: Coping with culture-related stressors. *The Family Journal: Counselling and Therapy for Couples and Families, 19*(2), 154–164. https://doi.org/10.1177/1066480711399723.

Caballero, C., Edwards, R., & Puthussery, S. (2008). Parenting 'mixed' children: Negotiating difference and belonging in mixed race, ethnicity and faith families. *Joseph Rowntree Foundation*. Retrieved August 15, 2011, from https://www.researchgate.net/profile/Chamion_Caballero/publication/265537866_Parenting_'Mixed'_Children_Difference_and_Belonging_in_Mixed_Race_and_Faith_Families/links/54b911660cf28faced626ac3.pdf.

Crippen, C. (2008). *Cross-cultural parenting: Experiences of intercultural parents and constructions of culturally diverse families* (Unpublished doctoral dissertation). University of New England, Australia.

Crohn, J. (1995). *Mixed matches: How to create successful interracial, interethnic, and interfaith relationships*. New York: Random House.

Falicov, C. J. (1995). Cross-cultural marriages. In N. S. Jacobson & A. S. Gurman (Eds.), *Clinical handbook of couple therapy* (pp. 231–246). New York: Guildford.

Frame, M. W. (2004). The challenges of intercultural marriage: Strategies for pastoral care. *Pastoral Psychology, 52*(3), 219–232.

Gaines, S. O., & Brennan, K. A. (2001). Establishing and maintaining satisfaction in multicultural relationships. In J. Harvey & A. Wenzel (Eds.), *Close romantic relationships: Maintenance and enhancement* (pp. 237–253). Mahwah, NJ: Lawrence Erlbaum.

Garcia, D. R. (2006). Mixed marriages and transnational families in the intercultural context: A case study of African-Spanish couples in Catalonia. *Journal of Ethnic and Migration Studies, 32*(3), 403–433. https://doi.org/10.1080/13691830600555186.

Globe Newswire. (2012, June 12). *When intercultural relations fail—What happens to the children? Bikel & Mandarano, LLP offers guidelines for American judicial system.* Retrieved January 6, 2016, from http://globenewswire.com/news-release/2012/06/12/479231/259017/en/When-Intercultural-Relations-Fail-What-Happens-to-the-Children.html.

Gonzalez, N. A., & Harris, T. M. (2012). Parenting in intercultural contexts. In N. A. Gonzalez, T. M. Harris, & A. Carlos (Eds.), *Mediating cultures: Parenting in intercultural contexts*, (pp. ix–xi). Blue Ridge Summit, PA: Lexington Books.

Heller, P. E., & Wood, B. (2000). The influence of religious and ethnic differences on marital intimacy: Intermarriage versus intra-marriage. *Journal of Marital and Family Therapy, 26*(2), 241–252. https://doi.org/10.1111/j.1752-0606.2000.tb00293.x.

Ho, M. K. (1990). *Intermarried couples in therapy.* Springfield, IL: Charles Thomas.

Hsu, J. (2001). Marital therapy for intercultural couples. In W. S. Tseng & J. Streltzer (Eds.), *Culture and psychology: A guide to clinical practice* (pp. 225–242). Washington, DC: American Psychiatric Publishing.

Hubber, T. (1998). *An exploration of intercultural parenting: The experience of Samoan & New Zealand-European couples* (Unpublished dissertation). University of Auckland, New Zealand.

Irastorza, N., & Devoretz, D. (2009). *Factors affecting international marriage survival: A theoretical approach.* Retrieved January 15, 2016, from http://www.sfu.ca/~devoretz/lecturenotes/sem9.pdf.

Keller, H., Lohaus, A., Kuensemueller, P., Abels, M., Yosvi, R., Voelker, S., & Mohite, P. (2004). The bio-culture of parenting: Evidence from five cultural communities. *Parenting: Science and Practice, 4*(1), 25–50.

Kenney, K., & Kenney, K. (2012). Contemporary multiple heritage couples, individuals and families: Issues, concerns, and counselling implications'. *Counselling Psychology Quarterly, 25*(2), 99–112.

Killian, K. (2013). *Interracial couples, intimacy & therapy: Crossing racial borders.* New York: Columbia University Press.

Luke, C., & Carrington, V. (2000). Race matters. *Journal of Intercultural Studies, 21*(1), 5–24.

Nakazawa, D. J. (2003). *Does anybody else look like me? A parent's guide to raising multicultural children*. Cambridge, MA: Perseus.

Owen, J. D. (2002). *Mixed matches: Interracial marriage in Australia*. Sydney: University of New South Wales Press.

Papps, F., Walker, M., Trimboli, A., & Trimboli, C. (1995). Parental discipline in Anglo, Greek, Lebanese, and Vietnamese cultures. *Journal of Cross-Cultural Psychology, 26*(1), 49–64.

Perel, E. (2000). A tourist's view of marriage: Cross-cultural couples-challenges, choices, and implications for therapy. In P. Papp (Ed.), *Couples on the fault line: New directions for therapists* (pp. 178–204). New York: Guildford.

Qian, Z., & Lichter, D. T. (2007). Social boundaries and marital assimilation: Interpreting trends in racial and ethnic intermarriage. *American Sociological Review, 72*(1), 68–94. https://doi.org/10.1177/000312240707200104.

Romano, D. (2001). *Intercultural marriage: Promises and pitfalls* (3rd ed.). Yarmouth, ME: Intercultural Press.

Sims, M. R., & Omaji, A. K. (1999). Migration and parenting: A pilot study. *Journal of Family Studies, 5*(1), 84–96.

Singla, R. (2015). *Intermarriage and mixed parenting, promoting mental health and wellbeing: Crossover love*. New York: Palgrave Macmillan.

Sullivan, C., & Cottone, R. R. (2006). Culture based couple therapy and intercultural relationships: A review of the literature. *The Family Journal, 14*(3), 221–225.

Ting-Toomey, S. (1999). *Communicating across cultures*. New York: Guilford.

Voas, D. (2008). Intermarriage and the demography of secularization. *The British Journal of Sociology, 59*(1), 83–108.

Waldman, K., & Rubalcava, L. (2005). Psychotherapy with intercultural couples: A contemporary psychodynamic approach. *American Journal of Psychotherapy, 59*(3), 227–245.

Wu, R. (2011, June 7–8). *A narrative inquiry into the lived experiences of Chinese-White heterosexual couples within a Canadian context*. Paper presented in Metissage, Mestizaje, Mixed 'Race' and beyond, 6th Critical Multicultural Counselling & Psychotherapy Conference, Ontario Institute for Studies and Education (OISE).

3

Cultures Coming Together

This chapter provides results and discussion pertaining to cultures coming together. Chapter 4 focuses on Themes 2, 3: Power Relations, Reverse Acculturation/Enculturation. Chapter 5 focuses on Theme 4: Making Intercultural Parenting Work. Chapter 6 discusses implications for theory, policy and practice, strengths and limitations of the study, and future research opportunities. The themes respond to the principal research question of the study that aimed to explore the lived parenting experiences of intercultural couples. Despite the fact that intercultural couples and parents developed their own internal relational and parental systems, they were also impacted by other systems such as their families and culture of origin, political, social, economic and legal systems. Systemic factors that greatly influenced the experiences of intercultural couples and parents included the ecosystem in which they lived, interpersonal dynamics in the relationship, and changes in the couples' system dynamics over time. The intercultural experience encompassed how participants perceived their cultural identities, relationships and the challenges and benefits they encountered as a couple and parent. The data revealed that intercultural couples, in particular immigrant

D. Bhugun, *Intercultural Parenting and Relationships*,
https://doi.org/10.1007/978-3-030-14060-1_3

partners, experienced culture shock and negative feelings, followed by gradual cultural adaptation and integrative acculturation within both realms of relational and parenting dynamics.

Summary of Themes Identified

The thematic analysis identified four major themes and twenty sub-themes from the narratives of the intercultural couples about their experience of parenting their mixed-heritage children. The main themes are outlined in Table 3.1.

The next section provides results and discussion pertaining to the principal theme "Cultures Coming Together" (Table 3.2).

Table 3.1 Main themes identified from data analysis

Themes	Sub-themes
1. Cultures coming together	1. Cultural identity 2. Culture shock 3. Racism and marriage disapproval 4. Cultural values and customs 5. Gender roles and beliefs 6. Language and communication 7. Similarities and differences in parenting 8. Contextual influences 9. Benefits and opportunities of intercultural parenting
2. Power relations	1. Righteousness and privilege of truth 2. Language and communication 3. Gender influence 4. Insider/outsider status
3. Reverse acculturation/ enculturation	1. Valuing ethnic heritage and host culture 2. Reciprocal acculturation 3. Global culture 4. Shift in parenting styles
4. Making intercultural parenting work	1. Individual sphere 2. Couples'/parents' sphere 3. Child's sphere

Table 3.2 Theme and sub-themes regarding cultures coming together

Themes	Sub-themes	Description
1. Cultures coming together	1. Cultural identity	Describes participants' experiences of their individual, couple, child, parent, family and religious identities
	2. Culture shock	Describes the participants' experiences regarding language, food, shopping, children's behaviour and parenting style
	3. Racism and marriage disapproval	Describes participants' experiences about the attitude of other members of the society towards them and their children and their relationship rejection by family and friends and the impact on their children
	4. Cultural values and customs	Describes participants' different experiences of customs and values when exposed to each other's cultural and social environment and the impact on their children
	5. Gender roles and beliefs	Describes the influence of gender dynamics in parenting and relational roles
	6. Language and communication	Describes participants' challenges with language barriers that created misunderstanding and conflict regarding their relational and parenting roles
	7. Similarities and differences in parenting practices	Describes participants' experiences of common and culture specific trends in parenting and the challenges and benefits associated with the parenting practices
	8. Contextual influences	Describes the impact of other socio-environmental contexts external to the family environment that influences parental roles and practices
	9. Benefits and opportunities of intercultural parenting	Reflects on the positive aspects of intercultural parenting experienced by participants and reported as enriching their children's and own lives

Cultural Identity

Individual Identity

In this study, participants self-identified as intercultural couples. They described their cultural identity in many different ways that were found to be quite unique to each couple. The most familiar and common cultural identity was related to the country where the participant was born. For example, Manuel, who was born and grew up in Uganda, proudly identified himself as African:

> I'm African. I was born in Uganda and I'm of Uganda birth right. (Manuel)

His wife Tammy concurred with his perception of cultural belonging:

> Obviously home is where the heart is. (Tammy)

Some participants identified themselves as bicultural as a result of the association between their country of birth and their sense of belonging to the newly adopted country. This is clearly demonstrated in Sarah's perception of her cultural identity:

> Having to migrate to Australia and having to assimilate to a different culture again… in a way now I am supposed to be Australian because I am also an Australian citizen now. But I still don't feel like I am Australian because I don't follow football, I don't follow your [husband] typical Australian kind of culture… for me I am kind of a mix bag and I always call myself that….mixed culture…which is good. (Sarah)

Sarah's husband Samuel concurred with her perception and experience of belonging to a mixed culture:

> I would say culturally English but Asian slant towards food. (Samuel)

An interesting pattern was apparent when participants were asked to describe their cultural identity. Immigrant partners were very firm about their cultural identity as being the country they came from, irrespective of how long they have been in Australia. In contrast, some Australian partners had difficulty in describing their own cultural identity. This may be partly because they seemed to take their culture for granted and therefore hard to explain. As Murielle said:

> What is Australian culture anyway? No one really has like, I don't know anyone that has 100 percent Australian, like what is it? Like you can't really pinpoint what exactly is an Australian culture because it is so mixed and so various where do you start to say that this is Australian and this is not. (Murielle)

Some host participants started to take notice of their cultural identity and differences when they were exposed to other cultures, including travelling to non-western countries and having a partner from another culture:

> From my travels to the Philippines… I could see the strong family ties and I could see a lot of things in the Philippines… people in some cases they had nothing but those two hats. Whatever they had…they made the most of it and with the things they had. I thought well it will be a good life choice. So pretty much I made up my mind before I met my wife… I would probably marry someone from that part of the world. (Jim)

Jim's example demonstrated a cultural point of reference where he was able to make an assessment of his own cultural background against the backdrop of another culture in the Philippines.

Identity as a Couple

Although this theme is distinct because it focuses on the experience of identity as a couple, and presented separately, it is linked to the experiences of intercultural couples in parenting their children because the experience of parenting is related to the experience of being a couple, especially in the intercultural situation. This theme is reflected in both contexts. Most participants described that when they are in the social arena, they can sense that people regard them as being different because of their looks and their mixed-heritage children. But they reported that this is not how they feel about or are even aware of themselves, unless this is drawn to their attention. Based on the responses, it was clear that a majority of couples did not see being in an intercultural relationship as a major concern. They did not deny that there were cultural differences. They all agreed that they were culturally different as parents, which will be comprehensively described in sub-theme two. Two participants reported that when they formed a relationship with their partners, they never looked at the partner from a cultural perspective, but rather as another person and human. As Simla explained:

> Yeah, it happened. It wasn't the fact that I was African or it wasn't the fact that he [Daniel] was Australian. It was the fact that we are connected as two people. (Simla)

In the above example, co-construction and negotiation of meaning was non-verbally acknowledged by Daniel regarding his wife Simla's interpretation about themselves as a couple.

Intercultural couples described that they became aware of their cultural differences when people drew attention to it, experienced language barriers, when they had children, and differences in customs and traditions. From the perspective of physical "racial" features, two participants reported that they were treated differently as couples and as parents when they were in a social situation.

Cathy sensed the perception of difference from people when she was in the public arena with her husband and children:

> Because I am white, blonde hair, blue eyes and they are black, I do get looks sometimes from people because they meet Will [husband] and the boys and he is like, "this is my wife" and people are like, "oh yeah". I would never have experienced that if I married a white guy. (Cathy)

Participants also reported experiences of perception of difference from their own extended family members, mostly as a result of differences in physical characteristics and language. This is reflected in Cathy's description of incongruent cultural identities as seen in her family by a member of her own extended family:

> When I had the boys, my aunty who is a barrister said to us, don't worry there's a lot of parents now that are having coloured children, that was only 13-14 years ago and I was like what? (Cathy)

Another important issue regarding couples' identity was the feeling and experience of being regarded as outsiders or insiders in each other's country. In this study, 'outsider' status was related to immigrant participants living in the host country. According to the participants, this experience was associated from living in the partner's country, speaking another language and having different customs and traditions. Malai described his perception of the experience of outsider status when his father-in-law criticised and complained about the cultural Thai food he cooked while staying with his host partner at her parent's home.

> Can you imagine that, yeah. He doesn't like my food, things smelled really weird. So it upset me because in my country food is number one thing for us and eating. (Malai)

His wife concurred with his perception of being considered as an outsider:

> Initially we were staying with my mom and dad. Malai wanted to still be cooking his food and, you know, you're used to that … sort of cooking in breakfast, lunch, and dinner. That's not how we do things here in Australia. So there were some challenges with my father. So my dad complained about it quite vocally. That was amazing. (Kylie)

However, the outsider status was not exclusive to the experience of the immigrant partner. It was also experienced as a two-way phenomenon, especially when the host partner travelled to their immigrant partner's country of origin to visit their relatives. One participant described how her perception of feeling like an outsider among her husband's family in his country of origin made her feel lonely and hard to take:

> And I guess me being Australian and seeing like the Indians as foreigners, sometimes I guess it felt like I was the foreigner because I was the only Australian in the group and sometimes that was hard to take… sometimes people weren't willing to talk and everyone just spoke in Hindi. No one would try to speak in English so, sometimes I found that difficult you know and I felt a bit alone at times. (Carol)

Two host participants described their perception of minority status within their own majority host culture and country. Gary related an experience of feeling the minority and outsider status within his own host culture because his wife Yan and her parents, who were staying at their home to help mind their daughter and with Yan's new pregnancy excluded him from any discussion about their daughter's health and spoke Chinese all the time:

> That's like I'm sitting in Asia by myself. (Gary)

Gary's wife Yan justified her act while also concurring with Gary's feeling of outsider status:

> Yeah and I didn't realize if he didn't complain. Also because my parents are here, I tend to speak more Chinese and sometimes just ignore him. If he didn't complain I wouldn't recognize it, I'd just keep speaking Chinese. (Yan)

Insider status related to the experience of the host participants who were born in the host country and spoke the majority language. For the purpose of this study, insider status related to the host participants' knowledge of the host culture and traditions regarding parenting. However, some participants also claimed the insider status from their experience of immersion in the Australian culture and society and through their relationship with their host partners. Two participants described their insider status based on the fact that they studied and worked in Australia before meeting their partners and marrying them:

> Well, when I met him I had been here for quite some time, since 1995. So I had already kind of friends who were Australians. So I knew exactly

> what people do, what my perception of the culture is… I had already been exposed a lot to the culture in some previous relationships, as well before this one. (Simla)

The insider/outsider status can have a dual effect on the couple's identity. Participants reported that the outsider status impacted negatively on their relationship and parenting. On the other hand, the insider status was reported as strength in the couple's identity because it commanded respect for them from having knowledge of and immersion in the host culture and parenting practices. The insider and outsider status can also be perceived as a power issue in intercultural parenting contexts and will be further elaborated on as a separate theme in Chapter 4.

Children's Cultural Identity

None of the participants in this study identified their children as belonging to one particular culture more than another. They identified their children as bicultural because of their cultural heritage from both sides of the family, and because they are aware of their racial and ethnic cultural background. They identified their children as Australian from a nationality point of view because "they have grown up in Australia" (Sarah), and were therefore automatically considered to be Australian from a nationality and citizenship perspective, which as much as it sounds contradictory, is how they perceived their children's identity.

Manuel and Tammy explained their children's identity as African Australian because they are being raised in Australia but still have cultural association with Africa:

> I would be saying that he's African-Australian, I suppose, yeah. (Tammy)

> They're Australian because they're being raised in the Australian society, but they have got the African blood… when it comes to food, you know when we go there, the mangoes, she loves the music, the dance, but she's used to the setting here. She's used to communicating in the culture here. She's used to the gadgets, the Australian gadgets. So yeah. (Manuel)

Sarah described her children as Eurasian because they are born and being raised in Australia and because of the way they look:

> Because they have grown up in Australia… they would probably be very much Australian in the way they see things and do things with their friends because they are educated here… but I think if someone asked them because of the way they look, very Eurasian, I think they know that there is a Filipino side to them. (Sarah)

Most parents also emphasised the choice of identity as belonging to the children themselves because of their looks, affinity and gravity towards a parent's culture and also to prevent confusion about their cultural identity among their peers and the social environment. Azumi described that her children perceived their cultural identity based on their looks:

> I think they feel confused. I ask them "which one do you want to be, Australian or Japanese?". Jessie she says Japanese and the little one says Australian. (Azumi)

Dharam: *And do they say why? Why would your first one say she's Japanese?*

> Yes because may be she looks more Japanese than Australian. (Azumi)

The parents' perception of their children's identity was reported to have impacted on their parenting practices. For example, most of the participants said that they encouraged and guided their children to be involved with and acquire the cultural characteristics of their migrant partners such as teaching them their language, bringing them on holidays to their partners' country of origin, and eating their cultural food. Michelle reported that she spoke her dialect and language to her children since they were young:

> When they were younger I used to talk to them in my dialect which is Ilocano. Ilocano is found on the northern part of Luzon. Even now when I get angry I express myself in my language…in Tagalong. They know I am angry and they know the meaning too. (Michelle)

Simla and her husband Daniel reported that they raised their son to be bicultural and are keen to see him become bilingual:

> I want him to know that he's from two cultures. He has an African culture and an Australian culture, and to respect both, and to feel comfortable with both... I keep saying that I will try with my Botswana because I would love him to know my language actually. (Simla)

> He will gravitate toward an African stranger before he would ever gravitate to a white stranger. So if he doesn't consider himself African, he certainly has an affinity toward that side of his culture, which is fantastic. (Daniel)

All the participants reported that by the very nature of being intercultural couples and encouraging their children to be bicultural and bilingual has benefitted and enriched their children's lives. The benefits and opportunities associated with children's cultural identity will be explored further below in the section regarding benefits and opportunities of intercultural parenting.

Parent Identity

According to the participants, parent identity was shaped by several internal and external contexts. Participants' perception of internal contexts included pride in their heritage culture, embracing cultural diversity, religious values, gender activities, socio-economic status and experience of own parents' parenting. Perception of external factors included the family and social environment, and growing up in collective societies in which parenting activities occur. These intricate factors influenced participants' attitude about parenting.

Regarding internal contexts, most parents, particularly migrant parents, were very proud of their heritage and cultural identity and encouraged their children to practice those cultural attributes, customs and values. One participant, for example, exposed her son to all the cultural activities of her diaspora community, so that he knows and learns about her mother's cultural identity, and has continuous engagement with her community and cultural activities:

> I want him to know that he's from two cultures. He has an African culture and an Australian culture, and to respect both, and to feel comfortable with both… I think the difference is the location… away from my close-knit family… perhaps it's the reasons why I'm involved a lot with the African community here. So I can actually create that village and networks around me that my son can also experience the wide range of people around me, the difference and the strength of a community, which is how I grew up. (Simla)

Simla's husband Daniel was very supportive of Simla in encouraging their son to also identify with his mother's heritage culture:

> But it's good because we were worried that he would just be dark skinned Australian. His friends are primarily from the white society. (Daniel)

Other parents considered themselves as bicultural and embraced cultural diversity as a rich experience for themselves and their children.

> So I'd say Australian slash Turkish, which is more of a historical sort of a bond which I'd like and intend to keep because of the religious values and stuff. (Murielle)
>
> I totally agree Turkish Australian. (Jeehan)

Parent identity was also demonstrated in terms of gender activities. One participant firmly believed that boys do not play with dolls and did not like his wife encouraging this behaviour in their son. This was described as a point of conflict in the family because his wife did not have a problem with their son playing with dolls:

> Men are supposed to be men and women are supposed to be women. He will see that part from me. I don't want him playing with dolls… I would have a problem. (Daniel)
>
> I think I would have a problem. He doesn't play with them you know… he thinks they're cute. He thinks they're his girlfriends. (Simla)

Parent identity was also apparent in participants' description of their socio-economic status. Three participants described that they did not achieve the educational and job status they desired because of personal and family situations, and did not want to see their children in the same situation. They wanted their children "to be better" than themselves and have a better lifestyle by encouraging and helping their children to be educated so that they can have better jobs, and economic and social status:

> I'm pushing her to become a doctor. I've been talking to her because there are certain things I've failed myself. I told her [daughter], "Look, I wanted to do this. I wanted to do that". So I'm trying to push her to see that she can do better than me and to do her best. (Manuel)

Manuel's perception of socio-economic status as an influential factor on parent identity was co-constructed as a reality by his wife Tammy:

> In African culture, study is so important… here you're not really looking to the future… how many 15 that sort of age really know what they want to do with their futures. They don't, not really and they don't know consequences. They don't where Manuel is from, it's so important to study if they aren't studying so they're nothing. (Tammy)
>
> Yes, that's why I want to go back and study. (Manuel)

Dharam: *What about yourself, what do you think*?

> I think it's important. I've even gone back to Uni now. I've stopped obviously when I had him, but I wish I would have done it when I was younger. (Tammy)

The participants' socio-economic status also defined how they approached their parenting styles and practices regarding, for example, discipline. Kylie reported that her job as a teacher gave her a better understanding of children's behaviour in their different stages of developmental growth and parented accordingly:

> The teaching that I did up until two years ago didn't really involve discipline because it was young adults, so now that I am dealing with children and teenagers I guess I am more aware of what works and what doesn't work with children. (Kylie)

Two participants reported that their parents' expectations of who they should marry was based on their own socio-economic status and assumptions. Their parents expected them to marry rich and educated men. This is exemplified in Cathy's case:

> I went to a private girls' school, I hung out with the church boys in Brisbane and the wealthy families and so mum and dad always expected me to marry someone that was going to be a doctor. Yes, so dad, so mum's family they lived in West End in Brisbane but they were all private school educated back… they all went to Girls Grammar… I wanted to be a hairdresser when I left school and that was not an option, there was no option it was "you are going to UQ and you are going to get a degree and you are going", you know. (Cathy)

In the above situation, it was evident that Cathy resented her parents' expectations which eventually impacted on her own parenting style. Cathy wanted her children to do what made them happy:

> I just want them to do whatever they want to do… and be happy with their life. I think because I was told that I had to go to University and all I wanted to do was be a hairdresser and now my mom says I probably had a salon… that's what I was told to do so for me like S [son] our 11-year old is very good at football, he wants to be a professional footballer player and I'm happy as long as he is. I want them to do what they want to do. (Cathy)

However, her view was not totally shared by her husband Will who believed that their children need to be educated for a better lifestyle:

> For me I think they really need an education, I really think they should want to strive for a better lifestyle…there is no future if your children don't have an education. I don't think football is enough, I was a

> professional football player and when that finished and you get an injury like I did, then your world stops, the money stops, you know what are you going to do. (Will)

Although some participants were against the idea of socio-economic status influencing their choices in life, this was not reflected in terms of their own parenting for most of those participants. The participants were keen for their children's education so that they could enjoy a better lifestyle, especially in view of the tough competition in the job market. As Yan and her husband Gary explained:

> Even I think that the most important thing is to get them to have good personality and have the love for nature and happiness in their life, and academics should be the second thing... if I was in China, I raise the kids there, I'd have to put the academic maybe first or the equal because everybody does that. If I don't do that my kids can only go to the worst school and couldn't go to university and couldn't get a job. (Yan)

> At A's [daughter] age you're expected to be able to quote poetry and to have a CV for when you go to preschool. If you don't have a good CV about the awards you've won, you won't get into a good preschool. (Gary)

External contexts such as the social and family environment in which parenting activities occurred also appeared to have influenced parent identity. The external contexts will be comprehensively described in the section regarding contextual influences on intercultural parenting.

Religious Identity

Most participants described religion as one of the influential factors determining the status of their relationship and how they raised their children. The findings in this study extended the interpretation of identity to that of one's religion. Participants from Muslim/Islamic backgrounds strongly associated their identity to religion. The religious identity dictated their socialisation values and hence their parenting styles and practices.

Rajack strongly emphasised his religious identity over cultural identity:

> I do not worry about the culture. The first thing I worry is religion… I am Muslim and she became Muslim… Before we got married we discussed me being Muslim and she said I will follow you. I said I do not want to force you to become Muslim and she was the one who converted into Muslim before we got married. I was worried about it because what about my children? (Rajack)

Rajack's wife Anya concurred with her husband's emphasis on religious identity, especially regarding their children's upbringing:

> Their upbringing! (Anya)
>
> Yes and we have one child…I started to worry about it….what are we going to do about it? So we moved to Bali to raise my son. (Rajack)
>
> We brought that religious culture and all those good quality back here… the way we run our family. Everything is the same as what we do over there. (Anya)

Likewise, Murielle made strong reference to her religious identity:

> I consider myself to be Australian, raised in Australia, initially the ideals of Australia but as a Muslim those ideals changed… my thing more isn't the fact that you live just culturally it's more important for me to live what with good values being those Islamic values… I don't consider my cultural values under that same umbrella as the religious values. I think cultures and religions are not the same thing. That's my view on it. (Murielle)

The participants' responses demonstrated that couples made meaning of their identity in terms of their relational, contextual situations and exposure to the culture of the host country. Identity can therefore be interpreted as more than just ancestral reference and needs to be looked at from the individual, couple, parent, children, and religious perspectives. In this study, Intercultural couples showed numerous and different levels of perceptions of their experiences, compared to some overseas studies that involved mostly Asian and black African people married to white Anglo partners (Hsu, 2001; Killian, 2001; Thomas, Karis, & Wetchler, 2003). For example, when discussing the perception of identity for intercultural couples and parents, many studies focussed on the individual, couple, child and parents' identity (Bratawidjaja, 2007; Cohen, 1982; Khatib-Chahidi, Hill, & Paton, 1998; Luke & Luke, 1998; Rockquemore & Brunsma, 2004).

Individual identity was related to one's ethnic, racial and national background, ethnic exposure and immersion, and one's personality and personal attributes. Couples' identity was related to how they are perceived in the social, familial, political and legal arena, such as societal and family approval or disapproval, racism, looks, perception of their partners, contextual and situational references such as being made aware of it, language limitations, differences in customs and traditions, and insider or outsider status. Children's identity was described in terms of the parental, societal and children's own perception of their identity, such as being primarily Australian, bicultural or mono-cultural. Parents' identity is shaped by internal and external factors such as parenting factors and attributes employed in their parenting role, and the socio-environmental and familial factors in which parenting activities occur.

This study confirmed the findings of those previous studies regarding individual, couple and children's identity. However, it also revealed other aspects of couples' identity, which are very important considerations for intercultural couples/parents. Regarding couples' identity, this study showed that minority status can be also experienced and felt by the host partners. For example, two host partners (Gary and Josh) related their perceptions of feeling the minority status when their migrant wives and in-laws, who were visiting at the time to mind their newborn children, were speaking Chinese and Vietnamese all the time. Gary described his experience as being in Asia by himself.

A study of Anglo-Asian Muslimah in Britain (Mogra, 2014), found that despite the demonstration of fluid identity regarding culture, ethnicity and race, the core identity remains that of being a Muslim. This was confirmed in the present study by two couples. The findings in this present study also extended the interpretation of identity to that of one's religion. Four participants from the Islamic/Muslim background defined their identity as their religion, which is Islam, instead of culture. Their social values and parenting styles and practices were guided by their religious identity and values, rather than being based on cultural assumption. The experiences of intercultural couples regarding religious preferences are further discussed in the next section.

Besides cultural identity dynamics, the participants in this study experienced several challenges such as culture shock, racism and rejection, language and communication problems, values and customs, and gender roles and beliefs in parenting practices. The challenges are described below.

Challenges for Intercultural Couples and Parents

Culture Shock

From the data gathered in this study, it was apparent that all couples faced challenges in their relationships and parenting practices. Some of the intercultural couples reported that their challenges were common to mono-cultural couples and parents. However, they encountered additional and unique challenges as a result of the intercultural dynamics. Most couples reported that they experienced culture shock due to a clash of cultural factors. Four participants described their experiences of culture shock regarding differences in children's behaviour, parenting styles, and family values. Manuel, for example, was shocked at the level of rights children have in the host culture:

> With Australia… this culture does that. It gives children rights and then it gives them the right to stand up to their parents. They don't have any respect. They end up burning factories or running out of the house when they are 14 or 13 and being in the streets which is not good. (Manuel)

Manuel's wife Tammy concurred with his opinion and thinks that parents are too soft with children:

> I think sometimes like we are too soft here. And I think they [husband] are all harder on the children. Here, if a child went without a meal, it would be the worst thing. There it happens quite frequently. (Tammy)

Another couple was shocked at people's lack of friendliness and attitude towards their family in the host culture, compared to the community attitude and friendliness in the migrant partner's society and culture:

> When you see the people on the street or your neighbour, I will be honest with you, I have been here a long time, they hardly say hello. We tried to say hello to our neighbours but they look at us as if we are stupid or strangers. (Rajack)
>
> In Indonesia, everybody is very friendly. (Anya)

Culture shock was also reported regarding the lack of extended family interaction in the host culture. Rajack and his wife Anya reported that they were shocked at the non-existence of extended family influences in their children and own lives:

> If I am in Bali I do not look after my children because they go with their uncles and other relatives. Everyone is offering to come for lunch or go here….go there. Otherwise everyday they are with their cousins. It is not like here…here it is very different. (Rajack)
>
> I have half brothers and sisters but I never see them, nor my cousins….it is quite different. (Anya)

Dharam: Neither your aunties or uncles!

> Yes. It is shocking. (Rajack)
>
> I don't see them either. (Anya)
>
> Even the children hardly know them. It is shocking to me. (Rajack)
>
> They would even hardly know them. (Anya)
>
> But in Bali you know every single person. In Bali you will know your relatives. (Rajack)

The narratives in this study revealed that participants were shocked at some of the cultural differences in family values as it impacted on some of the participant's parenting, relational and socialisation experiences. For example, what constitutes a family was a significant point of cultural difference. Five couples described that in ethnic groups or communities, the meaning of family goes beyond immediate family members and includes secondary and distant relatives, friends and the community. One participant was disappointed when her extended family members were not invited to her host partner's side of family functions. She viewed it as the reason why there are no strong family ties in the western culture. She was in conflict with the difference between the family values of her ancestral home to that of Australia, a view shared by her husband Jim as well:

> Our family does not only go with mother, father, daughter, sons, brothers, sisters and their boyfriend… with Asian family it has to be spread out… they will know that their family will not only be limited which is the Australian way or the western way. There is less interaction and less bonding. I find that one of the reasons why there is no family ties here because they limit and they become exclusive. I noticed that when we first married, when we get invited to his family [husband], straight away in my mind I said "am I the only one invited"… to me the invitation should be extended to me and to my family. Because I am now part of their family but I don't see that in his family. (Michelle)
>
> In other words they don't just get it. (Jim)

The above narratives demonstrated that intercultural couples/parents faced several challenges. Previous studies have described the challenges experienced by intercultural couples from a cultural perspective, such as culture shock (Crippen, 2008; Falicov, 1995; Romano, 2001), racism and rejection (Bhugra & De Silva, 2000), marriage disapproval (Cerroni-Long, 1985), divergent customs and values, religion, socio-economic status, food, communication, raising children (Romano, 2001), changes in family dynamics (Hsu, 2001), concerns about children's experiences (Hubber, 1998), gender roles and beliefs (Biever, Bobele, & North, 1998), and transnational processes (Singla, 2015).

The findings of this current study confirmed the findings of the above studies. Most of the participants in this study experienced some form of culture shock, because of such things as language and communication barriers, food culture, values and customs, gender roles, family dynamics, children's behaviour and parenting styles which negated their intercultural experiences, especially in the early stages of the relationship. Two couples stated that they did not experience culture shock to the same degree as the new immigrant partners because of their previous immersion in the host culture.

Racism and Marriage Disapproval

Some participants expressed experiences of rejection which could possibly be interpreted as racism. Rajack and his wife Anya were upset about the attitude of their neighbours and other people who refused to acknowledge them:

> I have to put up with it... we have been here in this area for fourteen years and we hardly know each other. (Rajack)
>
> They don't want to accept us. (Anya)

Cathy and her husband Will described how their children and they experienced negative racial comments, stereotypes, and rejection from friends. They perceived their friends and parents attitude about their relationship as discouraging and negative:

> It is hard isn't it? I have always been attracted to people of colour and it has never been an issue for me, but I came with him and my friends would say oh he will hit you he is a Maori, they always hit their partners eventually... oh are you sure, you will get comfortable, you won't be expecting it. (Cathy)
>
> The boys get bullied and called niggers by their peers at school. (Will)

Four participants experienced marriage disapproval from their in-laws. The marriage disapproval for three out of these four participants was from the parents of the majority host partner. Interestingly, in one case, it was from the reverse cultural perspective. Bill's wife Azumi was Japanese and her father did not want her to get married to a person from another culture. This highlights the fact that racism can be a two-way phenomenon:

> So I'll tell her I've got a ring here, see if that fits you and it did… so she is going to marry me, but her father won't let me because he doesn't like that kind of intercultural. He got sick and she had to go to Japan to help him. He couldn't feed himself. His hands became fixed and because she helped him feed himself he then changed his mind. (Bill)

Azumi concurred with her husband's assessment of her father's agenda regarding their wedding by nodding her head. In this situation, the discussion is not about equivalency in ethnic and or racial status because Azumi's father, as a member of the minority ethnic group rejected her daughter's marriage proposal from the majority host partner. In this case, it was more of an instance where some people are quite oblivious to the thought of intercultural relationships. However, it is also important to note that this case helps to bring another level of insight and reflection about majority and minority group discourse and understandings which predominantly assumed that majority groups always commanded power in relationships and other contextual domains. The findings in this study bring a different perspective to the notion of majority and minority discourse regarding power and superiority. The deficient perspective has usually been the focus on minority ethnic groups when in fact majority host partners can also experience rejection and racism in foreign contexts.

Oblivion of other cultures and the thought of intercultural relations was also apparent when one of the migrant participants went to his wife's house to seek permission from her parents to marry her. The father laughed it off:

> On my side, it became confrontational because I actually went there to my wife's house and I asked her hand in marriage from the father which is very unique so he laughed it off, "Ho, ho, ho, ho." He's like Santa Claus.

> So they had this culturally, very different view of how people should be and when I came into the picture I was like totally opposite of their lifestyle. So they had a bit of an issue. (Jeehan)

Jeehan's wife, on the other hand, perceived her father's objection to their marriage from fear of failure because of cultural problems:

> My family was more worried that there would be problems… but after three to five years of realizing that there weren't any massive problems, they're like, "Well you can't get much better". (Murielle)

Some participants experienced racism and rejection at a personal level, and reported that it was experienced by their children as well. According to Laszloffy and Hardy (2000), racism is "an act that denies a person or group humane treatment or a fair opportunity because of racial bias" (p. 35) and that "all expressions of racism are rooted in an ideology of racial superiority/inferiority that assumes some racial groups are superior to others" (p. 35). As such, discussions about racism are very appropriate and relevant in studies regarding intercultural parenting. Studies of mixed-heritage children (de la Peña, 2009; Driscoll & Nagel, 2008; Maxwell, 1998) found that children of mixed marriages experienced problems of acceptance in the cultural groups that were part of their heritage. The children's physical traits were identified as the factors that defined their differences. In this study four participants reported this problem, providing some support for Maxwell's statement. Two participants described that their children were racially vilified by their peers at school because of the physical differences to the point that they had to teach coping and defensive strategies to their children. Two other Islamic participants described that their neighbours were racist and would not talk to them and that other people on the street did not want to accept them.

In this study, the difference in the physical traits of participants and their children extended beyond the "black-white" concept, such as in American studies, because of the additional identifying physical characteristics of intercultural couples and mixed-race children from white Anglo-Australians to Asians, Indians, Middle Eastern, and

Pacific Islanders, and black Africans. Hubber (1998, p. 63) drew similar conclusions about the children of Samoan–New Zealand European relationships "who may experience different aspects of racism as the children may range in appearance from European to looking Samoan or Polynesian".

Olofsson (2004) found that intercultural couples struggled with how others in their environment, such as extended families, friends and the community perceived their differences. Cottrell (1990) also found that social stigma and society's intolerance towards intercultural relationships are expressed in the attitudes of families and friends. The findings of this study supported Olofsson and Cottrell's statements. Six participants experienced marriage disapproval from their parents and relatives based on racism and cultural differences. Two participants stated that their close friends strongly pursued them to end their relationship with their then boyfriend and current husband based on racial and cultural stereotypes and stigmas.

Another finding from this study is that racism and rejection doesn't necessarily come only from members of the majority host culture. Whereas the literature usually refers to racism and rejection of intercultural relationship from members of the majority culture host society (Tizard & Phoenix, 1993), this study found that it can sometimes be a two-way phenomenon. Some members of the minority ethnic groups equally oppose marriages to someone from another race or culture. Two minority ethnic immigrant participants stated that their parents, friends and members of their community opposed their marriage to someone from another race, which indirectly impacted on their relationship during family and social events. This study found that the individual and personal characteristics of those participants, such as perseverance, resistance, stubbornness, patience and commitment enabled them to restrain the negative attitudes and sustain their relationships.

Cultural Values and Customs

The narratives in this study revealed that cultural values and customs were significant points of difference that impacted on participants' parenting and relational dynamics. Many parents expressed concerns about the disappearance of important values among children such as respect for the family and society at large, and the need to resurrect those values. Manuel and his wife Tammy emphasised respect for elders and boundaries, which according to them is missing in the western culture.

> Respecting and being helpful to one another and being able to do their best… respecting people because that is what is lacking in this society. You'll find the kids on the train smoking, the fumes and the children are not respecting people, the elders and parents fighting with kids. (Manuel)

> We were always taught to be polite, say please and thank you and things like that. Obviously, it's different now. Society has changed a great deal. (Tammy)

Most couples emphasised moral values in association with religious values and believed that the lack of moral values impacts negatively on families. As Michelle and her husband Jim explained:

> A moral value is number one because this will be their [children] most important tool when they have their own family. It is like this is their principle that they have to follow as they get older. They will be good citizens if they have all these values. One of the reasons people, families deteriorate because there is no values in their family… it has never been emphasised. (Michelle)

> Looking after people, like in the new generation, that role seems to be handed over to other people, putting it off more and more. (Jim)

Cultural values regarding sex before marriage for children was another point of difference among two couples. They described that their values were connected to their religious values and beliefs, complementary to the family and social values. Although Michelle and her husband were staunch Catholics and inculcated strong Catholic values to their children, their perception about sex before marriage was very different. Michelle was strictly against sex before marriage for her children as opposed to her husband Jim who was more relaxed about it:

> When they were in high school I know that in the western world, girls specially will have sexual relationship at an early age. I have emphasised to them about that, to treat your body as a temple, to respect your body. I think they have realized that now because most of their classmates have been sexually active at such an early age. They talked about it now with STD and all that. And I think that is where we disagree that they are old enough to know what is right and wrong. But it is different from my point of view… to the point that I have to bring one of children to a doctor… and let her be aware of the pre-marital sex and be careful with the STD. Apart from the mind belief is my religious belief of being pure before marriage and all that. (Michelle)

> I thought of it more differently. If a child is in their teens… eighteen or twenty-one it will just happen. They are not anymore younger especially if they are with their friends after school. Some Australian kids are sexually active even as young as twelve. And the parents would be horrified with what is going on… but it is going on. (Jim)

In the above case, Jim respected his wife Michelle's perception regarding sex before marriage as a point of cultural difference and accommodation. However, he also accommodated and preferred his wife's cultural values and approach regarding parenting because according to him, they are better for children's well-being. This was reflected in Jim's answer to my probe about how the approach impacted upon their parenting:

> I would still go with my wife's model… I think the children have been brought up more to us as their mum's is the model. That is the model… that is the model from my wife. That is the best model I have… I think the children know what is expected of them from their mother. And we would respect whatever happens in their house. But whatever happens in their mother's house is a different thing. So the children know how to respect their mother and I will respect them. (Jim)

The above scenario regarding sex before marriage was not reflected in other couple's narratives. Society in general is less restrictive of girls and women lifestyle and become more acceptable of women's rights and social justice. Jim's approach could also be interpreted as a conflict resolution strategy. Respect and tolerance for one's partner's culture enhances relational dynamic.

Some participants were not very comfortable with certain cultural customs and values of their partners. Bill described how they had to take off their shoes when visiting his in-laws in Japan. He was very uncomfortable and unhappy about it:

> Well, we went to visit her family in Japan, we had to take the shoes off and then I had to put slippers on which were too small, and I'd be trying to walk inside the house and falling over these slippers… I hate taking off shoes all the time. It sends me bananas… I don't like walking around in my socks. I can't stand it. I'm not happy. (Bill)
>
> And you kept hitting your head all the time… he is tall. (Azumi)
>
> Yeah, so I had to bend down to walk inside their house. (Bill)

The above narratives demonstrate that respect for parents, families, elders and others in authority are important collectivist values embraced by many minority ethnic communities (Chao, 1994, 2000; Gonzales, Cauce, Friedman, & Mason, 1996; Renzaho, 2011). These values are often confused with the "authoritarian" parenting style as opposed to "hierarchical" parenting style, which is highly valued in many minority ethnic communities. Lindahl and Malik (1999) differentiated between authoritarian and hierarchical parenting style in that latter does not necessarily imply unresponsiveness as in the authoritarian style, but rather that elders command respect for their wisdom and experience and not questioned by subordinate members of the family or community in that respect. It also emphasises respect for parents and authorities and strong intra-familial boundaries. The findings of this study concur with Lindahl and Malik's statements. Most couples and particularly all the minority ethnic partners reinforced the hierarchical values in their parenting styles. Most did not agree with the way in which some children from the majority host culture disrespect their parents, elders, families and the authorities, are not interested in education and have poor work ethics.

According to the literature, cultural values and customs are quite resistant to change, and are ingrained in parents' values, beliefs and parenting practices (Gonzales et al., 1996; Keller et al., 2004; Renzaho, 2011). In order to adapt to cultural differences and succeed in their parenting roles, intercultural couples/parents adhere to the concept of mutual acculturation, a term developed by Falicov (1995), defined as a bidirectional adaptation process in intercultural relationships, wherein partners from both the migrant or minority and host or majority culture adjust to each other's cultural values. The process of mutual acculturation was evident in the findings of this current study. Besides learning about each other's language and food culture, most participants reported that they visited their immigrant partner's country so that both they and their children could have a better understanding, appreciation and direct experience of their partner's culture and associated parenting and relational behaviours.

Gender Roles and Beliefs

Couples also faced challenges due to culturally constructed expectations and differences in gender roles and beliefs in different cultural communities. For example, in some cases the husband did not read books to the children at night and did not do household chores because it was not a modelled behaviour from the country and family of origin. Kylie explained that she continues to read books to the children at night because her husband Malai was not raised to do that. As Kylie explained:

> When my husband's at home at night, I go, particularly when the kids were little and read them books and things, he would never do that. And I'd think, "Oh, gosh, he's only home a couple of nights a week, why doesn't he go and read stories to the kids?" But, it only dawned on me the other day that he wasn't raised to do that so why would he? It wasn't modelled thing for him to do that but it was for me, so that's what I do. (Kylie)

> I got to, got to agree because that's good thing for the kid… it's good thing to do. But I don't do it because it's different where I come from. (Malai)

However, there seemed to be incongruence between Kylie and Malai's culturally constructed perception in gender roles and beliefs, particularly about children's sickness. In her household when the children are sick, her husband cares for the children. As Kylie explained:

> But, you know one thing that's interesting when you talk about jobs and roles, when the kids are unwell, he is the one that is up there at night patting them down with a tepid cloth. They go to him, not me, because I'm like no fuss. (Kylie)

Gender roles regarding children's sickness were interpreted as a maternal responsibility among some migrant partners. Two participants reported that in China, when a child is sick, the mother always resorts to her own mother to help with the child's sickness. Interestingly, one male participant was very upset about not being involved in the medical decision-making process when his child was sick. His wife Yan reported that in the Chinese culture, the fathers are usually not involved in the care aspect of children. So she consulted with her mother when their child was sick. This was seen as a common gender practice among ethnic communities. As Yan explained:

> Just after she [daughter] was born my mother was here helping me. When she had something like got a fever and I and my mother worked together to try to gather information from Google, internet, anything and he was so angry because he said my kid, I should discuss with him, not with my mother. I think that may be the Chinese way because normally in China the father would not be involved… because that's women's thing. It's not a man's thing. (Yan)

Interestingly, this perception of gender role regarding maternal care was challenged by Yan's husband Gary. Gary was very upset about not being involved in the medical decision-making process when their daughter was sick:

> I'm also an experienced parent. I've gone through three children before that. I've been through temperatures, teething, nappy rashes, all these

> sorts of things and I think that I have a reasonable amount of input to have into that. (Gary)

Likewise, Daniel's expectations about his son's choice of toys and his views of men and women were very definite and static. He expected his son to be rough and messy and expected men and women to be gender appropriate:

> He's a boy. He likes doing boy things. He's rough, he's naughty, he's messy. His masculinity comes out regardless if you want to go around actions or cultures. I expect men to be men, and women to be women. I don't particularly like androgyny or masculine women, or feminine men… He will see that part from me. I don't want him playing with dolls, for instance. (Daniel)

Daniel's wife Simla disagreed with his gender perception of their son regarding playing with dolls because she perceived their son's interest with dolls differently:

> I will not say that he plays with dolls, but you know like you see the doll, there's a doll there. It's a beautiful African type of doll. Sometimes he picked it up and actually quite liked it and then he said that's mommy. (Simla)

Naomi vented her frustration at having to do everything from looking after their son to doing all the house chores. Her husband Pravin acknowledged that he is less involved in the parenting process and house chores, but reported that it was due to the demanding nature of his work as a restaurant owner. The inference here was that both of them work and needed to share their parental and domestic roles, but the husband was less involved:

> I do everything. Like everything, that's very simple, that answers that, I do everything… I still take him to day care, I do all the housework, I do all the cleaning and the cooking, the folding, the washing, the ironing. I do everything like that. (Naomi)

> Yeah she does most of the things… I still take him to day care… Mondays the whole day he's with me because she's at work. I'd say there isn't a day that he's with her all day from morning to evening. Most of the fun day, Monday, I do that. And on top of that I've been a little busy for the past year and half because I just put up a restaurant and it's demanding there, you can't just leave the business as you know. (Pravin)

Gender roles and expectations are reported to be more rigid in collectivist cultures as opposed to the flexibility of roles in individualist cultures, especially regarding different rights and responsibilities between male and female (Kellner, 2009). Another recent study in Denmark (Singla, 2015) found that "the gender-related responsibility for primary parenting seems to be among women deeply engrained, irrespective of ethnic belonging" (p. 121). Negotiation of gender roles and expectations presents common challenges and reflects the power position in any relationship. However, it was exacerbated for intercultural couples because of the unique characteristics they bring into the relationship, such as dominant discourses of especially upper class South Asian males, who do not want to share household chores (Rastogi & Thomas, 2009). Interestingly, this current study suggested that gender roles were not too much of a challenge for most of the intercultural couples. Three participants reported challenges in gender roles regarding management of the family finances and activities, sleeping patterns of children, and boys' choice of toys. One participant stated that he could not fully execute his parental roles and obligations because of the nature of his work and external commitments. Most participants wanted their relationship and parenting experiences to be positive and therefore engaged in collaborative processes. The shift in parental roles and obligations by minority ethnic partners can be interpreted as an adaptive process to reduce conflict in the context of the majority host culture. Two of the minority ethnic, male partners stated that they would more likely revert to their homeland traditional male roles and expectations if they went back to live in their country. This can also be interpreted as a power dynamic.

Language and Communication

Several participants perceived language and styles of communication as significant challenges and issues, especially for those in relationships with partners from Asian and non-English speaking backgrounds, when it came to communication and interpretation of daily parenting and relational activities and interactions. Three couples often misunderstood and misinterpreted what their partners said because of the cultural way of communicating a message or intention such as the tone used, abbreviations, time taken to think about something and silence.

Gary and Yan described how communication between them became quite volatile because of language issues regarding parental and daily domestic activities:

> We've identified a lot of the issues with language, with speaking, like the way Chinese talk and the way we talk are very different. Chinese tonal language to westerners is foreign and is shown in your speech also usually in first emotion, particularly when English is a second language to my dear wife. Actually I think it was more in misunderstandings that we see the cultural differences. Mandarin is a very different language. It's tonal. If you don't get the tone right, they've got no idea what you're talking about… when we got upset or frustrated about something Yan gets a little bit flustered and her English goes downhill very rapidly. When she gets angry, I wish she would speak Mandarin instead. (Gary)

> I think it's so unfair. I try but he just keeps talking, talking and I couldn't. Sometimes even just several arguments is about could I, could you, or can you just this sentence. I just use can you do something? (Yan)

Five participants described that although their migrant partners spoke English, their style of communication caused misunderstandings and conflicts for the couples. An example arising out of the style of communication is reflected in Gary's family regarding dinner time:

> So when it's dinner time it's chīfàn which means eat food. That's the sentence. There's especially if you use the wrong tone when you're saying stuff, people understand that quite differently and certainly that's what

> happened between us. I would understand quite differently what she was saying. I felt that she was being really short with me and very abrupt, and I thought that was her fault… I felt like she was being rude to me. (Gary)

Manuel and his wife Tammy described communication and interpretation challenges between themselves because of decision-making time frames about family and parenting issues. Manuel takes a long time to make decisions, which frustrates Tammy:

> I take a long time to make a decision and this is because I'm from another culture and then coming to a different culture. So I'm thinking back home I would be doing this like this, how do I do it here. I'm confused because I don't know what the Australian culture is. So it takes me longer and Tammy is waiting, "what have you decided?" and I'm like "I'll get back to you". (Manuel)

> And sometimes his understanding of what I have said is different and then he'll get annoyed. And then I'll talk to him and he will say no and you said this. I'll say no that's not what I meant and I have explained what I meant or what I said and he does take that as an offence and sometimes he thinks she's saying this horrible thing to me when it's not what I meant. (Tammy)

Silence was also reported as another form of challenge in communication style. Manuel and his wife Tammy experienced communication challenges regarding silence when an issue, such as cultural parenting customs and traditions, became too overwhelming for Manuel, but not for his wife who liked to resolve issues as they occurred:

> Yes if something is too much for me, I just keep quiet. (Manuel)

> That makes me cranky with you because I like to resolve things. (Tammy)

In the above situation, there is tension because Tammy's partner's communication style is culturally different to her own. However, despite the communication problems, misunderstanding and subjective interpretations, both Manuel and Tammy reported that they were interested in understanding each other's culture and integrating it with their own.

The motif here can be interpreted as the willingness for Manuel and Tammy to embrace difference and belonging through the conception of "*mixedness*". Participants regarded their partner's cultural dynamics as rooted in their identity.

Some of the differences related to the mode of communication with the children. For example, Cathy didn't agree with the way her husband ordered the children around the house.

> But I will often say to Will, "don't talk to them like that", like he will go out and say "get dressed" and P will say "I'm watching this", and he will say "I said now, do it now" and I say "why don't you just say how long has that show got? Okay in five minutes we are going to switch that off" and Will would be like "because I'm the father and I'm trying to do it now". And, because I'm a teacher probably as well, I know you have got to sometimes give kids a bit of time to say, he needs to stick to a routine, he needs to be told. (Cathy)

Cathy's husband Will agreed with his wife's concern about the way he communicated with the children, but reported that it was a learned behaviour from the way his parents communicated with him and his siblings:

> The way I was brought up your father said stop, you stopped, your mother said no more you stopped, you know go and do that, go and you know, go and get your brothers and sisters ready for dinner you know, I never had "I'm watching TV" and then I guess your way of handling it, I have learned that, the way that I used to fly off the handle and try to be assertive and say look I expect you do this when I tell you to do it and I don't understand there is never, there is no excuse not to. (Will)

This study has shown that language barriers have serious implications for intercultural couples. Barrett et al. (2005) contend that "any language directly impacts how people who speak it understand the world. It affects what we do and don't think about, whether or not there are words for some experience" (p. 57). Romano (1998) also stated that language can contribute to misunderstandings between intercultural couples. Two other studies (Reiter & Gee, 2008; Tili & Barker, 2015) suggested that lack of or avoidance in communication in intercultural relationships results in distress, and "when compared to intra-cultural relationships, individuals in intercultural relationships were more likely to report conflict" (Reiter & Gee, 2008, p. 553).

This study revealed that communication style was a parallel challenge entwined with language problems. Some participants had problems with their partner's communication styles, which led to major misunderstanding, arguments, withdrawals and unhappiness. For example, one immigrant partner, in particular, resorted to his cultural ways of dealing with problems such as silence, withdrawal, time and thought processes, whereas his host partner wanted immediate answers and dealing with problems straight away, thus imposing a western "individualist" cultural value on the minority immigrant partner. Hall (1976) refers to these styles of communication as being typical of "high-context" and "low-context" cultures, respectively.

High-context and low-context communication refers to how much individuals rely on non-verbal cues to communicate a message. According to Hall (1976), high-context cultures prefer harmony and consensus, and are less governed by reason than intuition and feelings. The words are not as important as context, which might include the sender's tone of voice, facial expression, gestures and posture. Many things are left unsaid, with the assumption that the internalised cultural context will indicate what is meant. Low-context cultures, on the other hand, are ones in which information is explicitly stated in the communication. Explanations are expected when statements or events are not clear, and meanings are derived from the situation or event, rather than from an internalised cultural understanding. Hall's interpretation of "high-context" and "low-context" cultures clearly reflects the communication styles of participants in this study. This is exemplified in Manuel and his wife Tammy's case. Tammy, who is classified as low-context culture, from being an Anglo-Australian, wanted immediate answers and resolution, as opposed to her husband Manuel, who is classified as high-context culture and takes time to think about his answers and responses.

However, current empirical research regarding high-context and low-context styles of communication suggests changes regarding disclosure of information in high-context communication style. Hammami, Al-Jawarneh, Hammami, and Al Qadire (2014) examining "reasonable" patients' perception of norms in a high-context communication culture, revealed that (1) even in an overall high-context communication culture, extensive and more information than is currently disclosed is perceived as the norm; (2) the focus of the desired information is closer to benefits and post-procedure's issues than risks and available alternatives; (3) male, post-procedure, and older patients are in favour of more information disclosure; and (4) male, older, and more educated patients may be particularly dissatisfied with current information disclosure. This perception of norms in high-context cultures was not evident in this current study.

The findings in this study support the statements of the above studies. Five participants stated that language barriers and communication styles such as tone, abbreviations, time taken to think and silence created lot of misunderstanding of what was said or intended, thus leading to conflict, especially for those in relationships with Asian and non-English speaking background partners. However, the remaining participants did not report as much of a problem with language and communication, partly owing to their work or study immersion experience in the host country, or because they learned and spoke English in their homeland. This study also found that language and communication were reciprocal challenges for the majority host partners when they visited their minority ethnic partner's country because they could not speak the local language or communicate with their partner's relatives.

From the above narratives, language and communication styles were also perceived and interpreted in terms of power dynamics. For example, mastery of the English language by the host partner during arguments and conflicts, often ended up in decisions being made in favour of the host partner because the immigrant partner experienced difficulty in communicating his/her opinions and thoughts about an issue clearly and effectively. Power has been identified and interpreted as a discrete theme in this study and will be explored in Chapter 4. The power dynamics regarding language and communication will be further explored in that chapter.

Similarities and Differences in Parenting Practices

In this study, participants described their parenting experiences as both similar and different to those of mono-cultural parents because of the uniquely specific characteristics that were associated with their intercultural background. It is therefore important to elaborate on those similarities and differences. The interviews clearly pointed to the fact that common fundamental values and practices were at the core of the relationship and parenting experiences. However, the point of difference was how couples managed and achieved those fundamental values and practices to prevent conflict. The similarities and differences were described for both couples and parents. The primary aim of this study was to explore the parenting experiences of intercultural couples. As such, this section focusses on the similarities and differences in the parenting dynamics of intercultural parents. The similarities and differences in parenting practices are described from an internal and external perspective. The internal perspective addresses the dynamics between the couples/parents regarding parenting, whereas the external perspective addresses the outside dynamics that impact on and influence couples/parents parenting practices.

Similarities

Participants overwhelmingly acknowledged that although there are differences between their cultures of origin, there are also lot of similar parenting dynamics between them such as family values, parental roles, approaches and practices, and parental support. These dynamics were identified and described as essential ingredients for healthy and successful intercultural parenting. As Daniel and his wife Simla pointed out:

> I think that there are a lot of commonalities within our parenting culture. We have a good, loving relationship and love our children, and pretty much I think agree on how we intend to raise our children… we want him to experience a lot and to have an open mind, and any chance for community engagement is very much encouraged so he has a fairly holistic wide range of upbringing. (Daniel)

> I would not really want him growing in one way just thinking it's very individualistic, so he thinks it's just me, me, me. That's why we want that bridge clearly defined so he is aware of others out there. (Simla)

All the participants reported that their parenting practices were influenced by the experiences of their own parents' parenting style and practices, such as what may be termed the "no and yes factor". Some participants modelled their parents' positive style of parenting and others rejected the parenting styles that impacted negatively on them. One participant described how he never experienced a "yes" answer from his father whenever he asked for something that he liked or wanted. The answer was always "no", which made him feel sad or not loved. As a result of the negative experience, the participant described how he never wanted his son to feel like that and provided him with things that he wanted. On odd occasions when he said no to his son, he felt guilty and bad about it:

> If he told me to do something and I don't do it, he was very, very strict. I'm not that strict with my son. Maybe that's why, because sometimes he was strict with me for no reason… if like [son] would want a toy just to give you a rough example, my dad would tell me, no you don't need that. And no means no, end of story… so when he [son] says I want to get that thing Daddy, and I'm thinking if he doesn't get it he will remind me for 10 days. So I just go do it… so I actually learned from that, basically, this is how I'm different to my dad. (Pravin)

However, his wife Naomi had a different and positive experience of parental love and affection. She reported that her parents, especially her mother always showed lot of warmth and had plenty of time for her, which she liked and wanted to provide that parenting experience to their son:

> My mum was, I'm one of 5 children, so she was a very maternal person. She's a very affectionate mother. She had a lot of time for us kids. It was always her intention to always be there for us all the time. All I can remember is mum being home after school every day, you know, she's always there, milk and cookies. In a lot of ways I really embrace that and remember the specialness of that and wanted to provide that for [son]. I do smother him with a lot of affection. (Naomi)

As described earlier, the participants reported religion as one of the influential factors determining the status of their relationship. The religious identity dictated their socialisation values. According to most participants, common religious values among the couples also influenced and helped them in implementing common parenting practices based on their common religious affiliations, values and beliefs. The common religious values regarding parenting were interpreted as being helpful in resolving parenting and relational-cultural differences among the couples. This is explicit in Gary and his wife Yan's case:

> I think maybe the church helps because the church we go is like a multi-cultural thing. (Yan)
>
> Okay, the church that Yan is talking about, we've got a group of people that share values, we're raising children with the same values. I guess they're important for me because of my own religious beliefs. (Gary)

All the couples interviewed expressed common goals for their children. The most common goals included providing the basic welfare needs of children, education, respect for others, and moral and religious values. From the data gathered, it appeared that the welfare and education of their children were the main goals of the participants. Jeehan and his wife Murielle described how important and serious a job it was for them to provide for the welfare of their children first:

> We put aside our own personal desires and wants and stuff like that and became selfless for the sake of the kids, which gives us, you know, I suppose a beautiful thing back there too because we try to do things to make them happy. (Jeehan)
>
> Yeah, we just argue on the spot and try to come to a resolution and the kids see that too. (Murielle)

Most of the participants were adamant regarding education for their children. The focus on education for the children was not only for the personal success of the children in life, but also for the overall good of the community that they belong to and can serve. This was manifested in Daniel and his wife Simla's enthusiasm about their son's education:

> He'll be given a very high level of education. We intend giving him private schooling throughout high school. He will be expected to do university. (Daniel)

Simla agreed with her husband Daniel's views about education and commented on the importance of education for success within a globalised world:

> Because it's a global society now… We believe those things give you the best chance of success in life… that also contributes to the society that you come from, the better person you'll become… We have that ground plastered and solid, then whatever he does out there in the world he will be a model citizen. (Simla)

All the participants described the family and extended family as an integral and important source of stability and support for the children. However, the level of engagement and support, especially from extended families, was a point of differentiation that will be discussed comprehensively in the cultural differences section:

> My family is very strong, aren't they, which is probably not unique for you [husband], because you've got grandparents and aunties and uncles, all living around the same area, we don't have that. I'm really lucky because we have a lot of support from my family. My mum is always there to pick up the kids or look after the kids. She'd be the first person that I always call… I've always respected and admired Malai for his family value and instilling that value of respect for each other, the way he installs that in the children when they fight with each other. He always goes back to them saying, "This is your sister, she is your blood." (Kylie)

Kylie's husband Malai echoed her sentiment about the important role of the family and extended family in children's upbringing:

> So that's good thing for the kid to see that. (Malai)

Kylie and Malai's perception was also echoed by other participants:

> I think family is still a big answer, I mean I have always had strong family in mind but I think it is even stronger on the Vietnamese side, like extended family especially because there is more involvement and I am sure if we lived closer to her extended family we would see them all, all the time. (Josh)

A common issue among parents was parental role and approach to discipline. All parents agreed about disciplining their children but how it was done was a point of disagreement. Most of the female participants described themselves as soft and more moderate and considered the fathers to be too harsh, albeit more effective disciplinarians. Three host partners thought that their husbands were too harsh on the children. This is well reflected in Kylie and her husband Malai's case, where Kylie is quite soft regarding discipline as opposed to Malai who believed that discipline needs to be conducive to the children's conduct, which is also a belief from the way he was disciplined by his parents:

> There have been moments where I thought that Malai is being little bit harsh in the way that he's been reacting to different situations. Because you always say to the kids, "Oh, you know, don't push me there or you won't like it." Like I think they fear him whereas they don't fear me. (Kylie)

> But I know it's pretty much like that in the area, the way I grow up… the kid go la la. I say do it now or I will wreck it. But we can play when it's play time. We play like buddies. So they can know, oh this time it's not playing. (Malai)

> That's true. I think that's really clear, like the kids know when they are having fun with Malai, when he's been playful with them and having a good time but then when he's the father, things certainly are meant. (Kylie)

The data collected in this study highlight an important point about discipline influenced by gender. All couples reported that when it came to disciplining the children, the fathers were more effective or more listened to than the mothers. Fathers were reported as being the "boss". As some participants described it:

> I think the father is more the boss. (Yan)

Dharam: *Why do you say that? Is it a gender thing or what?*

> He's always the one who has a high authority. If I couldn't get her to listen to me, her father could… I think mothers always tend to be soft and fathers are stronger… yeah, the boss of the family. Even the dog knows. (Yan)

Most couples also reported that discipline needs to be implemented based on age appropriate factors. Gary, who is a father of two grown-up children from his previous marriage, described this perception of age-appropriate discipline based on his long term experience as a parent:

> I believe that the children need to learn self-discipline. I believe that they do that through discipline initially. But as they get older, you do reason with them. I don't think that you can reason with a 1-year-old too much because I think your words are falling into space… I strongly believe if you use discipline with children when they're younger, you teach them self-discipline. They learn how to control, how to be self-controlled and self-disciplined and then as they get older they don't need that. (Gary)

Manuel and his wife Tammy expressed strong parental attitudes and responsibilities regarding discipline and children's responsibilities, because according to them, the economic conditions, lifestyle and children's roles are different to Australia:

> I would be most strict. I would use the cane obviously when it's really necessary and we'll go to the field and dig. You know, like teach them more hard work because there is no Centre link… and respecting, teach them to say Mister whereas here it doesn't work they use the first name, so yes it would be different and teaching them to respect the extended families. (Manuel)

> They have to do things around the home, they have their role around the home and the boys have a different role. So that would change in a way. (Tammy)

The data also revealed that many couples supported and believed in smacking as a disciplinary measure. Some participants described the positive effect of smacking on themselves by their parents when they were children. Three participants reported that they smacked their children when they played up, but strongly maintained that it is different from beating children, which they don't agree with:

> We believe in smacking, both of us have always agreed on that kind of thing. We've tried the old counting one, two, three when disciplining the children, we haven't really done too much of the time out option because we found that it wasn't very effective kind of thing. (John)

John's wife Rula concurred with John's belief about smacking but explained that disciplinary patterns of children have evolved as the society's belief about discipline has changed with time:

> I think you try your best and then I know society now is different, everyone, and your kids are going to grow up in the world that is different, everything is just so different from yours. I guess we just try to implant those things to them and hopefully they grow up and they choose to be good. (Rula)

Another migrant participant believed that smacking from his parents had positive effects on him because he did things that he would otherwise not do:

> Yeah, my parents used a cane not once, not twice, which was really good with school. At certain times it just gets you to do certain things that we don't do. Out here, the cane is not allowed, which is bad. You can't smack the kids. You can't do anything. But then at the end of the day if the kids burn the factory or burn the cul-de-sac at the end of the street, they're going to ask, "Who are the parents of this kid?" But really you are trying to tell them, discipline them… but out here, you can't touch the kids. (Manuel)

Manuel's wife Tammy concurred with her husband and believed that discipline in the form of smacking is different from beating a child and is appropriate when necessary:

> You can, but you can't beat them. There's a difference and I think every child, when it's called for they do need a smack, I really think. (Tammy)

All couples, except one, said that they had the full support of their spouses in terms of parenting and family roles. A lot of the support was divided between the working and study hours of their partners and sometimes according to the sphere of influence and what is convenient at the time. One participant described that he did not provide adequate support to his wife regarding parenting because of heavy business commitments. The data gathered also revealed that most mothers looked after the educational component of the children. Fathers, in contrast, were more involved in the socialisation process of the children, such as sporting and outdoor activities, which explains the sphere of influence factor, that is, parents take on responsibilities that they are more skilled at.

> We don't have traditional solo jobs like I guess I do now and Malai often worked at night. During the day, if he can take the kids to school, he will take the kids to school. But we've chosen a lifestyle where we just help each other out where there's a need… He does a lot of cooking when he's home. (Kylie)

> Because my Aussie wife doesn't cook Thai food (laugher)… Okay. I'll tell you about it. When they were a little bit young, we take turns, but pretty much like put them to bed, but because they're big now, I don't put them to bed. K put them to bed, read the book. Oh, it's a good thing, I agree with that. (Malai)

John was also explicit about his particular skill in his family. He did not want to be stereotyped as the typical Australian man marrying an exotic foreign wife so that he does not have to do anything, but at the same time he recognised his weaknesses such as cooking and his strength such as gardening and therefore they have a mutual agreement as to who does what according to their skills:

> I'm aware and I am conscious of being stereotyped by my fellow Australians. I don't want to be perceived as the white man who's married the exotic foreign wife and he just sits back and does nothing and the wife does everything and that's why he married in that culture. At the

> same time I also recognise my strengths and my weaknesses. My weakness is cooking. In that case I believe not so much culturally, but we sort of accept as individuals where our strengths are. Rula mowed the lawn today because I was at work. It needed doing so she did it, but predominantly we stick to our roles and that suits me and it seems to suit her. (John)

John's wife Rula agreed with his description of their respective roles in the family:

> Yeah. (Rula)

Interestingly, from the data collected, it was evident that most immigrant partners, in the event of them going back to their home country, reported that they would revert to the traditional and customary parental roles and values of their home country. This was especially noted in relation to gender, where there was a shift in the male immigrant partners' roles out of necessity and because of what was conducive to the environmental, contextual and situational influences. As Malai explained:

> Because this is Australia, I have to fit in this culture. But in Thailand, I might not do what is considered a woman thing... no cooking, no washing clothes, because of my environment... here if we disagree even like my daughter or my kid, I wouldn't go like with the strong word to them even I'm angry. But in Thailand I might do it. See the difference? (Malai)

Malai's view was confirmed by his wife Kylie:

> He hangs the clothes out and he hangs out the women's underwear which is what he wouldn't have done in Thailand. (Kylie)
>
> We wouldn't do that in Thailand. (Malai)

Another common dynamic among parents was the socialisation process of children. Parents were very concerned about the lack of respect and negative social attitudes displayed by children and did not want their children to be exposed to that. As Rajack and his wife Anya explained:

> The culture is very funny here… the kids are running away, smoking on the street, kissing and stealing. May be my kid does not want to do that but it depends on who he is hanging with and that concerns me. (Rajack)

Rajack's wife Anya agreed with her husband's perception and concerns regarding the socialisation of children:

> I think that there is a part of me that I would want to raise my kids differently anyway. Living here in Australia because you look at so many things differently, like children at age of twelve or thirteen they are already going out and I do not want my kids to be like that. (Anya)

Differences

Intercultural parents/couples described that they also encountered additional and different cultural experiences because of the differences in their cultural values and beliefs, which in most cases were not discussed or were dormant until they had a child that triggered the cultural differences. The couples/parents' differences in cultural and personal dynamics impacted on their parenting practices. Intercultural couples described differences in intercultural parenting practices such as discipline; sleep patterns; cultural taboos and traditional medical practices; children's socialisation process; education; language and communication style; role of children, and the role of extended families.

Most of the participants described that they did not think about parenting issues when they formed their relationship. This was partly because they were more focussed on the relationship. Their cultural differences about parenting emerged when the children were born, thereby prompting them to discuss and negotiate the differences, which will be described in chapter four. Two couples said that they researched the literature on parenting before becoming parents.

Most migrant parents reported that they were very serious about discipline, a characteristic they modelled from the way they were parented as described in the earlier part of this chapter. All the migrant participants said that they did not agree with the way children are disciplined in the host society and believed that parents need to be stricter on the children. For example, Malai thought that his wife needed to change her tone when the children are disobeying her, whereas his wife argued that the child's behaviour can be related to the kind of day he/she had, such as tiredness and was therefore responding appropriately:

> Totally different the way the children in this country grow up. I totally not agree. (Malai)

Dharam: What sort of things are you referring to?

> Like example, say the kid does a thing differently than what you tell them to do and you call that kid and say you are naughty. For me, I don't grow up and sit in the chair watching the television for five minutes… the time out thing… and another thing is, when the kid damaged something they say, "Oh sweetie don't do that. Can't you hear me?" And for me I don't agree with that because we warned them already. (Malai)

> I think he doesn't take into consideration which I probably do because I'm the mother, particularly with our son, he gets very, very tired and I know when he gets really tired, he gets really stuffy and actually gets a bit, sort of rude and verbally abusive, not nice. But, I guess I would make allowances for that but Malai won't make allowances for that and so I think that's a little bit harsh sometimes. (Kylie)

This case demonstrated a clear example of subjective interpretation where one person relied on cultural references for the style of parenting as opposed to the partner's individual and western authoritative approach to parenting, thus triggering the difference.

Intercultural couples described the sleep patterns of children as another area of strong cultural differences. Two participants were more inclined to have the baby in bed with them or at least in the same room as opposed to their Australian partners who wanted to train the child to sleep in a separate room. Both mothers expressed the need to nurture the child in close proximity and breastfeed them whenever required. This also meant that they did not have to leave the comfort of their room to feed the child. Their Australian partners were more concerned about sleep training by having the child in another room and letting the child cry. They also did not want to be disturbed in bed and have their sleep disrupted. This is exemplified in Josh and Ng's case:

> Around his sleep and stuff and the cot sleeping like I brought our son into the bed and I think that might be a cultural thing, I might tend to justify the close sleeping. In most of the world they sleep in the same bed as the parents whereas here it's different… I don't know I didn't feel comfortable with that and also I like feeding him to sleep, just like holding them and nurturing. I think controlled crying and stuff that is very western thing it's not really like I think in Asian cultures or other cultures, if they cry you just feed them or your comfort them. So I think the controlled crying is really hard. (Ng)

> The transition to the cot, yeah it's hard because he has to sleep in a cot but you don't want him to have bad habits. But because sleeping was a bit of a cultural thing, it was just a dilemma… he cries at like 4:00 in the morning and then comes and sleeps in our bed for a few hours and kicks us and we can't sleep, so that's just frustrating sometimes. (Josh)

Breastfeeding was another point of tension among couples and among the extended family. Manuel reported that in his African culture, mothers always breastfeed their children. He expected the same for his children and was very upset when his wife Tammy started to bottle feed their son when she went back to work:

> There was an issue there with breast feeding because I went back to work and he didn't want to feed anymore, and my milk dried up. He wasn't very happy about that and his mom wasn't very happy either. It took me a while to explain to him and for him to understand. If I'm going to work five days a week and he's having a bottle five days a week, he's not going to want to be breastfed. (Tammy)

Manuel and Tammy went on to describe other points of differences regarding cultural parenting practices, such as traditional medicine, umbilical cord and nappies. Manuel and his mother were not happy about Tammy's lack of understanding of their cultural practices.

Both Manuel and Tammy had to explain each other's cultural practices extensively until a compromise was reached:

> I'm not going to just talk on my behalf but on the people who come from a different culture like this baby is supposed to be washed in a certain herbal medicine but Tammy doesn't understand. I brought the medicine from home… But she's asking me, "Why is he showering in this thing?" But that is what is important in my culture that is supposed to be done. Then there is another thing of keeping the umbilical cord. If you don't keep the umbilical cord from my culture, the kids will just loiter around they don't become anything, so yeah. (Manuel)

Dharam: It sounds like that is the point of parenting when you started to notice the differences?

> Yes, I like explaining because I've got different background and I have got to explain myself to Tammy, say, "This is why we are doing this because of this". (Manuel)
>
> One of the things, the boys don't wear nappies and I said well no and the way that we do that is different. We can't have him around without a nappy and going to the shops… it's just not something that is well so I got him in nappies. (Tammy)
>
> Yes. It's for these problems, the way you do that and my mom is telling me, "Oh has he got a nappy? If he's at home don't put on the nappies". I'm thinking, oh, she's my mom, she knows she raised me. So I come to Tammy and she says, "Why are we doing this?" (Manuel)

In this situation, Manuel experienced conflict between his ancestral and his wife's parental practices and how he would be perceived among his extended family and community for adopting his wife's western practices against his cultural parenting practices. Under the circumstances, Manuel and his wife had to communicate and compromise on their parenting practices.

Another area of difference among intercultural couples was the socialisation process of children. Three participants did not agree with their children going out with friends or sleeping over, arguing that they care more about what is best for the children as opposed to their Australian partners who believed in trusting and giving responsibilities to the children. Rajack was very protective of his children as opposed to his wife Anya's idea of building trust in the children:

> With his friends, I want to go to the beach with my friends, I just want to catch the bus, I want to watch a movie. Of course it is not in my culture... I will not let him go. It is not something that children do outside that we do not know. I did not grow up like that. (Rajack)

> I would be asking the questions "who are you going with? What time are you going to be picked-up, things like that". You have to let them go and trust them. You have to give them responsibility to do the right thing. If you keep them locked up behind and pamper them, what will happen when they become adult. Are they going to be wild? And that hurts. (Anya)

> That hurts... that is our culture. I do not worry on everything I just want what is best for my children. (Rajack)

All the parents in this study described that they were keen about their children's education, but migrant parents seemed to put more emphasis on education, both for themselves and the children. When prompted as to why they focus so much on education for the children, they responded that it was: (1) an important value to boost the children's job opportunities, future well-being and better lifestyle; and (2) they did not want their children to be doing what they are doing because of the lack of or missed educational opportunities. As Michelle, Manuel and Tammy explained:

> That is one thing I notice in the western world they leave the kids at year level 11 and let them do what they want and follow the dream. I really don't approve of that and I tried to tell my workmates that. (Michelle)

> I'm pushing her to become a doctor. I've been talking to her because there're certain things I've failed myself... So I'm trying to push her to see that she can do better than me and to do her best. (Manuel)

Manuel's wife Tammy described the disparity in the perception and importance of education between her husband's native country and the host culture:

> In the African culture, study is so important. Here you do not really know when you're at that age. You're not really looking to the future ... or how many children 15 that sort of age really know what they want to do with their futures. They don't know consequences... for us here it's not pushed so much that it's so important. (Tammy)

The above narratives clearly demonstrate a culturally constructed perception of the importance of education and parental concern regarding socio-economic status. According to Leyendecker, Harwood, Comparini, and Yalcinkaya (2005) and Hoff, Laursen, and Tardif (2002), socio-economic status has an impact on how parents raise their children. Most of the parents in this current study strove for a better education for their children and themselves, and some couples wanted their children to be in better jobs than themselves, thus reinforcing social class attitudes. This study showed that minority ethnic partners, especially Asian and African partners were more committed to their children's and their own educational achievements and job opportunities. This attitude was based on the premises that: (1) they did not have the opportunities and financial means to achieve higher education in their homeland; (2) they did not want their children to be in the same situation as them in a country like Australia which has plenty of educational and job opportunities; and (3) that education, better jobs and higher status in society reduces racism and social exclusion. Three participants from the majority host culture stated that they did not worry about what kind of jobs their children have, if the children are happy in what they are doing.

Earlier, differences in parents' beliefs about children's socialisation such as autonomy, trust and responsibility, were discussed. This section will look at parents' description of children's role, specifically children's gender role relating to household chores and children's rights and responsibilities in the family context. Most migrant parents still believed in and ascribed to gender-related roles. For example, according to his

Kylie, her husband Malai still believed in gender-related roles in his family:

> But I think Malai probably expects more jobs from his daughter than he does from his son. Wouldn't you say? So particularly at meal times, he'll ask her to clear the table rather than, I think it's just a default position that you just go to the daughter. (Kylie)
>
> Yeah, because it's a girl thing and boy things are different. (Malai)

Another migrant participant went further in her cultural attitude towards gender role by emphasising and defining the domestic household chores for her children:

> Funny I've heard myself say to my son, you know you're outside, you mow the lawn, it's a man's job. My daughter inside, now she's washing the dishes and cooking. Come and watch cooking, I don't want my son to cook. When I see my husband outside mowing the lawn, I say to my son, pull your boots on, outside. (Rula)

All migrant parents believed that children should be taught hard work and responsibilities alongside rights:

> So I would be teaching them hard work and that is what is important raising the children here… another thing with Australia I think the culture here is to bring up rebels. Children are too much opinionated… this culture does that. (Manuel)

Manuel's wife Tammy disagreed with him that children in Australia are too opinionated:

> Sometimes that's where we might clash because I always say what I think I don't hold back, obviously with respect in mind. So sometimes it can cause issues but I'm not going to sit and say nothing and then be unhappy. Therefore I think we need to discuss things and then come to a medium where both parties are happy. Otherwise what sort of relationship or marriage would that be if one is always unhappy all the time and having to give into everything? (Tammy)

Interestingly, Azumi described how children are not praised for being good or successful in her Japanese culture, compared to Australian parents who praise children and regarded same as positive parenting attributes.

> The way he said my daughter is a first for (inaudible) or something. It's not happening to Japanese parents. Japanese parents never say their children are the best. Oh my children are the best or beautiful or anything like that, but Australian people they admire their children. That's good part, expressive, tell the people like this, but never in Japan will you say like this. People think "ojai baka"... Ojai means appearance, Baka is the fruit. You are two fruits, you can't see. (Azumi)

Besides the internal dynamics impacting on intercultural parents/couples, intercultural parenting also appeared to be influenced by contextual factors. A social constructionist approach attempts to understand participants' experiences of a phenomenon based on individuals' lived experiences and the impact of contextual influences on those experiences. The contextual influences on intercultural parenting are explored in the next section.

Contextual Influences

Social scientists (Bronfenbrenner, 1979; Parsons & Bales, 1955; Rockquemore & Brunsma, 2004) suggested that society is a system of relationships that creates the structure of the society in which we live and that determines one's life and character. According to Bronfenbrenner's (1979) ecological theory, human beings develop within distinct interconnected systems such as the parental system. In this study, the responses from the participants demonstrated that parenting experiences were significantly influenced by broader systems and socio-environmental contexts external to the family environment and intimate relationships. Two participants described that their parenting style was influenced by their interconnected rather than just cultural attributes. Contextual influences that impacted their parenting practices included the environment, extended families, friends, personality/individuality and transnational processes.

Environment

All the couples described the environment, such as their neighbourhood and community as having an impact on their parenting experiences regarding safety and trust. Some participants also described how living and interacting in a culturally diversified environment had a more positive impact on their family and parenting experiences, thus safeguarding their children against racial prejudice:

> We actively engage in the local Tongan community. We have a lot of interaction in the ethnic communities. We also have our church, which is multicultural, and Rula has got some family living here... so they've had exposure to both cultures in terms of the language...Sunday school, the whole thing, church. So our kids are therefore exposed to that as well. Most of the Tongan community events we go to are centred around churches anyway, different denominations. And I guess also what we see in other couples from different cultural backgrounds. We see what other couples do and how they've adapted and then we try and embrace a bit of that. (John)

Other participants said that they altered their parenting attitudes in order to be conducive to the environmental circumstances in which the children are raised so that their children's safety and achievements are optimal. Malai and his wife Kylie described that the physical and social characteristics of their neighbourhoods impacted on the decisions they made about their children's activities:

> In Thailand, the environment is different than here. Maybe it's more about safety and trust. (Malai)
>
> Yes, because we would be eating out on the street more often. You probably spent more time outside there than what you would be doing at home. Yeah, because there would probably be more freedom than what there is here. You spend a lot of time around adults. (Kylie)

The environment impacted on the decisions made by some participants regarding sleepovers by children. Their decisions related to safety and trust in other parents they befriended in a new environment. As Carol and her husband Jay explained:

> We found ourselves in a new environment. We didn't know the parents. We didn't know the kids and we just had an abundance of people coming who we just didn't know who they were. (Carol)

> So if we were back in Wollongong, where we came from, and where we knew and were friends as parents, I don't think a sleepover would be that stressful. Four and a half years ago, I mean when we first came here and I guess the Gold Coast has got that perception of being dodgy and then you let them go and then you think, "Oh, okay. Where are they going?" you know. (Jay)

Manuel described how he had to build resistance and survival mechanism in his children by teaching them to be tough in a tough Australian environment:

> I'm still thinking because this is a very, Africa is rough but I think Australia is too rough. So I'm thinking I might teach him how to become rough as well because if I'm teaching him to be soft, respectful and whatever, will that be enough? (Manuel)

Parental role seemed to be also influenced by the evolving demographics of the society. The very fact that Australia is becoming an increasingly multicultural society and many children are from mixed families seems to bring a degree of commonality among them and less need to get stressed. Also, their children were surrounded by other intercultural students and families at school and their social environment. As Sarah and her husband Samuel explained:

> It is just living in Australia but most of the other cultures are having families really and bringing them up the Australian way. Which is really Australia is a multi-cultural society…in a way we kind of fit that way. It does not seem odd or anything but for me there are no more values or anything from my culture that are a hindrance or advantage or anything… I think being in a school that has different cultures means they

> do see other cultures it is not just Australian. It is a good way that they see other cultures. (Sarah)

> And the culture is not strange to most kids anymore. There are a lot of kids who have mixed culture. They generally do not look different…they have the Asian shape and eyes. But they are not surely being picked as Japanese or Filipino kids. (Samuel)

The literature on intercultural relationships and parenting emphasised that contextual, ecological and systemic factors greatly influence couples and parenting experiences (Belsky, 1984; Crippen, 2008; Crippen & Brew, 2013; Le Vine, 1988; Rockquemore & Laszloffy, 2005). Kotchick and Forehand (2002) also reported that factors outside the family shape parenting generally. The findings in this study strongly supported the literature review findings. Participants mentioned contextual and systemic factors as influencing factors impacting on their relationships and parenting practices. All the participants described how the environment, including positive and negative physical and social characteristics of their neighbourhood, impacted on their experiences of safety, trust and community living and the decisions they made about discipline and their children's activities. Four couples reported that because Australia is becoming an increasingly pluralistic and multicultural society, with many mixed families and children at school and in the social environment, they do not feel like being outsiders anymore, and they are not stressed about it.

Extended Family

The intercultural couples emphasised the importance, contribution and significant role extended families play in the lives of their children and described this as the strength of the collective society. Intercultural couples described getting financial, moral and physical support from their extended families. Most of the migrant participants were raised in collective societies and valued the contributions of extended family members, especially grandparents, in their upbringing. In this study, participants were seen to be encouraging and facilitating the external parenting facilitators. For example, grandparents from overseas visited and supported them during pregnancy, childbirth and well after childbirth:

> The grandparents are here for a year at the moment... also, we plan to apply for my parents to immigrate here... we hope after or even before that, my parents live with us and she [daughter] the little one will see how we treat my parents with respect old people, respect other people and they will learn that because that's Chinese culture. (Yan)

However, the data showed a significant and consistent disparity about the level of involvement and support intercultural couples received from their migrant partners' extended families compared to their white Australian counterparts. A clear differentiation of the extended family influence, as described by most couples, is exemplified in the following description by Pravin and his wife Naomi:

> In one way it is different compared to here. Because there you have a lot of relatives, everybody is around you, like you've got your grandmother, your grandfather, and all other relatives. Having a kid in India as you know is kind of a specialty... my mother never felt like she had a kid because of all the help all the time. (Pravin)

> I guess it's not so close knit. My parents actually moved away from Brisbane, where all the extended families are, my Nana, my aunts... I remember when I was about 4 years old we moved to the Central Coast. Mum says to get away. But I don't remember ever being, I was never left in the care of my aunt or... we visit, we spend Christmas together, but that would be it. (Naomi)

Michelle described how she got financial, moral and physical support from her extended family and was shocked at the attitude of her Australian in-laws when she asked for help:

> I was sick and getting worse. I just told his [husband] mum how I wish Jim can help me so that I can have some rest because I had twenty-four seven, I had twins. What I got from her, trust me, "look listen he is an

> electrician and he needs his sleep". Wow, to get that from my mother-in-law was something that I never have expected from her. That sort of shocked me. I was also in my post-natal depression at that stage. So that kind of support I will never get from his side. (Michelle)

Michelle's disappointment was shared by her husband Jim who added some insights into the contrasting extended family support they experienced in their parenting exercise:

> We used to live on a boat…Mary got a lipodystrophy…she was sick and her sister came and stayed for a week. She cooked broth and so mostly she came to help. (Jim)

Lack of support from the host extended family regarding child care was described as disappointing by several participants because it made it hard for them to juggle between work and their parental responsibilities. The disappointment is reflected in Tammy and her husband Manuel's statements:

> My mum and I think in general, the Australian, the older generations they're more selfish now. They don't want to be looking after the children while we're off at work. A lot of kids are in day care rather than being with their grandparents or their extended family. (Tammy)

> That's a shock to me. Now we don't have anybody if he's in day care, he's sick. Since I took him to day care he's been sick. If I leave the job the government is not going to support me. It's just a conundrum. (Manuel)

Distances between countries and states were also seen as impacting on parental support and cultural exchanges. Most of the immigrant participant's extended family members live in other countries. Simla described how the distance makes it difficult for her son to experience the African extended family culture. However, although her husband Daniel has extended family members in Australia, it saddens her to realise that the Australian extended family is not involved in their son's life:

> It doesn't exist in terms of the Australian extended family. Even though they're here, it's not that very far, but it's never because his family just grew up like that. People do their own thing... yeah, it's a very small family and very individualistic family. So our son doesn't have as much connection with his extended family apart from Face Book. (Simla)

Daniel concurred with his wife's disappointment:

> It's not... my family is 2,000 kilometers away. S's family is back home in Botswana, so we're all orphans in some way. (Daniel)

Although most intercultural couples reported that they enjoyed positive extended family influences, one couple indicated that extended family members can also have negative influences regarding parenting. Rula and her husband John described how Rula's sister was a negative influence when Rula tried to discipline the children:

> I'm glad that we're actually away from my family. Because then I can keep control over my kids. If I was in New Zealand or Tonga, my kids would not listen to me. I had that experience of my sister coming to live with us for a year, my son was so different. He wouldn't listen to me, he was really sulky... Because my sister was here and every time I tried to discipline him my sister would take him away. My sister would have a lot of say in the way I discipline my son. (Rula)
>
> He runs to the auntie for everything. My parents, they may be see things we do that they don't agree with but they won't say anything. (John)
>
> My family will. (Rula)
>
> Which gives us that autonomy as a couple to make our decisions and find that balance, whereas T's family would be boisterous in front of us to do things. (John)

Previous studies reported that Intercultural couples struggle with extended families' stereotypes and intolerance towards intercultural relationships (Bhugun, 2016; Cottrell, 1990; Crippen, 2008; Crohn, 1995).

The findings in this study supported those findings. However, the findings of this study added another dimension of strengths perspectives to the context of extended families. The narratives demonstrated the importance of the extended family support, notably the contributions of the extended family towards participants' experiences of parenting. There appeared to be a divide between the level of involvement and support provided by extended families from the minority ethnic partner's side of the family, and that provided by the majority host partner's extended family. The participants stated that the extended family members, including mothers, fathers, sisters, brothers and aunties from their minority ethnic immigrant partners were very involved in their children's lives and upbringing. Some family members even flew to Australia and helped with their pregnancy, childbirth and caring for the children for several months and this was seen as a very positive contribution to the parenting experience.

Except for two couples, all participants stated that the involvement and support of extended family members from the majority host partner was very limited, and in some cases non-existent. Distance, family conflict, intolerance for intercultural relationships and lack of interest were revealed as some of the reasons for lack of extended family involvement and support. The literature refers to extended family dynamics in terms of "individualistic, collectivist, high-context and low-context" social attributes (Hall, 1976; Hofstede, 1980; Molina, Estrada, & Burnett, 2004). More research needs to be done on why extended family members from the dominant white host culture are not very involved in their children's lives and upbringing.

Friends

The data gathered demonstrated that friends were important source of support and influence in relational and parenting dynamics. Most of the immigrant partners described that living away from their home country, including family members, friends, community, and customs and traditions, left them with a feeling of sadness, isolation, loss, and lack of support in the host country or the new environment they live in. Couples described how they developed new socialisation processes to minimise those feelings of loss and support. Friendship was described by some couples as a significant socialisation process for continued support and enhanced relational and parenting dynamics. The meaning of "family" extended to friends who were seen as family members due to the distance or lack of involvement of family members. Simla described how in the absence of her extended family members, her friends and the community she engaged with became her family:

> That's the way it is here. Family is not blood anymore. When you come from one country and citizen in another country your friends become your family. And so we've created our own networks of people that are friends and family, as well. One of my friends who I've been here with for a very long time, she knows everything. I see her as my sister and my other friends, they are the same. They've known him [son] since he was young. They are his aunties, not blood aunties, but his aunties. He has uncles everywhere. (Simla)

Simla's husband Daniel concurred with her interpretation of friends as family members given the situational context:

> A lot of the people that Simla spoke about, most of them have refugee backgrounds. And sometimes reaching out to others creates your own family network even if it's not blood. It creates a communal family atmosphere. (Daniel)

John described how he modelled his own experience of friends as families to his children.

> I myself have lived with a Samoan family for over 10 years and they're kind of like my second brothers and things. So with our kids we're kind of everyone's uncle and auntie, even the church pastor and they called the wife auntie and so on. (John)

Participants also described their friends as role model for parenting styles and important source of parental tips and advice. As Sarah described it:

> Your friendship will have an impact too. The way other parents discipline or don't discipline and sometimes you think that you are not too strict or too relaxed. So when you see someone else with children go off the rails and how they react to it and makes you think of your own role. (Sarah)

This study showed that besides strong family influences, friends were another significant source of support and influence in the relational and parenting domain, and reduced their feeling of loss and sadness. This feeling of loss and isolation is supported by Cottrell's (1990) and Crippen's (2008) findings about the challenges of living far away from families and relatives. In this study, participants reported that they turned to friends to minimise those feelings of loss and support. Migrant participants described that the friends and the community they engaged with in their new country of residence became their family, thus extending the theoretical meaning of family. The concept of "friends as family" can be related to the concept of "fictive kin" (Chatters, Taylor & Jayakody, 1994; Lee, 2013; Voorpostel, 2013). Fictive kin are referred to as people to whom one considers to be related but who are not necessarily related by blood or marriage (Chatters et al., 1994). These authors referred to the family like relationships that African-Americans have been reported to form with non-related close friends. They argued that African-Americans defined the boundaries of their families flexibly so as to include more distant kin and collateral relatives so as to expand their network. Further research into this concept of friends as family would enormously benefit intercultural families and couples living in another country, far away from families and friends.

Personality and Individuality

The narratives revealed that personality and individuality were other sources of influence on parenting. Some parents related their experiences to their personality type and individual events in their life as opposed to culture. According to Simla, it is just about who they are as individuals:

> For me, I haven't looked at it as a different culture. It just has been about who we are. We were together for a little bit before we had him [son]. We got to know each other first before we became parents. It was a good thing because I knew what kind of things to expect from him. (Simla)

Simla and her husband Daniel also explained the individuality perspective in relation to the daily activities and chores in her family.

> I would never really explain it as culture. It's not that thing being a woman for example, or perhaps an African woman and they should be cooking and doing these things. For me, it's never been a dominant thing in our relationship or parenting. It's just been part of who we are without having to express it. (Simla)

> We both get things done as collective and spend equal time. There's no hierarchy and there's no masculine/feminine structured relationship... we're both quite liberal and well educated. (Daniel)

The narratives identified flexibility as an important personality characteristic that facilitated the incorporation of partner's cultural values and hence a vehicle to reduce conflict. Participants from both the host and migrant context reported that they tried to understand and accommodate certain cultural practices of their partners.

> Certain thing like this baby is supposed to be washed in a certain herbal medicine, but T doesn't understand that... she's working on it... If it wasn't T [wife], if it was a different person who is strong-minded, they would refuse him to shower in that. (Manuel)

> One of the things, they don't wear nappies... and I said well no and the way that we do that is different. We can't have him running around without a nappy and going to the shops... it's just not something that is well. I got him in nappies. But if we were to live over there obviously, then he wouldn't be wearing a nappy. (Tammy)

Other participants believed in their own self-attribute and drive for successful outcomes in life. As Jay described it:

> I think with me, I tend not to focus on too much outwardly, like I don't really feel pressure from my family or friends or anyone. It's me, it's the drive within me, I've got… If it's to do with the household or the finances or education or kids, it's my drive. (Jay)

The belief system was also seen as an important construct in guiding how participants raised their children. Gary, for example, described that his parenting style was influenced by his belief system:

> I think more it's my belief system than my culture. I'm not sure that there is a set cultural way of bringing up western children. It's very ad hoc… I believe that I have a responsibility to mould them and I need to use tools that I have to do the best that I can to mould them. That's not my culture. It's just what I believe and what I strongly believe since I had my first child. (Gary)

Childhood negative experiences seemed to have an impact on individuality patterns and behaviours of some parents. For example, Gary's individual perception of how to bring up his children was also influenced by his own negative experiences as a child:

> What happened to me has influenced me in how I raise children. I've always been a parent with a purpose and a single-minded purpose. What I'm envisioning is the end product and I'm trying to achieve an end product almost with my child and that's a child that I don't care if they want to be garbage collectors, but it's important that they're happy and they are fulfilled in what they're doing. (Gary)

The narratives in this study showed how the socio-environmental contexts shaped the participants' parenting process. In all sociocultural contexts, parenting appeared affected by both past and current situations that dictated which parenting styles and practices were most effective. Self-confidence, degree of safety and trust in the community, and support from friends contributed to the participants' positive parenting experiences.

Transnational Processes

As mentioned in the introduction, the concept of transnationalism refers to multiple links and interactions linking people and institutions across the borders of nation-states. When immigrants engage in transnational activities, they create "social fields" that link their original country with their new country or countries of residence. These social fields are the product of a series of interconnected and overlapping economic, political and sociocultural activities. Intercultural couples and parents live within broader social context outside their relationship in both the country of residence and their immigrant partner's country of origin. In this study, broader social factors included migration, political and religious concerns. Migration concerns involved language and communication, and racism and discrimination problems. Within a transnational environment, immigrant partners described challenges they encountered in negotiating their belongingness. As Rajack and his wife Anya explained, despite the fact that they have been living in their suburb for fourteen years, their family has been the subject of racism, Islamophobia, exclusion and negative attitudes because of their Muslim and religious identity:

> I did see the difference… when you see the people on the street or your neighbour… I have been here a long time… they look at us as strangers. (Rajack)
>
> I suppose people keep to themselves… don't they? (Anya)

Other host partners described how their families were gazed at in public places and comments made about their children and husbands because of their visible differences:

> Because I'm white blonde hair, blue eyes and they are dark, I do get looks sometimes from people… I would never have experienced that if I married a white man. (Cathy)

Both Cathy and Anya were very sensitive to the exclusionary processes experienced by their immigrant husbands. Cathy was particularly sensitive to the exclusionary process based on the ideologies of colour and racism towards her husband and children.

However, participants also described their positive transnational experiences, especially within the diasporic environment. For example, Simla described her positive experiences as a facilitator in helping her African communities to integrate the African network and social environment, and adapt to the host society. This integrative style of acculturation helped intercultural couples and parents to maintain their cultural affiliation, while at the same time being part of the larger host society:

> It's reflected in the work I do with the African (inaudible) Council… It is very reflected in the work that I do working in the multicultural sector… it's the reasons why I'm involved a lot with the African community here. So I can actually create that village and networks around me that my son can also experience the wide range of people around me and the difference, the strength of a community, which is how I grew up. (Simla)

Simla's integrative acculturation activities demonstrate her agency in the host society contrary to societal myths as victims of circumstances, such as socio-economic dependence.

As demonstrated in the above narratives, transnational processes have a significant impact on the experiences of intercultural couples and parents. According to Singla (2015), the problems experienced by intercultural couples are anchored in what she called "outside circumstances as well as inside ones. Politics is perceived as an outside circumstance but in close proximity to the inside one" (p. 145). The positioning of the immigrant partner as the "victim" of the political and social system demonstrates the interplay between outside and inside circumstances (Singla, 2015). This study confirmed Singla's inside and outside circumstantial assertions. Participants experienced migration concerns such as language and communication barriers, discrimination, exclusion, and public gaze. Within a transnational environment, immigrant partners described challenges they encountered in negotiating their belongingness. The host partners in this study expressed sensitivity towards the exclusionary processes of outside forces against their immigrant partners.

According to Singla (2015), changes in the political landscape of Denmark have been marked by polarised ethnic groups, Islamophobia, exclusion and negative attitudes towards multiculturalism. The findings in this study confirmed and extended Singla's arguments. Although Australia officially embraces multiculturalism, the political landscape and public opinion have been recently increasingly marked by polarised ethnic groups, Islamophobia, exclusion and negative attitudes against immigration and refugee settlement, especially those from Islamic faith backgrounds.

Transnationalism, however, also had some positive effects on immigrant participants' experiences such as diasporic community social engagement, adaptation and integrative acculturation. For example, two immigrant partners actively engaged in their diasporic community events and functions to sustain their cultural identity, beliefs, and customs and values, as well as promoting same to their offspring and host partners. The immigrant partners also utilised the transnational process as a vehicle to utilise their human capitals to assist members of their diasporic communities to adapt to the host society. In this study, most of the immigrant partners were highly skilled, had good jobs and enjoyed good socio-economic status, thus challenging the myths and stereotypes that immigrant partners are victims of circumstances, passive and economic dependents. The next section discusses benefits and opportunities of intercultural parenting.

Benefits and Opportunities of Intercultural Parenting

The positive elements of intercultural parenting were apparent in all the participants' exciting descriptions of how their experiences enriched their lifestyle and family life. The positive experiences intercultural couples encountered in their relational dynamics were reported to impact on how they raised their children. Given the extent of the benefits and opportunities identified, it was important to recognise those as the strength of intercultural relational and parenting dynamics. The benefits to parents/couples and children will be described separately to allow an in-depth understanding and appreciation of the extensive benefits and opportunities intercultural families experienced and enjoyed. This section will describe the perceived benefits to parents, followed by benefits to children.

Benefits to Parent Couples

Benefits and opportunities for intercultural couples were reported as richness of both worlds, learning another model of parenting, holistic family life, and cultural competency. Participants described how fascinated they were experiencing the richness of travelling to their migrant partner's country, meeting their extended families and participating in the local culture and traditions. This fascination was exemplified in Kylie' statement:

> When I went to his family, I was just fascinated because it was a place where not many foreigners or in fact, no foreigners, had ever been before. I got to learn about how to make exotic cakes. Your mum was making banana food with banana leaves. I love all that creating sort of stuff. It seemed a very simple sort of life and to me it was very appealing. And everyone was very friendly and lots of people were coming, and it was all about food and talking and socializing [laughter] I mean it brings more richness to my life and my children's lives. (Kylie)

Kylie's husband Malai shared her jubilant emotions:

> Over there they say every day is happy day… it is like this in our culture. (Malai)

The food culture of migrant partners was reported to be more appealing than that of the host partner, which was interpreted as enriching the host partners' lifestyle. Samuel and Gary described their excitement about being able to share their migrant wives' food culture:

> My food culture was very plain and boring, just an Aussie steak and veggies. Whereas that really impacted on the way we like to eat Asian food and live our lives now. (Samuel)

> Food, to me it's food. I love food from different cultures. It was really good. Enjoying food together, steamed buns, and all sorts of stuff. I love Asian culture. I love the food. I love the variety of food. I could go to China and go from restaurant to restaurant. We both miss the Chinese food from China. (Gary)

The intercultural relationship was viewed as creating opportunities for intercultural parent couples to be exposed to other forms of parenting. Most parents reported that they learnt another way of parenting which added value to their own and children's lives. Gary and his wife Yan described how they experienced and learnt about the dimensions of softness and discipline in parenting from each other:

> I think Yan brings an incredible softness in A [daughter]. She's a very soft person and I think that that has an impact on our daughter. Yan is an incredibly soft and gentle natured person. I think that that puts another dimension into the parenting that I don't have that softness because I am single-minded, I am focused and I'm trying to achieve something within her… It's a learning experience for me in being soft and having that sort of nature. It's something that I'm not used to. I didn't grow up with any of that. (Gary)

> One thing for me from his side [husband] is discipline. Discipline is a big thing I've learned. Yeah, it's like love is not the only thing you have to do. When you discipline them you love them for the future. (Yan)

Azumi explained the benefit she gained from marrying an Australian in terms of gender role limitations in her culture of origin when it comes to parenting. In Japan, she reported that women are solely responsible for raising children. She was able to experience a negotiated parenting role with her Australian husband as opposed to strict cultural values and expectations about gender roles when it comes to parenting in Japan.

> I think because maybe Japanese men always working hard and then I can't do everything, no time. So here Bill, he's more involved with education or concerned about children. So that is my benefit for being married to an Australian guy. (Azumi)

Cathy described how her husband Will learnt new ways of communicating with the children based on his own negative childhood experience. Will was brought up in a very violent and authoritarian family setting and had a tendency to parent the same way, especially with the boys. Cathy convinced Will to communicate instead with the boys, which resulted in better parenting outcomes:

> I think the boys are well rounded. They have learnt to communicate because you didn't use to communicate a lot did you, like your family weren't really communicating in that way, so they have learnt to talk things through and to communicate more. (Cathy)

> They voice their opinion which was never in any of our household. (Will)

Participants reported that they found other positive aspects of parenting and living that they never experienced in their own environment and upbringing. Tammy described some aspects of parenting different to her own:

> Yes, I think the way that they are just encouraging study and work ethics, not be lazy, they see things differently… I think people would work harder if Australians took a leaf out of that book. They would have more qualifications for better jobs. (Tammy)

Perception of holistic family life was of concern among some host participants when exposed to and compared to their migrant partner's upbringing. Three participants described that they did not grow up in healthy family environments, compared to their partner's rich family life. They experienced poor or non-existent family life in their own upbringing. They really got a sense of healthy and holistic family life when they formed their own intercultural relationships and were exposed to healthy dynamics in their partners' parent's relationships.

Daniel described how being with a partner from another culture made his family more complete and holistic.

> For me, I think, having Simla's cultural influence about family has made me or made our family perhaps more complex. (Daniel)
>
> Not in a bad way. (Simla)
>
> No. Not in a bad way. Complex and holistic, and perhaps more inclusive and wide-scoping than if it had just been a typical Anglo-Saxon upbringing. (Daniel)

Josh and his wife Ng echoed Daniel's sentiment about acquiring strong family values, which was lacking in Josh's environment.

> I mean I have always had strong family in mind but I think it is even stronger on the Vietnamese side, like extended family especially because there is more involvement and I am sure if we lived closer to her extended family we would see them all, all the time. (Josh)
>
> Yes, strong family values drawing that from the Vietnamese side. (Ng)

Intercultural couples described that the exposure to their partners' world, people and other cultural entities gave them cultural ascendency and competency over those in mono-cultural relationships. They described the positive cultural attributes they gained such as sensitivity to, empathy and tolerance of cultural dynamics, adaptability and flexibility and open-mindedness. John described how he now understood why his wife does things the way she does:

> In terms of being more bicultural in the way I approach things, understanding sometimes things that frustrates me, that may be Rula might do. But I sort of sit back and think that she's Rula and she's not raised the way I was raised, don't worry too much about it. (John)

Samuel explained how he became more open-minded and thought outside the box:

> Also for me, it opens my mind like an outgoing Aussie and never thinks of going to Asia. But meeting an Asian girl I have been to Asia a lot. The Asian arts, I guess from that in mind, I am going that way, going towards Asian influence with arts, food, travel and we go to Asia more often than we have been to Europe. I did not have that influence before. (Samuel)

Anya described how tolerance for each other's culture enhanced her relationship with her husband:

> I think as you said you know, you have an open mind, you have the benefit of referring back to that type of culture. You can give and take in different things. We get along because I agree so much for his culture. (Anya)

Benefits to Children

Parents perceived that their children benefitted enormously from belonging to an intercultural family and being brought up by intercultural parents. The benefits were described as unique benefits unknown to children from mono-cultural families, including: best of both worlds; job opportunities, adaptability/tolerance/acceptance/open-mindedness, and food culture. Naomi and her husband Pravin reported that by encouraging their son to be bicultural has benefitted and enriched his life:

> I think it's wonderful that he's [son] being not just exposed to another culture, but learning about another culture and how daddy grew up... He talks about India and points to it on the map. He knows that's where Nana lives. That's an experience for a child who grew up in Australia doesn't have. And he even said to me the other day when we were at a shopping centre "mommy they're speaking Punjabi. It's a foreign language". So I think it's been not just a wealth of knowledge for him, but a beautiful experience to really share in another culture and that's going to benefit him throughout his life, not just as a child. (Naomi)

Naomi's husband Pravin concurred with her view and elaborated further that their son's exposure to two different cultures was benefitting him in his developmental growth as he was able to take the positives from both cultures. For example, growing up in the Australian context gave their son the tools to be strong and independent, and exposure to the Indian culture taught him the notion of positive love:

> The positive in Australia is that he's been given the tools to grow up to be a strong independent young boy, and the positive from the Indian culture is that he continues to be shown a hundred percent positive love, he will know that he'll never be alone, we're not going to kick him out when he's 16. (Pravin)

Two other participants reported that exposure to other cultures taught their children about non-materialism, and respect for people. As Tammy explained:

> But they also get to see the other sides where life is not about materialism, but life is about being kind to people, respecting people and helping… If you have only one culture, for example just Australian culture, they don't know what else is out there in the world. (Tammy)

There was a perception among most of the participants that mixed-race children are more beautiful and it increases their chances of getting jobs. This viewpoint is related to the biological phenomenon termed hybrid vigour, which suggests that cross-breeding produces children who are genetically fitter than their parents. According to Ziv (2006), cross-bred individuals show qualities superior to those of their parents. Also, mixed-race people are biologically different and prettier than non-mixed (non-white) people by nature. Gary was very adamant about the hybrid vigour phenomenon and its associated benefits to his daughter:

> So I think that being incredibly beautiful because of her mixed race, she's just going to have a fantastic life. I think because while looks aren't everything, and whether we like it or not, apparently studies of employment have shown that you're more likely to get a job if you're good looking. (Gary)

Gary's observation can be interpreted from a strength-based perspective against societal negative stereotypes about mixedness and discourse regarding mixed-children. It could also be in keeping with the ethos of the global elite. However, hybrid vigour does not just apply to the biology of sex, and not all crosses between genetic backgrounds have positive outcomes. There are also instances where *crosses* between genetic backgrounds may have negative consequences. Many adverse and damaging recessive alleles are masked in people of hybrid origin. This does not mean that science is fiction. It's just that the cultural narrative framework puts pressure upon how we interpret scientific propositions and assertions, especially in areas which require personal expressive frankness and honesty. Besides the biology of sex, vigour can also be contributed to the environment and one's socio-economic status, such as geographic areas, hygiene, financial capacities, beauty products and changes to physical looks and attributes from cosmetic surgeries such as in Asia and among the elites. In real terms, genetics are basically a foundation to one's health. As Ziv (2006) also postulated, besides genes, other factors such as discipline, dedication and near obsessive training, proper nourishment, free from toxins, and regular exercise' contribute to a healthier disposition.

Gary went further to describe that his daughter being bilingual enables her to establish business and employment opportunities in the emerging economies of countries like China where her mother's side of parents and grandparents are from:

> There's 1.4 billion Chinese. Being able to speak Mandarin is going to be an incredible asset for her as she grows up… with China being the emerging world economy, she'll be able to facilitate business over there if she wants to because she can go over there and speak Chinese and English fluently, and sort of be interchangeable between the two. (Gary)

Gary's wife Yan concurred with her husband that their children being bilingual is beneficial for their future:

> She can go and work there and speak the language. (Yan)

Children belonging to intercultural families and relationships were reported to be more adaptable, tolerant, accepting and open-minded to other cultures. All the participants reported those qualities in their children from belonging to two cultures. As Michelle and her husband Jim explained:

> They are more adaptable because they are exposed to two cultures… They have built tolerance from knowing themselves as culturally different and assimilated well. What matters to others would not matter to the children. We came from a different world. We light a candle for the night, whereas if the electricity went out with an Australian couple, they would say what kind of holiday is this. (Michelle)
>
> Absolutely. (Jim)

Jeehan and Murielle described how their children became accepting of everybody:

> They're more worldly, like even the teachers have said that the kids are very worldly, they're very accepting of everybody that they don't, you know, they're not judging. (Jeehan)
>
> If you look at our kids and their friends, like my son's best friend was a Chinese kid. My daughter is best friends with a Lebanese girl and it's like her best friend is like an Australian girl. So it's allowed them to see the class, a different class of people, a different diversity of cultures and be accepting to them so they can be friends with anybody. (Murielle)

Children belonging to intercultural families were also reported to benefit from the food culture of their intercultural parents. Azumi described the benefits of the food culture for her children:

> I think they can have both cultures and different foods, better. Because the other children didn't know nourishment, (inaudible), they couldn't eat. My children it doesn't matter anything they can eat. They can eat Australian food or Japanese sushi, or rice bowl, anything. Beans, pickles, or anything they can eat but other Australian children can't eat because it's from when they were born they get both things. So more variety for anything that is edible. (Azumi)

Much of the literature on intercultural marriages and mixed-heritage children has focused on the challenges and constraints couples and children encountered within such domains. Given the increasing globalised world and multicultural relationships and mixed-race children, more research is now emerging showing the benefits of being intercultural (Bhugun, 2016; Bratawidjaja, 2007; Crippen, 2008; Keller et al., 2004; Molina et al., 2004). Bratawidjaja (2007) stated that intercultural couples "found themselves to be stronger individuals and couples because they focussed on their strengths instead of their weaknesses and the uniqueness they brought into both the marriage and parenting" (p. 184). Keller et al. (2004) claimed that the process of parenting enables the transmission of cultural values. Molina et al. (2004) argued that intercultural relationships facilitate a richness that is less likely to occur in mono-ethnic couples. Crippen (2008) identified opportunities that extended to both parents and individuals such as access to other models of parenting, plasticity of roles and enhanced cultural competency. Plasticity of roles refers to increased flexibility in gender roles in intercultural relationships.

Hubber (1998) argued that a child who has been socialised into a family which has successfully negotiated culture differences, "is uniquely prepared to deal with issues relating to those dimensions of difference between people, culture and other group comparisons, as well as the discrimination society accords to the minority groups differing from the 'norm'… and that this ability would be less likely to be fostered in a family which is 'mono-cultural' because cultural difference is not a salient issue" (p. 69). The findings of this study concur with statements by Bratawidjaja, Crippen, Hubber, Keller et al. and Molina et al. However, this study could not develop the ideas of the above researchers regarding benefits and opportunities experienced by the mixed-race children because they were not involved in the study. The participants' perception of their children's positive experiences was based on their own observational assessment of the children's activities, developmental growth and socialisation processes within the family, and outside the family.

Participants in this study reported that their children inherited the richness and best of both worlds and have ownership of two different cultures. The fact that the children developed cultural competency, spoke another language and inherited "hybrid vigour", that is, they are beautiful from being mixed-children (Lewis, 2010; Ziv, 2006), increased their job opportunities in Australia and globally. Participants reported that the food culture was a rich experience for the children as they were exposed to and could enjoy so many different dishes, compared to mono-cultural children. Participants also reported adaptation, acceptance, tolerance and open-mindedness as other positive characteristics that the children developed from being bicultural.

All the participants reported that they also enjoyed the above benefits experienced by their children, as well as other benefits and opportunities as intercultural couples. The benefits included other models of parenting from being exposed to parenting in other cultures, and holistic family life from being exposed to healthy family environments in their partners' culture, compared to the poor or non-existent family life in their own upbringing.

This study also highlighted the benefits and positive effects of partner selection and relationship standard, whereupon couples selected their partners based on characteristics that they found attractive, such as exotic characteristics and other factors that they had in common such as having similar faith and family values. The context of partner selection based on relationship standards and commonalities were found to reduce intercultural conflicts and motivated couples to manage any relational and parenting issues. For couples who have been in long term relationship, partner selection and convergence on relationship standards helped to achieve (a) easier parenting dynamics, (b) better relationship satisfaction, (c) less stressors, and (d) facilitates positive integration/adaptation processes. This finding supported previous studies regarding relationship standards in partner selection (Hiew, Halford, Van de Vijver, & Liu, 2015) revealing that almost all cultural combinations of partners shared greater similarity on standards. Also, across cultural combinations, high agreement between partners on both standards, predicted high relationship satisfaction.

According to the participants, the experience of being an intercultural couple and raising mixed-children was a rich intercultural phenomenon. From the above narratives, it was clear that all intercultural couples encountered positive experiences for themselves and their children as a result of their unique cultural affiliations. The differences were regarded as strengths and benefits that superseded mono-cultural parenting experiences. This study identified some other important issues that impacted on parent couple's experiences regarding parental and relational dynamics such as power relations, reverse acculturation, and negotiation of differences. These are described in the next chapters.

Summary of Cultures Coming Together

This chapter described participants' experiences as intercultural couples and parents. The major theme included: cultures coming together. The experiences were described as both similar to parenting dynamics and different because of the intercultural characteristics. All couples encountered internal and external challenges regarding relational and parenting dynamics. Internal challenges related to identity issues, culture shock, racism and marriage disapproval, cultural values, gender roles, language and communication, and differences in cultural beliefs and parenting practices such as values regarding children's socialisation and developmental processes.

The external influences such as the environment, community, friends, extended families, personal attributes and transnational processes played a significant role in intercultural couple's lives and parenting processes. The degree of support they received from their environment, social network and the family determined the quality of their experiences as intercultural couples/parents.

The narratives showed that despite the challenges that intercultural couples experienced, they and their children also enjoyed many benefits and opportunities from their intercultural relationship. The benefits and opportunities for intercultural parent/couples were reported as richness of both worlds and cultures, exposure to other models of parenting, cultural competency, and a holistic family experience. The benefits and opportunities for their children were reported as belonging to two cultures, cultural awareness and competency, job opportunities, open-mindedness and the food culture.

Interestingly, many of the couple's experiences were also impacted by other internal and external dynamics such as power, mainly regarding parenting and relational issues, acculturation processes, how they negotiated differences, and will be described in the next chapter.

References

Barrett, S., Chin, J. L., Diaz, L. C., Espin, O., Greene, B., & McGoldrick, M. (2005). Multicultural feminist therapy: Theory in context. *Women & Therapy, 28*(3/4), 27–61. https://doi.org/10.4324/9780203047125.

Belsky, J. (1984). The determinants of parenting: A process model. *Child Development, 55*(1), 83–96. https://doi.org/10.2307/1129836.

Bhugra, D., & De Silva, P. (2000). Couple therapy across culture. *Sexual and Relationship Therapy, 15*(2), 184–192.

Bhugun, C. D. (2016). *The experiences of intercultural parenting in Australia* (PhD thesis). Southern Cross University, Australia.

Biever, J. L., Bobele, M., & North, M. W. (1998). Therapy with intercultural couples: A post-modern approach. *Counselling Psychology Quarterly, 11*(2), 181–188. https://doi.org/10.1080/09515079808254053.

Bratawidjaja, A. (2007). *The experience of being parents of mixed-heritage children: Phenomenological analysis* (Unpublished doctoral dissertation). Kansas State University, Kansas.

Bronfenbrenner, U. (1979). *The ecology of human development.* Cambridge, MA: Harvard University Press.

Cerroni-Long, E. L. (1985). Marrying out: Socio-cultural and psychological implications of intermarriage. *Journal of Comparative Family Studies, 16*(1), 25–46.

Chao, R. K. (1994). Beyond parental control and authoritarian parenting style: Understanding Chinese parenting through the cultural notion of training. *Child Development, 65*(4), 1111–1120. https://doi.org/10.2307/1131308.

Chao, R. K. (2000). The parenting of immigrant Chinese and European American mothers: Relations between parenting styles, socialization goals, and parental practices. *Journal of Applied Developmental Psychology, 21,* 233–248. https://doi.org/10.1016/so193-3973(99)00037-4.

Chatters, L. M., Taylor, R. J., & Jayakody, R. (1994). Fictive kinship relationships in black extended families. *Journal of Comparative Family Studies, 25*(3), 297–312.

Cohen, N. (1982). Same or different? A problem of identity in cross-cultural marriages. *Journal of Family Therapy, 4*(2), 177–199.

Cottrell, A. (1990). Cross-national marriages: A review of the literature. *Journal of Comparative Family Studies, 21*(2), 151–169.

Crippen, C. (2008). *Cross-cultural parenting: Experiences of intercultural parents and constructions of culturally diverse families* (Unpublished doctoral dissertation). University of New England, Australia.

Crippen, C., & Brew, L. (2013). Strategies of cultural adaptation in intercultural parenting. *The Family Journal: Counselling and Therapy for Couples and Families, 21*(3), 271–263.

Crohn, J. (1995). *Mixed matches: How to create successful interracial, interethnic, and interfaith relationships*. New York: Random House.

de la Peña, M. (2009). *We were here*. New York: Delacorte Press.

Driscoll, A., & Nagel, N. G. (2008). *Early childhood education, birth–8: The world of children, families, and educators*. Boston, MA: Allyn & Bacon.

Falicov, C. J. (1995). Cross-cultural marriages. In N. S. Jacobson & A. S. Gurman (Eds.), *Clinical handbook of couple therapy* (pp. 231–246). New York: Guildford.

Gonzales, N. A., Cauce, A. M., Friedman, R. J., & Mason, C. A. (1996). Family, peer, and neighbourhood influences on academic achievement among African American adolescents: One year prospective effect. *American Journal of Community Psychology, 24*(3), 365–387.

Hall, E. T. (1976). *Beyond culture*. New York: Doubleday.

Hammami, M. M., Al-Jawarneh, Y., Hammami, M. B., & Al Qadire, M. (2014). Information disclosure in clinical informed consent: "Reasonable" patient's perception of norm in high-context communication culture. *BMC Medical Ethics, 15*(1), 3.

Hiew, D. N., Halford, W. K., Van de Vijver, F. J. R., & Liu, S. (2015). Relationship standards and satisfaction in Chinese, Western, and intercultural Chinese-Western couples in Australia. *Journal of Cross-Cultural Psychology, 46*(5), 684–701.

Hoff, E., Laursen, B., & Tardif, T. (2002). Socioeconomic status and parenting. In H. Bornstein (Ed.), *Biology and ecology of parenting* (pp. 231–252). Mahwah, NJ: Erlbaum.

Hofstede, G. (1980). *Culture's consequences: International differences in work-related values*. Beverly Hills, CA: Sage.

Hsu, J. (2001). Marital therapy for intercultural couples. In W. S. Tseng & J. Streltzer (Eds.), *Culture and psychology: A guide to clinical practice* (pp. 225–242). Washington, DC: American Psychiatric Publishing.

Hubber, T. (1998). *An exploration of intercultural parenting: The experience of Samoan & New Zealand-European couples* (Unpublished dissertation). University of Auckland, New Zealand.

Keller, H., Lohaus, A., Kuensemueller, P., Abels, M., Yosvi, R., Voelker, S., & Mohite, P. (2004). The bio-culture of parenting: Evidence from five cultural communities. *Parenting: Science and Practice, 4*(1), 25–50.

Kellner, J. (2009). Gender perspective in cross-cultural couples. *Clinical Social Work Journal, 37*(3), 224–229. https://doi.org/10.1007/s10615-009-0214-4.

Khatib-Chahidi, J., Hill, R., & Paton, R. (1998). Chance, choice and circumstance: A study of women in cross-cultural marriages. In R. Breger & R. Hill (Eds.), *Cross-cultural marriage: Identity and choice* (pp. 49–66). Oxford: Berg.

Killian, K. D. (2001). Reconstituting racial histories and identities. *Journal of Marital and Family Therapy, 27*(1), 27–42. https://doi.org/10.1111/j.1752-0606.2001.tb01137.x.

Kotchick, B. A., & Forehand, R. (2002). Putting parenting in perspective: A discussion of the contextual factors that shape parenting practices. *Journal of Child and Family Studies, 11*(3), 255–269. https://doi.org/10.1023/A:1016863921662.

Laszloffy, T., & Hardy, K. (2000). Uncommon strategies for a common problem: Addressing racism in family therapy. *Family Process, 39*(1), 35–50. https://doi.org/10.1111/j.1545-5300.2000.39106.x.

Lee, C. (2013). *Fictive kinship: Family reunification and the meaning of race and nation in American immigration*. New York: Russell Sage Foundation.

LeVine, R. A. (1988). Human parental care: Universal goals, cultural strategies, individual behaviour. In R. A. LeVine, P. M. Miller, & M. Maxwell West (Eds.), *Parental behaviour in diverse societies* (pp. 3–12). San Francisco: Jossey-Bass.

Lewis, M. B. (2010). Why are mixed-race people perceived as more attractive? *Perception, 39*(1), 136–138. https://doi.org/10.1068/p6626.

Leyendecker, B., Harwood, R. L., Comparini, L., & Yalcinkaya, A. (2005). Socioeconomic status, ethnicity, and parenting. In T. Luster & L. Okagaki (Eds.), *Parenting: An ecological perspective* (pp. 319–341). Hillsdale, NJ: Lawrence Erlbaum.

Lindahl, K. M., & Malik, N. M. (1999). Observations of marital conflict and power: Relations with parenting in the triad. *Journal of Marriage and the Family, 61*(2), 320–330. https://doi.org/10.2307/353751.
Luke, C., & Luke, A. (1998). Interracial families: Difference within difference. *Ethnic and Racial Studies, 21*(4), 728–753. https://doi.org/10.1080/014198798329847.
Maxwell, A. (1998). Not all issues are black or white: Some voices from the offspring of cross-cultural marriage. In R. Bregger & R. Hill (Eds.), *Cross-cultural marriage: Identity and choice* (pp. 129–152). New York: Berg.
Mogra, I. (2014). Anchoring identity in faith: Narrative of an Anglo-Asian Muslimah in Britain. *The Qualitative Report, 19*(3), 1–22.
Molina, B., Estrada, D., & Burnett, J. A. (2004). Cultural communities: Challenges and opportunities in the creation of "Happily Ever After" stories of intercultural couplehood. *The Family Journal: Counselling and Therapy for Couples and Families, 12*(2), 139–147.
Olofsson, E. (2004). Review of cross-cultural marriage: Identity and choice. *Transcultural Psychiatry, 41*(2), 300–301.
Parsons, T., & Bales, R. F. (1955). *Family socialisation and interaction process*. New York: Free Press of Glencoe.
Rastogi, M., & Thomas, V. K. (Eds.). (2009). *Multicultural couple therapy*. New Delhi: Sage.
Reiter, M. J., & Gee, C. B. (2008). Open communication and partner support in intercultural and interfaith romantic relationships: A relational maintenance approach. *Journal of Social and Personal Relationships, 25*(4), 539–559. https://doi.org/10.1177/0265407508090872.
Renzaho, A. M. N. (2011). *Parenting in a new culture: A challenge for African migrant families*. Retrieved September 14, 2011, from http://www.deakin.edu.au/news/2011/260711africanmigrants.php.
Rockquemore, K. A., & Brunsma, D. L. (2004). Negotiating racial identity: Biracial women and interactional validation. In A. R. Gillem & C. A. Thompson (Eds.), *Biracial women in therapy: Between the rock of gender and the hard place of race* (pp. 85–102). New York: Haworth Press.
Rockquemore, K. A., & Laszloffy, T. (2005). *Raising biracial children*. Landham, MD: Alta Mira Press.
Romano, D. (1998). *Inter-cultural marriage*. Yarmouth, ME: Intercultural Press.
Romano, D. (2001). *Intercultural marriage: Promises and pitfalls* (3rd ed.). Yarmouth, ME: Intercultural Press.

Singla, R. (2015). *Intermarriage and mixed parenting, promoting mental health and wellbeing: Crossover love*. New York: Palgrave Macmillan.
Thomas, V., Karis, T. A., & Wetchler, J. L. (2003). *Clinical issues with interracial couples: Theories and research*. New York: Hawthorne Press.
Till, T. R., & Barker, G. G. (2015). Communication in intercultural marriages: Managing cultural differences and conflicts. *Southern Communication Journal, 80*(3), 189–210.
Tizard, B., & Phoenix, A. (1993). *Black, white or mixed race? Race and racism in the lives of young people of mixed parentage*. London: Routledge.
Voorpostel, M. (2013). Just like family: Fictive kin relationships in the Netherlands. *The Journal of Gerontology, 68*(5), 816–824.
Ziv, A. (2006). *Breeding between the lines: Why interracial people are healthier and more attractive*. Fort lee, NJ: Barricade Books.

4

Power Relations, Reverse Acculturation/Enculturation

The previous chapter focussed on the first theme identified in participants' experiences regarding relational and parenting dynamics: cultures coming together. This chapter focusses on the themes of Power Relations and Reverse Acculturation/Enculturation. Table 4.1 summarises descriptions of the two themes. More detailed descriptions of the sub-themes comprise the remainder of this chapter.

Power Relations

Most of the time, intercultural parents and couples try to achieve a balance in how they manage their intercultural relationship and parenting experiences. However, some parents and couples still experience prejudice regarding power dynamics throughout different phases of their relational and parenting experiences. In the context of intercultural parenting and relationship, power is described in different ways, such as attempts by some host partners to exercise authority over their migrant partners by claiming the privilege of truth regarding parenting practices. However, some migrant participants report that they also experience

D. Bhugun, *Intercultural Parenting and Relationships*,
https://doi.org/10.1007/978-3-030-14060-1_4

Table 4.1 Themes and sub-themes regarding power relations and reverse acculturation

Theme	Sub-theme	Description
2. Power relations	1. Righteousness and privilege of truth	Describes power issues regarding the privilege of truth in parenting practices
	2. Language and communication	Describes how command of the host language influences communication, behaviour and decision-making processes regarding parenting and relational issues
	3. Gender influence	Describes the influence of gender in decision-making and cultural preferences regarding parenting
	4. Insider/outsider status	Describes participants' perception of how power is exercised from being the host or immigrant partner regarding parenting
3. Reverse acculturation/ enculturation	1. Valuing ethnic heritage and host culture	Describes how migrant partners revert to their heritage culture whilst also embracing the host culture regarding parenting practices
	2. Reciprocal acculturation	Describes how host partners also value and adopt their minority ethnic partner's parenting values
	3. Global culture	Describes how shifts in the global culture towards a more cosmopolitan culture which values the coexistence of inherent differences and tolerance for diversity impacts on children and relationship
	4. Shift in parenting styles	Describes several participants' preferences and shifts from authoritarian to authoritative parenting styles

power dynamics such as inner status in the host partner's country from immersion and acculturation, and a sense of belonging from being married to their host partner. The emergent sub-themes about power dynamics experienced by intercultural couples are described below.

Righteousness and Privilege of Truth

In this study, the issue of power was not always evident or obvious until it was brought up by one partner, usually by the migrant partner. The host partners seem to consciously or unconsciously communicate with their partners in ways that reinforce their own cultural patterns of thinking and values. Gary, for example, described that he was "always right" and privileged in his cultural view about the sleeping patterns of children, because he had parenting experiences from his previous marriage. He believed that children should not be sleeping with parents and that they should be left to sleep-cry. His wife Yan was opposed to that method and wanted the child to sleep in the same bed as them so that she could nurse her. But Gary was very firm about his belief:

> Basically, we tried a sleep-cry type method. This is how we do it here. And mum goes "oh she's crying. I can't let my little angel cry". Her strategy was to get up and my strategy was to try and stop her. (Gary)

Dharam: So how did you resolve that?

> Most of the time I just tend to go his way. (Yan)
>
> Because I am always right. (Gary)

Likewise, Bill was very stubborn about what recreational activities children can or cannot go to. He did not agree with his wife's cultural views about recreational entertainments for their children because he was not interested in those forms of entertainment and mindful about the associated costs. In this situation, Bill exercised power over resources because he had absolute control over the family finances. As a result, his wife gave into his ways most of the time:

> I know what's in the bank and she doesn't. She doesn't know how to do banking. (Bill)
>
> I always obey his idea. That's the way… he is a boss. (Azumi)

> Because I'm right. I am a straight person and if I don't like the idea I am not movable. I will not change my mind. I am fixed. I don't need help. I am a very confident person. She needs help… but sometimes she will interpret the help I give her as not helpful and that's her problem. (Bill)

From a social constructionist perspective power is seemingly present in all phases of intercultural relationship and parenting. According to Pare (1996) "power is seen as playing a central role in privileging some voices or stories while silencing others" (p. 5). In other words, power grants the privilege to have one's truth prevail and establish knowledge supremacy over others. This interpretation of power concurs with the above participants' narratives in this current study. Host participants Gary and Bill were absolute in the righteousness, supremacy and privilege about their own cultural "truth" over that of their partner's cultural values, especially regarding parenting practices. Gary believed that he was "always right" and had the privilege of his own truth regarding sleeping patterns of children, referred to as "sleep-cry", because of the way it is done in the western culture and parenting experiences from his previous marriage. Although the participant referred to the privilege of truth from his cultural perspective, it can be also interpreted as a power issue from a gender and personality perspective. Power therefore plays a role in any form of negotiation where individuals strive to have their voices and stories heard.

Language and Communication

In this study, power regarding language and communication was evident when some participants reported that they tried to control their partner's behaviour or thoughts. It was apparent that there was a complex interaction between power and language and communication. Some of the male participants from the dominant host culture appeared to dominate in the interaction with their partners because they spoke their own host language, promoted their own culture and thus became the judges of appropriateness and righteousness. For example, when Gary had fiery arguments with his wife Yan, he used his language ability to exert power in the communication:

> When we would disagree about something, her English would decline very rapidly because she can't think quick enough in English. So her mind would revert to Chinese, so she's lost her words and I am on fire. (Gary)

> The way I speak and annoy him or the way he speaks, I think it's challenging and he tried to persuade me to go the western way. (Yan)

Gary capitalised on the strength of English being his native and host language to dominate and pursue his arguments whereas Yan lost grip of her arguments because she was trying to translate from her native Chinese to English. Frustration then made her turn fully to her native Chinese language and as Gary said he was "on fire", thus a creating a power imbalance. In this situation, Yan being from the non-dominant culture and less proficiency in the English language, reported that she felt less powerful.

Romano (1998) stated that language barriers can create misunderstandings between intercultural couples. The findings in this study concur with Romano's suggestions. Power regarding language was manifested when some participants tried to control their partner's behaviour or thoughts. Two participants stated that language barriers made it difficult for them to win a plausible argument with their host partners as the latter overpowered them with the command of the language, which eventually led to frustration, emotional distress and unhappiness. Another participant found it difficult to communicate properly with her children in her first language because the children have assimilated into the host culture and did not want to speak their mother's language. All the participants encouraged their children to learn or speak some of the immigrant partner's language so that they could communicate with their extended families and members of the ethnic minority community.

Power is most of the time present during communications with each other even if it is not necessarily evident. The intercultural partner perceived to have the most power often determined the communication pattern in the relationship. The relationship between communication and power in intercultural relationships is not often explored in the literature and as such was a focus of this study.

Gender Influences

In this study, most of the male partners appeared to exercise more power than the female partners regarding discipline and socialisation processes of the children. All the female participants believed that their husbands had more power when it came to disciplining the children. As Kylie described, the kids know when her husband is playful and when he is the father:

> I think they fear him whereas they don't fear me… they know when he is playing with them and when he is the father' (Kylie)

Kylie's husband Malai reported that his approach to disciplining their children was effective because he used his disciplinary tone appropriately according to the children's behaviour, contrary to the soft tone used by his wife:

> What happens sometimes is the tone, the talking. If you're (wife) not happy with what they're doing you should change your tone a little bit… Like for me, I can change, different all the time… when I say do this and they're laughing I change my tone. (Malai)

Interestingly, gender power to males was also linked to religious values and beliefs. Rula described how she submitted to her husband's lack of understanding of her culture because of their religious values, where the man is regarded as the "higher authority":

> He says he understands my culture, but sometimes there are things that he could really never understand. That's when I think our faith comes in and there is a bit of a submission in our stuff. We have to kind of I have to submit to him. And so, "okay, I have to let go". It's painful, but…. (Rula)

However, power is not a not a one-way dimensional process. Some male participants reflected on how they lost power when it came to gender roles in the intercultural family context. Although men and women had defined roles in certain ethnic cultures, the inference was that men were still regarded as the authority in the family and ultimate decision-making processes. According to the narratives, this view of power status was compromised as a result of marrying into a western culture, which promotes equal gender power and rights. For example, Malai reported that he never cooked, washed and put women's clothes on the clothes line. But in Australia, he started to cook, wash and hang clothes out to sustain a healthy relationship and family:

> He cooks all the time so that's not what would happen in Thai culture. I think it's just a survival thing because here like you said to adapt… he hangs clothes out and he hangs out the women' underwear which is not what he wouldn't have done in Thailand. (Kylie)

> No, no cooking a well… I have changed big time… like Kylie said in our culture the man never hangs women's undies, bras, etc. on the clothes line… because this is Australia, I have to fit in this culture. (Malai)

According to the narratives, it appears that the shift in power dynamics is also related to the fact that most women work in either full-time or part-time and therefore the husbands have to share the family and parenting responsibility. Also, the lack of parenting support from extended family members in Australia as opposed to the support in ethnic families back home, forced the men to share the family and parental role:

> I think it has to be shared a lot of the time because I'm working, he is working and we are trying to juggle school drop offs… if he is not working during the day, he will be at home and look after the kids. If I was at home and I wasn't working, I would be doing the majority of the care. (Tammy)

Tammy's views were shared by her husband Manuel who agreed that he was doing more house chores because Tammy was also working:

> I changed being taught how to cook now and I'm not good at that. (Manuel)

Keller (2009) suggests that there is a clear power differential in collectivist cultures. Women are regarded as having loyalty to men, rather than relying on their own potentials and success. Gender roles are more rigid wherein the rights and obligations of men are significantly different to that of women. This study confirms Kellner's findings and goes further by revealing that power dynamics also exist in intercultural relationships among men from individualistic cultures in the host society. For example, all the female participants stated that their husbands, irrespective of their cultural backgrounds, exercised more power than them regarding discipline and socialisation processes of the children.

Outsider/Insider Status

In Chapter 3, perception of outsider/insider status was reported in terms of the experiences of identity as a couple. In this chapter, however, the outsider/insider status is described in terms of power dynamics and transnational processes in the participants' parenting and relational experiences.

From a parenting perspective, some migrant partners described feeling powerless from being treated as outsiders regarding their parenting practices, such as sleep patterns. Most of the time, immigrant partners report that in their culture and country, newborn children sleep with the parents in the same bed, but are disappointed when their host partners insist that the children should sleep in separate rooms. The immigrant partners felt powerless because the sleeping pattern of the host culture was imposed on them. This was apparent in Yan's case, whereupon her husband Gary imposed the sleeping pattern of the host culture:

> He was like, "Just let her cry," and I just couldn't endure the crying. (Yan)
>
> Mum couldn't endure. That's where they need to be guided. (Gary)

However, host partners are not immune from the feeling of outsider status and being powerless. Host participants can also feel powerless from being treated as outsiders within their own host culture when their wife's parents visit and stay with them to look after their children. As one host partner explained, when their child became sick, he was excluded from the care process, because according to his wife's culture it's a "woman's business" to care for a sick child. His wife consulted with her mother about the medical needs of the child instead of him:

> To me relationally we should be resolving things as a family unit like we have, called family unit, you and I, and out from that whereas I guess part of the Chinese culture is you and your mother or me out of here. That's the circle… (Gary)

Gary's wife Yan acknowledged his frustration.

Likewise, Anya reported that she and her children felt a sense of outsider status from being marginalised in her own Australian culture. Anya converted to her husband's Islamic religion of her own free will before they got married and felt that her family was rejected by people on the street and neighbours:

> They just reject us. (Anya)

The power dynamics regarding insider/outsider status have important implications for the participants' experiences of parenting. For example, when the host partners visited their migrant partners' heritage country and were exposed to the way of parenting in that country and culture, they reported that they got a better understanding of why their migrant partners parent and behave in a particular cultural way, and thus allowing for flexibility in their own parenting practices. As Naomi and her husband Pravin explained:

> There's a focus here on children need to grow up quickly, they need to be independent, they need to be strong individuals, whereas in India I think the culture is more, this is a child, we're going to treat them like a child until they become an adult. (Naomi)

> I still think he is a kid. And even if he's just close, I just want him to be a little of an Indian touch, that kind of experience that I had. (Pravin)

> I think having R's parents over 3 months every year so I get to see how she I guess interacts with JV as well and that impacted some of my parenting style. (Naomi)

Many migrant participants also experience power dynamics such as insider status from becoming a citizen of the host country and having children who are born in the host country. As Sarah explained:

> I am now an Australian citizen… they [children] have grown up in Australia. (Sarah)

However, some host participants also experience power dynamics from what can be termed reverse insider status in their migrant partners' countries, local communities and political and cultural associations. For example, knowledge of their migrant partner's language and culture was inferred to as a privilege for insider status. This was exemplified in John's family case:

> We had some Tongans come here on Aus-Aid scholarships, that I was able to be around and got exposed to the language, and that is when I became interested in learning about the Tongan language and got a little bit of an insight, I guess, from an outsider looking in about the Tongan culture. I travelled with my family to Tonga when I was 13 years old… I got very much involved in the local Australian-Tongan community, Tongan community ethnic radio here in Brisbane. I made an effort with our daughter from a young age. I actively read her Tongan storybooks for children to try to expose her to the language. I spoke to her a lot more in Tongan, I sang her songs in Tongan. (John)

Insider/outsider status was also influenced by participants' experiences of transnational processes, that is, influences of broader political and social attributes external to their intimate relationship such as exclusion, learning a new language and negative stereotypes. Cathy and her husband Will described how they had to protect and build resistance in their children against racist attitudes at school because of their race and colour:

> I try and build resilience into the boys. I don't know if that is, it is like if I had married a white man there wouldn't be a, I wouldn't have to deal with any racist element in the children's lives. [Son] has been called a pooh at school before and a nigger. (Cathy)

> We try and build resilience that you don't just become a victim and go I have been called a nigger, you stand and be proud of yourself. (Will)

Sarah described her experiences of negative stereotypes when she is in the public arena with her host partner:

> Years ago it was a hard thing when they looked at you…I know in the early times people looked at me….thinking is she a Filipina bride. (Sarah)

Cottrell (1990) found that intercultural couples tend to conform to the cultural practice of the dominant host culture. Seto and Cavallaro (2007) also found that the place of residence impacts on couples' power distribution in a relationship. The findings of this study support the arguments of these authors. In this study, immigrant partners perceived themselves mostly as "outsiders" because they live in the host country and therefore the need to conform mostly to the host culture. In the context of the intercultural relationships, the concept of "outsider status" refers to the partner who migrates to the host country and lives in the partner's home country. Most of the immigrant partners also experienced power imbalance, from being isolated from their relatives, lack of extended family support, loss of their culture and experiencing language and communication problems. One immigrant participant gave up on some aspects of her cultural values and traditional recreational activities for her children in order to minimise conflict with her host partner, who was adamant about his values.

The host participants experienced insider status power dynamics from belonging to the majority population and race, speaking the majority language and having an overall knowledge of the Australian society and culture. However, some immigrant partners also felt a sense of power from immersion in the host culture and "belongingness" from being married to the host partner. Interestingly, this study revealed that some majority host partners in intercultural relationships can also experience the feeling of minority status. As one host partner described, he felt completely ignored when his wife's extended family members were visiting, and completely immersed themselves in their homeland language and traditional practices. Another participant from the majority host culture felt the same when she was visiting her husband's native country and all his relatives spoke in their local language. She felt powerless and lonely. Two other host partners described how they were the subjects of racism, rejection and ignored in the social arena because of their marriage to minority ethnic partners in Australia.

The narratives also revealed that acculturation was not a one-way process but was dynamic and fluid in many instances, based on the couple's immersion, experiences and preferences of each other's cultural processes. The process of reverse acculturation is described below.

Reverse Acculturation/Enculturation

Kim and Park (2009) defined reverse acculturation as the cultural practice wherein a country's fully acculturated minority member introduces the heritage culture to the majority host society. In this study, it was evident that reverse acculturation was facilitated by factors such as globalisation, mobility, multiculturalism and multi-layered advances in technology. From the narratives, reverse acculturation/enculturation was manifested in multiple domains such as use of language, identity, food, values, behaviours, cultural knowledge and social affiliation and activities. Reverse acculturation was attributed to both the individual and societal level. From the individual perspective, reverse acculturation occurred when participants from the minority group reinforced their cultural heritage in the relationship and parenting processes in the host society. From the societal perspective, the cultural exchange was manifested at the centre of the host society itself, wherein the society was tolerant of cultural coexistence or multiculturalism. Given that this study explored the intercultural parenting experiences of participants, reverse acculturation was described mostly at the individual level of parenting and relationship dynamics. The following sub-themes evolved from the participants' narratives of reverse acculturation/enculturation and are described below: (1) Valuing ethnic heritage and host culture; (2) Reciprocal acculturation; (3) Global culture; and (4) Shift in parenting styles.

Valuing Ethnic Heritage and Host Culture

All the migrant partners expressed strong sentiments and willingness for integration between their native home and host culture, including traditions, beliefs, values and connections. The following statement by Manuel suggests that he considers himself to be both African and Australian and values the integration of the two cultures in his family:

> I am an African… and now I am an Australian. I became an Australian citizen. She is an Australian. She is learning about the African culture… You know the meals she cooks, African meals. She's been to the country. Actually, she's [daughter] Australian, but when it comes to food when we go there the mangoes and she sees the people, then she's African. I'm teaching her the language. I'm teaching both of them and getting them to eat African food, as well. (Manuel)

Manuel's wife Tammy agreed with his statement and added how she and the children value Manuel's heritage culture:

> She does – she loves the music and things like that … I have learned a lot of his culture, as well. (Tammy)

Simla on the other hand, while valuing the integration of the two cultures, emphasised the importance of the diaspora communities, in her case the African community in the host country which allowed her family, especially their son to have continued association with her home culture and community connections. Her husband Daniel supported her and their son to be involved with the African diaspora community and culture:

> I take him to events… it's often kind of fun things that he comes along to when I do African events and that kind of stuff. His Africaness is so much formed and it's forming his identity. (Simla)

> We were worried initially that he wouldn't perhaps understand his cultural background. But as it turns out he more clearly identifies with that African side of his background. (Daniel)

Reinforcement and incorporation of the migrant heritage culture was evidenced in partners from both the ethnic minority and dominant group. All the partners from the ethnic minority group were strongly in favour of reinforcing their home cultural values and goals such as respect, discipline, strong family, work ethics, education and community engagement for their children. This was emphasised in Malai, Pravin, Manuel and Michelle's narratives. Malai described an example of incompatible host culture to his homeland traditional Asian parenting style, referred to as "filial piety", such as respect for and unquestioning obedience to parents. Malai reported that unlike many children in Australian society he was brought up to respect all of his people and family, and reinforced those values in his children. His wife Kylie supported his views about family values and the way he reinforces it in their own family:

> I grew up with the respect for all our people like family, you know uncle, aunty. Number one is respect… the way children in this country grow up, I totally not agree… and these will become bigger in the future when they become teenagers because there is no respect, there is no fear of the parent, nothing… That is why I'm really reinforcing that with my children. (Malai)

> To be honest, I've always respected in him that family value and instilling that value of respect for each other and your members of your family. I've always admired him for that and I've often just sort of sat back and observed him and the way that he installs that in the children. (Kylie)

Pravin, likewise, believed that the values and emotions instilled in his child should come from the Indian side because it is missing in Australia:

> The values and emotions should come from the Indian side because I kind of don't like what it is here. I only learned it slowly and slowly, because before in the last 2, 3 years, I am looking into it more deeply... I kind of get scared, because when you see other kids, I don't want my kid to be like that. No way in the world. (Pravin)

Pravin also described his preference for the strong family values and support for children in his home country of India:

> I like the way things are done there than here. Like how close they are to their family. I don't know whether [son] will be like that to us in the future. I would like him to be. I don't want him to think that if he can't afford anything I will say "get out of my house, I have nothing for you". I am not that kind of person. (Pravin)

Pravin's wife Naomi concurred with her husband's feelings and fears, but she also referred to the strengths of both cultures, which would benefit their son:

> Not as much respect for their parents... but I think the benefit for [son] is that he can take the positives from both the cultures. (Naomi)

Rajack and his wife Anya explained that they have acculturated to the Australian society, but when it comes to cultural values and customs, they wanted to raise their children with their homeland cultural values and work ethics.

> We stayed in Bali for couple of years to understand the culture. My son will know which one is his grandmother and grandfather. I was worried about that. (Rajack)

> Yeah, it's very important for them. (Anya)

Kim and Park (2009) reported on reverse acculturation among Korean-American immigrants who introduced the heritage culture to the host nation. Miller (2010) refers to enculturation as adopting attributes of the new country they migrated to whilst retaining those of the heritage culture.

Both these dynamics of reverse acculturation and enculturation were apparent in the findings of this current study. The findings on reverse acculturation reported by Kim and Park (2009) and this present study bring a different perspective to Berry's (1997) formulation, and to current acculturation theory (Cleveland & Laroche, 2007), which state that acculturation is unidirectional and that immigrants eventually relinquish their heritage culture and adapt to the host country's culture and values. Whilst this may be true for some immigrants, defined within contextual realities, such as fleeing war-torn countries and political and religious persecutions, it does not necessarily apply to migrants who immigrate to different regions of the world because of the effects of globalisation and a plural metropolitan society. It certainly did not apply to me either because I migrated to Australia for economic benefits.

Diaspora communities were also considered as an important mechanism to sustain cultural ties with the heritage culture and local members of the relevant minority ethnic communities (Bhatia & Ram, 2009). Diaspora communities are currently matters of debate and concerns in the public and political arena in Australia (Beech, August 19, 2013) and other countries embracing multiculturalism. The positive contributions of such communities to society in general, particularly in the context of intercultural dynamics, should not be ignored (Chan, 2013). Recent global shifts towards a more cosmopolitan culture also reinforce the concept of reverse and reciprocal acculturation/enculturation. As the participants in this study described, the willingness on their part to embrace aspects of other cultures enhanced their lifestyle and opportunities in both the heritage and host cultures.

The current study found that participants from the minority ethnic group engaged in both reverse acculturation as well as enculturation processes by reinforcing their cultural heritage in the relationships and parenting practices. The phenomenon was amply demonstrated in multiple domains, such as family values, language, identity, food, values and goals, behaviours, cultural knowledge and social affiliation and activities. Two particular participants also went back with their children to their heritage country for a couple of years in the early stages of parenting, to inculcate and immerse their children in their heritage culture because they did not like the western way of raising children. This is a phenomenon that is beyond the scope of this study and needs further exploration and study as a discrete phenomenon.

The narratives revealed that reverse acculturation was not just a unidirectional, but also a "reciprocal process" (Bhugun, 2016), which is further explored in the next section.

Reciprocal Acculturation

The narratives in this study demonstrated another dimension of acculturation, where some participants from the dominant culture in the host society were also influenced by, preferred and adopted their partner's minority group cultural processes. In other words, the influence shifted from an ethnic minority partner to the partner of the dominant host culture. I termed this process as "reciprocal acculturation" (Bhugun, 2016). Reciprocal acculturation is different to the concept of mutual acculturation (Falicov, 1995), as latter is about adjustment of dysfunctional patterns wherein couples must negotiate cultural conflicts, make mutual accommodation and develop new cultural codes.

According to the host partners, they were important values that were missing in their own upbringing and in Australian society. This was reflected in John's description and supported by his wife Rula:

> They are lucky in the values and morals. I would prefer more of the Tongan cultural values and morals because I like the fact that the brothers and sisters, the man, the brothers don't walk through the house with no shirt on and expose themselves in front of their sisters. I like that there's boundaries and there's definitely respect for the elders and what they say, whereas Australian kids would tell their parents where to go at any age… when our daughter grows up, I think my wife would not approve of her wearing a mini skirt or short length dress when she is a teenage girl. The expectation is that she dresses more modestly, with more self-respect and all that. (John)

> They really dig into us the importance of staying as a woman and keeping yourself pure, of being a respectful person, and with your brothers and sisters in my culture, the girls were not allowed to be with the brothers,

> or go to the brother's room or watch a movie with your brothers. I think that's quite special growing up because I learn to respect my brothers and my brothers learn to respect me. I think my decision for the kids was based on my upbringing really. (Rula)

Jim described how his travels and encounters with other cultures exposed and heightened his preferences and adherence to the minority group cultural processes, such as family values and education:

> From my travels to the Philippines, I could see the strong family ties. So pretty much I made up my mind before I met my wife…I would probably marry someone from that part of the world… It seems like we do not have many values in this country like the immigrants. They work hard, they get educated and become moral citizens. I think on my side, the children have been brought up more as their mum's the model. That is the best model I have… yes the kids getting good marks from the early days. I see it from my wife and kids. (Jim)

Michelle confirmed and supported and her husband's view of family values in the Asian culture:

> I notice that the family life in the western world is different from the Asian family life. The mothers specially are the prime mover. She will be responsible for the moral value. The moral values in the western world, the religious values and the family values, I think I am grateful that they are now experiencing or realizing the values that I have taught them. (Michelle)

Samuel and his wife described the influence Asian food had on the way they eat and live their lives in his family:

> I guess the one thing that follows is the food part from culture that we eat more Asian food. Cooked a lot of Asian food… My food culture was very plain, boring just an Aussie steak and veggies. Whereas that really impacted in the way we like to eat and live our lives now. (Samuel)

Gary described how globalisation and the emergence of China as a world economic and cultural power influenced him to encourage his daughter and himself to learn his wife's Chinese language and culture, so that his daughter could benefit from the Chinese global job opportunities:

> I think that she is going to have an incredible benefit, with China being the world emerging economy... she will be incredibly placed to take advantage of it... she will be able to facilitate business over there if she wants to because she can go over there and speak fluent Chinese and English. (Gary)

Gary's wife Yan concurred with his views:

> It's good that they have the Chinese culture in their blood and they could use the Chinese language. (Yan)

Gary's description of globalisation, and seeing the world as an integrated whole, was manifested in the narratives of several participants. This phenomenon of a global culture is examined below.

Global Culture

The narratives in this study clearly demonstrated that reverse acculturation was occurring because of shifts in the global culture towards a more cosmopolitan culture which values the coexistence of inherent differences and greater tolerance of diversity. According to the participants, the heterogeneous global culture and the willingness on their part to embrace aspects of other cultures enhanced their children's lifestyle and opportunities in both the heritage country and host cultures. These sentiments are reflected in Gary's perception:

> There are no borders anymore. It's incredibly easy to travel worldwide. The world is increasingly a multicultural society. That's what we are trying to do with our children... For me, I see that I have two Chinese-Australian children. To me, it's very important that they learn aspects of both cultures and that they learn both languages ... to really try to get the best out of both worlds for them. (Gary)

Yan concurred with her husband's views:

> I think because our kids were born here, we will grow up here. I think it's absolutely Aussie, but if they have more culture its good for the future… I think Western culture is good for kids because they are more happy, but there are some good things in our culture like respect for old people and good work ethics. (Yan)

Daniel described how Australia is a multicultural country and most Australians are outwardly thinking. For that reason his wife Simla was encouraging their son to be part of the global society and be connected:

> Like most, more liberal-minded Australians are culturally aware because we are a country where almost 50 percent of the population was either born elsewhere or their parents were… Australians are multicultural and outwardly thinking. We're also widely travelled. (Daniel)
>
> So I would really want him to feel as part of the wider culture. And that's how we are raising him… it's about the connectedness. (Simla)

Jeehan reported an example of global culture where what he called his "tribal communities" were starting to accept the western culture because they are increasingly exposed to and changing their views about other cultures. He related the experience to his own Turkish parents, who opposed his marriage to someone from a western culture, but gradually changed their views when they witnessed the positives and commonalities between the two cultures. The positive shift in the global cultural attitude and acceptance of intercultural relationship can be interpreted as enhancing positive family relations and children's relationship with their extended families:

> My family were very tribal, very ignorant in their own ways. They had a big identity crisis when we got married. "You are not going to eat that horrible food. What are you? Is that food? What are you guys doing?"… They didn't really see too much of the world other than their own community. But once I got married into the Australian culture, my brother was the

> same also, they started to say, "wow there's uniqueness in this. These people are different to us and they are not bad as what we thought, and we've always alienated these people, but really they accept others and we have so much in common". So it allowed our intermarriage, allowed the rest of the family to see that it can actually work with cross cultures. (Jeehan)

Jeehan's wife Murielle concurred with her husband, and stated that globalisation also enabled them and their children to interact with friends from different cultures and nationalities, thus making them feeling globally connected:

> So I think because we've got friends from such a broad cultural base too that they [children] see someone from Tanzania that is, you know, one of our friends, or Gambia I think I've got friends from every nation. I could go on holiday around the world … I think we're kind of the world's global culture which is good for the children. (Murielle)

Globalisation exposed intercultural parents and couples to different styles of parenting which helped them to reflect on their own parenting experiences and the parenting styles they preferred for their own children. This is reflected in the next section below.

Shift Towards Authoritative Parenting Style

Most immigrant partners described their preferences for the Australian cultural concept of independence and authoritative parenting styles because according to them, it makes the children happier. Asian participants, in particular, reported that they did not like the authoritarian parenting style of their parents regarding discipline and educational expectations and hence adopted the authoritative parenting style towards their children. For example, Yan described how she felt sad and lacked self-confidence because of her father's authoritarian style of parenting when it came to educational achievements. She did not want her children to go through the same experiences and feelings:

> My father was always like a "discourage". It's like when I got the top mark, may be top three score in the class, my father was like, "why didn't you do harder? You could be the top one" and always made me sad… my father is an engineer and he wanted me to be an engineer. That job is not interesting for me. I don't want to force my kids to do what I want. I try to encourage my kids. I don't want them to feel that way because in my whole life I always think "Oh, I'm not the best. Always somebody is better than me", lack of confidence. (Yan)

Yan's husband Gary concurred with her feelings, and disagreed with the Chinese cultural and authoritarian parental expectations regarding education:

> I tend to disagree and I think it's an old saying that goes all work and no play makes Jack a dull boy. I'm not sure that as a result of all the education that the Chinese go through that they're that much further advanced than western people are educationally, although all they've got is a depersonalized drilling system where people are forced to rote – do stuff by rote over and over, and over again for 18 hours a day. I'm not sure it's benefiting that much. (Gary)

Likewise, Pravin reported that he did not like his experience of very strict discipline from his father, as a consequence of which he softened his approach towards his son:

> If he told me to do something and I did not do it, he was very, very strict… For my dad, no means no, end of story… sometimes I resented him for lot of things. I actually learnt from that and may be that is why I am not very strict with my son. (Pravin)

Communication and enabling expression of feelings from children seemed to be elusive among some ethnic minority groups. Azumi expressed disappointment about her parents not communicating and spending enough time with her because they were too busy working hard till late to make money. She had many questions for her mother but the latter never had time for her questions. Azumi did not want her children to suffer the same way:

> They were always busy. So they didn't read me a book or anything... they never said to me to study... I couldn't play outside or they didn't take me to the parks or to amusement parks... had many questions to ask my mother but she had never time for my questions and she died too early. I tell my children and do not want them to suffer like me. (Azumi)

Her husband Bill witnessed and described his wife's pain and disappointment, which according to him, led her to parent their children differently to her own upbringing:

> Well, she didn't have a good feeling about her parents. From what I've heard, [wife] told me that there are many questions that she wanted to ask her mother about, and her mother never had time for her to ask questions... so she's bitterly disappointed. She suffered and she doesn't see how that was fair and she doesn't want her children to suffer the same way. (Bill)

Likewise, Sarah described how nobody talked about their feelings in her homeland family and wanted to reverse that cultural attitude:

> For me, going back to my family, nobody talked about their feelings. So my way of doing things are very emotional and I have to get them to tell me how they are feeling about something. (Sarah)

Another participant described his upbringing as tribal, and did not want his children to grow up in a similar parental context. He wanted his children to grow up differently within the context of an evolving parenting style and civilised society. He was supported by his wife in the wish that their children need a different upbringing from his.

> I look at the wrongs and limitations that we had within that tribal culture [Turkish] and I think "well, I'm not going to do that to my kids". I want them to expand, understand and be educated. I want them to be wise and diverse and be accepting of everybody's culture. (Jeehan)

> And to look at people's culture and accept them and love them. Different foods, different occasions and also look at things that causes people, like societies from these cultures to go backwards. (Murielle)

The debates over parenting styles have been well documented over the years, with consensus, mostly in the western and individualist cultures, for the authoritative style of parenting (Baumrind, 1967, 1971), which emphasises responsiveness alongside demandingness. On the other hand, and as described in the literature review, most collective cultures, especially Asian, African and Middle-eastern cultures, embrace and justify authoritarian parenting. However, there seems to be a shift towards an authoritative parenting style in the Australian context, among intergenerational parents and some new migrants. In this current study, in the context of intercultural parenting, participants from the African culture were found to be practising a mix of authoritative and hierarchical styles of parenting. As mentioned in the literature review, Lindahl and Malik (1999) differentiated between authoritarian and hierarchical parenting styles, in that the latter does not imply unresponsiveness in the same way as authoritarian parenting style. They suggested that hierarchical parenting styles promote respect for elders, parents and authorities and strong intra-familial boundaries.

In two separate studies on African migrant families in Australia, Renzaho, McCabe, and Sainsbury (2011) and Sims and Omaji (1999) found that many African and Arab speaking migrant families struggled to reconcile the parenting styles and practices of their country to the legalised parenting practices and policies in Australia. Renzaho et al. (2011) found that "migrants tend to come from collectivist cultures where an authoritarian parenting style (where obedience to authority is valued) is the norm, yet they find themselves in a new continent where individuality (valuing self-maximisation, self-reliance, individualism and autonomy) is the norm" (p. 417). This current study, which includes the parenting experiences of some African migrants, reveals an evolving perspective on their parenting styles because of the intercultural parenting dynamic. The African participants in this study were keen to make their relationship work, and as such have adopted some strategies, including flexibility, compromise and negotiating their parenting styles. In the context of intercultural parenting within Australia, it appears that African participants have shifted from an authoritarian to a combined hierarchical and authoritative parenting style.

Four out of five participants from Asian cultures have shifted from their parents' authoritarian parenting style to that of the "authoritative" parenting style. However, the four Asian participants were female and therefore gender considerations in the way they were parented may have also influenced this shift. Unfortunately, there were no male Asian participants in this study to corroborate or challenge the changed pattern of parenting styles among the Asian participants. According to the participants, the reason for the shift in their parenting style was based on three factors. (1) Dislike of their parenting experiences from their parent's authoritarian parenting style, particularly regarding discipline and educational expectations. The participants described that their parents were never happy with their study results and demanded better performances, thus making them feel sad, inadequate and lacking in confidence. (2) Lack of communication about children's feelings. According to one participant, Japanese parents never say their children are the best. (3) Exposure to other styles of parenting where children seem to be happier. As one participant described, in the Chinese culture parents speak to children like a leader or treat the children as if they are workers, as opposed to Australians who were perceived as speaking to children on the same level. This is an interesting phenomenon revealing current and emerging changing attitudes about parenting styles among Asian communities in the Australian context.

The findings of this current study challenge current thinking about parenting in collectivist cultures. The assumption is that the collectivist culture embraces and promotes authoritarian parenting style. This assumption, as revealed in studies by Chao (1994, 2000) bears substance in Asian homogenous collectivist societies, but may not be entirely relevant to members of the collectivist society who have migrated to other western countries. The assumption is also challenged following another study (Cheah, Leung, Tahseen, & Schultz, 2009) in which immigrant Chinese mothers of pre-schoolers favoured the authoritative parenting style, because it predicted increased children's behavioural abilities. This current study adds to the debate about assumptions regarding authoritarian parenting based on the findings of parenting within an intercultural context and a western society. Similar to the African context mentioned above, this study revealed an equally evolving perspective on the parenting styles among immigrant Asian participants, because of the intercultural parenting dynamics. The Asian participants in the intercultural relationships were equally keen to make their relationship work and as such have adopted some strategies, including flexibility, compromise and negotiating their parenting styles. In the context of intercultural parenting, within Australia, it appeared that the Asian participants have also shifted from an authoritarian to authoritative parenting style.

The results of this study also challenge the assumption that parents parent the way they were parented (Santrock, 2007; Tanaka, Kitamura, Chen, Murakami, & Goto, 2009). This was not fully demonstrated in all the parenting experiences described by the participants. Asian participants, in particular, did not like the way they were parented and as a result shifted from their parent's authoritarian parenting style to an authoritative parenting styles. The shift in parenting style appeared to have been influenced by the context of the environment they lived in and exposure to new styles of parenting. The narratives revealed that whilst migrant participants valued their homeland cultures, they were also willing to integrate them with the host culture to obtain a balanced and healthy intercultural parenting experience.

Summary of Power Relations and Reverse Acculturation/Enculturation

This chapter presented two themes with in-depth descriptions of participants' experiences about intercultural parenting: Power Relations; and Reverse Acculturation/Enculturation. Participants reported that parenting issues, language and communication, gender and insider/outsider status influenced the power dynamics in their relationships. Also, most of the minority immigrant participants demonstrated their engagement with both the acculturation and reverse acculturation processes, wherein values and traditions of the heritage culture were introduced to the host culture and partner. Likewise, some of the host partners described "reciprocal acculturation", wherein they showed preferences and engagement of their immigrant partners' cultural values and practices.

This study also revealed another important finding regarding parenting styles. Some immigrant ethnic minority partners described their preferences for the authoritative parenting style because of certain negative aspects of the authoritarian parenting style they were subjected to in their own upbringing.

Intercultural parents had their own subjective understanding and interpretation of parenting based on the cultural parenting values, beliefs and traditions they were raised in their homeland and host culture, personal/individual style of parenting and contextual influences. The cultural differences in parenting sometimes led to conflict among the parents. However, intercultural couples and parents made considerable efforts to resolve the differences which are described in the following chapter.

References

Baumrind, D. (1967). Socialisation processes associated with dimensions of competence in preschool boys and girls. *Child Development, 38*(20), 291–327.

Baumrind, D. (1971). Current patterns of parental authority. *Developmental Psychology Monograph, 4*(1, Pt. 2), 1–103. https://doi.org/10.1037/h0030372.

Beech, H. (2013, August 19). I am Australian. So Am I. *Time Magazine, 182*(8).

Berry, J. W. (1997). Immigration, acculturation, and adaptation. *Applied Psychology: An International Review, 46*(1), 5–34.

Bhatia, S., & Ram. A. (2009). Theorizing identity in transnational and diaspora cultures: A critical approach to acculturation. *International Journal of Intercultural Relations, 33*(2), 140–149. https://doi.org/10.1016/j.ijintrel.2008.12.009.

Bhugun, C. D. (2016). *The experiences of intercultural parenting in Australia* (PhD thesis). Southern Cross University, Australia.

Chan, L. L. (2013). *Reverse acculturation: A global rebalancing phenomenon or driven by globalised diaspora* (Unpublished doctoral dissertation). Gordon Institute of Business Science, University of Pretoria, South Africa.

Chao, R. K. (1994). Beyond parental control and authoritarian parenting style: Understanding Chinese parenting through the cultural notion

of training. *Child Development, 65*(4), 1111–1120. https://doi.org/10.2307/1131308.
Chao, R. K. (2000). The parenting of immigrant Chinese and European American mothers: Relations between parenting styles, socialization goals, and parental practices. *Journal of Applied Developmental Psychology, 21*, 233–248. https://doi.org/10.1016/so193-3973(99)00037-4.
Cheah, C. S. L., Leung, C. Y., Tahseen, M., & Schultz, D. (2009). Authoritative parenting among immigrant Chinese mothers of pre-schoolers. *Journal of Family Psychology, 23*(30), 311–320. https://doi.org/10.1037/a0015076.
Cleveland, M., & Laroche, M. (2007). Acculturation to the global consumer culture: Scale development and research paradigm. *Journal of Business Research, 60*(3), 249–259. https://doi.org/10.1016/j.ijintrel.2008.12.008.
Cottrell, A. (1990). Cross-national marriages: A review of the literature. *Journal of Comparative Family Studies, 21*(2), 151–169.
Falicov, C. J. (1995). Cross-cultural marriages. In N. S. Jacobson & A. S. Gurman (Eds.), *Clinical handbook of couple therapy* (pp. 231–246). New York: Guildford.
Keller, H. (2009). Gender perspectives in cross-cultural couples. *Clinical Social Work Journal, 37*(3), 224–229.
Kim, Y., & Park, S. (2009). Reverse acculturation: A new cultural phenomenon examined through an emerging wedding practice of Korean Americans in the United States. *Family and Consumer Sciences Research Journal, 37*(3), 359–375. https://doi.org/10.1177/1077727x08330758.
Lindahl, K. M., & Malik, N. M. (1999). Observations of marital conflict and power: Relations with parenting in the triad. *Journal of Marriage and the Family, 61*(2), 320–330. https://doi.org/10.2307/353751.
Miller, M. J. (2010). Testing a bilinear domain-specific model of acculturation and enculturation across generational status. *Journal of Counselling Psychology, 57*(2), 179–185.
Pare, D. A. (1996). Culture and meaning: Expanding the metaphorical repertoire of family therapy. *Family Process, 35*(1), 21–42.
Renzaho, A. M. N., McCabe, M., & Sainsbury, W. J. (2011). Parenting, role reversals and the preservation of cultural values among Arabic speaking migrant families in Melbourne, Australia. *International Journal of Intercultural Relations, 35*(4) 416–424. https://doi.org/10.1016/j.ijintrel.2010.09.001document.

Romano, D. (1998). *Inter-cultural marriage*. Maine: Intercultural Press.
Santrock, J. W. (2007). *A topical approach to life-span development* (3rd. ed.). New York: McGraw-Hill.
Seto, A. C., & Cavallaro, M. (2007). Cross-national couples in the Mainland United States. *The Family Journal, 15*(3), 258–264. https://doi.org/10.1177/1066480707301315.
Sims, M. R., & Omaji, A. K. (1999). Migration and parenting: A pilot study. *Journal of Family Studies, 5*(1), 84–96.
Tanaka, M., Kitamura, T., Chen, Z., Murakami, M., & Goto, Y. (2009). Do parents rear their children as they were reared themselves? Intergenerational transmission of parental styles (warmth and control) and possible mediation of personality traits. *The Open Family Studies Journal, 2*, 82–90.

5

Strategies for Making Intercultural Parenting Work

Intercultural couples face unique challenges because of their cultural differences in parenting styles, beliefs, values and traditions. As such, it was important to elucidate how intercultural parents negotiated and resolved their parenting differences. All the parents were very keen to make their parenting journey a positive experience. In order to achieve that goal, intercultural parents negotiated their cultural differences by developing several conflict resolution and management strategies.

The narratives are conceptualised into three spheres to capture the significance and importance of the strategies. The three spheres are described as (1) individual sphere, (2) couple's/parents' sphere; and (3) child's sphere. These three spheres overlap because of the close interactions between the spheres. It is also important to discuss the strategies from the individual, couple and child's sphere, because it helps to generate deeper insights about the experience from their different perspectives. It also enables insights into the interactions between the three domains that are dependent on each other for successful experiences of the phenomenon. Strategies in the individual sphere includes: respect, flexibility, patience and perseverance, acceptance and tolerance and open-mindedness. Strategies in the couple's/parents' sphere includes: communication, compromise, spheres of influence, asymmetric decision-making, cultural

D. Bhugun, *Intercultural Parenting and Relationships*,
https://doi.org/10.1007/978-3-030-14060-1_5

literacy and embracing partners' culture, having a plan and preparedness for minority feeling. Strategies for the child's sphere includes: not imposing culture on child, encouraging multiculturalism, listening and respecting children, consistency in parenting and teaching children values. The three spheres are described below and outlined in Fig. 5.1.

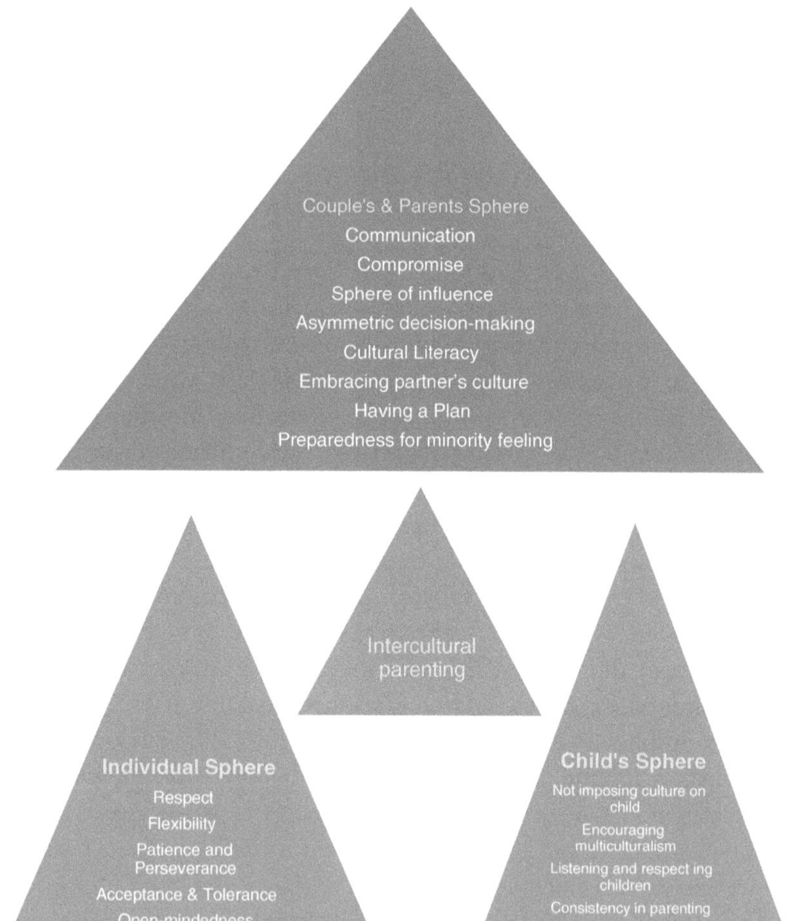

Fig. 5.1 Conflict resolution and management strategies of intercultural couples/parents (*Source* Developed for this study)

Individual Sphere

The success of intercultural relationship and parenting depends partly on the parents and couple's individual behaviour and characteristics within the cultural context. The most common reported individual characteristics are identified as respect, flexibility, patience and perseverance, acceptance and tolerance and open-mindedness.

Respect

All the participants agreed that while there were cultural differences in their parenting style and practices, they respected each other as another person and the qualities they brought to the relationship and the family. As Kylie and Malai explained, they respect each other in the way they do things and who they are:

> He respects me in the way I do things. (Kylie)
>
> I think I'm pretty lucky. I am a lucky man. We get along very well, like good partner and we know each other for a long time and we have children together and she does a good job, you know. She is easy. (Malai)

Manuel described how he grew up in a traditional African way, but has changed his attitude towards women and respects his wife equally. He was even surprised that his wife could cook African food and show interest in his culture:

> I thought it was going to be hard. Of course, she wasn't from Africa. Knowing food, (inaudible) eating the foods, I was shocked she could cook very good food… she learned how to cook African and expressed an interest in my culture, sort of respecting one another… I grew up in a very traditional way, but I've come very far, as well. I respect, I believe in equality between man and a woman. I'm not a misogynist (laughter). (Manuel)

Manuel's wife Tammy echoed her husband's cultural view of traditional African man and eventual adaptation to the host culture's view about woman and emphasised that he had to make compromises for them to be happy:

> I don't know if this is too much of a stereotype, but African males, they're very different to Australian men. The way that they have been brought up is different. Their view of women and what women should be like and what their role is and what my role is, is a lot different to modern Australia... but I think you do have to make compromises at times to both be happy, like you do have to... don't you. (Tammy)

Simla and Daniel explained that in fulfilling their daily obligations towards the family, they focus primarily on being respectful of each other and their cultural differences come second to respect:

> It's not being conscious of their culture first and foremost. It's being respectful of the other person and the culture becomes secondary to the respect in the relationship, and of the family network. We're both quite liberal and well educated, and intelligent people. And whatever cultural expectations may have been relevant in the past, we don't see as relevant now. (Daniel)

> Daniel loves to cook and he takes care of us in terms of feeding us, the family. We both work so that is never an expectation that Daniel will do this, I will do this. It's who comes home first and when we're home together we both do things. (Simla)

Flexibility

All the participants explained that there are certain issues that can never be resolved and the best strategy to survive them is flexibility and tolerance. Manuel explained how, after several explanations, his wife Tammy was flexible in incorporating his cultural traditions of washing new born babies in certain herbal medicine and keeping the umbilical cord:

> Like I said before, we had problems with washing the baby in herbal medicine and keeping the umbilical cord. If it wasn't Tammy, if it was a different person who is strong-minded, they would refuse him to shower in that yet the culture says he's supposed to shower in that. We agreed me and her, so we kept that but in different culture with a different person they would refuse. (Manuel)

Malai described how he became flexible in his cultural gender roles, such as hanging women's clothes on the clothes line, because he lives in Australia and has to fit with his partner's culture. Malai's wife Kylie confirmed before that he would not hang out clothes in Thailand because it is considered a women's job.

> For example because like my wife said before, in our culture, the man never hangs women's undies, bras, etc., on the clothes line. We don't do that in Thailand or in my culture. Because this is Australia, I have to be flexible to fit in this culture, in this country. (Malai)

Carol echoed Malai's experience, and according to her, it is also an overall learning and adaptive process.

> You have to be flexible, because you know it is two cultures meeting, and even though we didn't have to sort lot of things out, there were certain things that we have to get used to both cultures, especially all the Indian things and the language and you are going to a party and I am the only Aussie there. (Carol)

Patience and Perseverance

Being in an intercultural relationship requires patience and perseverance, and allowing oneself the opportunity and time to understand the different ways one's partner do things. It also allows others to see things differently. This is echoed in Anya's perception of patience and tolerance:

> It's true. We know some Australian people they want to marry Indonesians but they are like these you know, they don't give themselves enough time to know the partner. You have to have a lot of patience, you have to be tolerant. Otherwise you end up fighting like two bulls because they have different ways of doing something. (Anya)
>
> Especially in the cooking. (Rajack)
>
> I cook the pasta and things like that. He cooks the rice. (Anya)

Kylie explained how her husband's personal attributes of patience and peaceful way of doing things helped to resolve and bring peace to everyone in the family. This was acknowledged by her husband Malai who also attributed it to possibly his personality type and helpful attitude:

> I would have been out shopping or something and I'd be racing to get home on time but I would get home with say 10 minutes to sort of hand over… we had one car at the time. I would get there and he would just be patient, peaceful and calm. Here's the key and off he would go. Whereas if the situation was reversed, I would be like, "Where are you?" I'd be frantic and stressed. So he has this inner peace, relaxed kind of attitude from his culture that I think you know helps not only to resolve things, but it just flows to everyone in the family. (Kylie)
>
> That may be my personality as well. I believe anything can help. (Malai)

The narratives also demonstrated that perseverance and persistence against parents and societal negative attitude towards intercultural relationships and marriage were important determinants that helped the survival of intercultural relationship. Most parents finally accept the relationship after they witness the success of the relationship, which nullifies their stereotyped beliefs about other cultures. This was demonstrated in Jeehan and Murielle's case:

> Well, because we lived in Sydney among a big Turkish community, we were very Turkish grounded. We were very isolated from Australian people … we were like taught it was us against them… my family was very tribal. They seem to marry only in their own faith and in their

own identity. But once I got married into the Australian culture, they started to say "they're not as bad as what we thought". So it allowed our inter-marriage. (Jeehan)

My family thought it was excellent. They were like "Yay!" initially. (Murielle)

Acceptance and Tolerance

The narratives in this study demonstrated that personal attributes of acceptance and tolerance were key determinants for the success of inter-cultural relationships and parenting. Moderation between values and tolerance of each other's culture benefitted the children because they can relate better with their parents from sharing their cultural values. As Naomi and her husband Pravin reported:

Some moderation between adhering to your values and some education about the different culture would provide the child with opportunities to relate better with the parents because they've got an equal acceptance and understanding of both cultures so there's an equal appreciation there of each parent. (Naomi)

Yeah. In that way I think we've done well there. (Pravin)

Michelle and her husband Jim described the need to accept and tolerate their partner's culture, but they would be more conservative in their parental approaches if there are risks involved:

Yes I became more tolerant to my husband's western culture. You have to live in the western world. You can't be just pedantic. You have to live in harmony. (Michelle)

Unless it comes down to safety… If we can see that the children want to do something and it is peer pressure, the Australian way or whatever, then if there is a risk we pull back and say no… like schoolies. Unlike Gold Coast parents, we will go and pick up the kids every night…we don't get them out of sight. (Jim)

John and his wife Rula reported the need to accept and tolerate each other's culture without too much expectation because they were raised differently:

> I guess in terms of being more bicultural in the way I approach things, understanding sometimes things that frustrates me, that may be Rula might do. But I sort of sit back and think that she's Rula and she's not raised the way I was raised, don't worry too much about it. (John)
>
> He claims he's Tongan, he changes and I think my expectation is not there for him to kind of understand it, without me saying things. (Rula)

Open-Mindedness

All the intercultural couples described that being open-minded and knowledgeable of their partner's culture before and during the relationship, and the diversity that the intercultural relationship brings, helped their relationships and allowed them to see things in a different way. Otherwise the relationship and parenting process won't work. The notion of individual open-mindedness is exemplified in Anya and her husband Rajack's narrative.

> If you have an open mind, you have the benefit of referring back to that type of culture. You can give and take in different things. We get along because I agree so much for his culture that is the benefit. If you have only one culture, for example just Australian, if you are only brought up in that environment, you don't know what else is out there in the world. (Anya)
>
> You don't change people…we are not here to judge people. We hang around with anybody…we make friends with anybody. (Rajack)

Sarah and Samuel echoed Anya and Rajack's notion of open-mindedness and hoped that their children develop the same notion:

> I always keep an open mind and very accepting of people…it does not matter what background or race they come from. It is good if the kids are being the same and try not to be prejudiced and say hateful words. (Sarah)

> Also for me it opens my mind like an outgoing Aussie. I never thought of going to Asia. But meeting an Asian girl I have been to Asia a lot. (Samuel)

The next section describes making intercultural parenting work from the couple's/parents' sphere.

Couple's/Parents' Sphere

Intercultural parents resolve their cultural and personal differences in parenting by actively engaging the principles of communication, compromise, sphere of influence, asymmetric decision-making, cultural literacy, embracing partner's culture, having a plan and preparedness for minority feeling.

Communication

Communication is described mainly as talking about feelings and issues, and listening to partners in order to understand each other and reach positive outcomes. The following cases exemplify a pattern reported by most intercultural parents:

> Obviously I'll voice what I think and then he also voices what he thinks, as well. Neither of us sits back and sort of goes (inaudible)… I don't think that we just go by his culture or just by mine either. Yeah, if there is an issue we discuss it and come up with what would be the best outcome for our family and for our children… there was an issue with breast feeding because I went back to work. He was not happy about it. It took me a while to explain to him and for him to understand. We had to talk about it. (Tammy) I tell her this is how we do it in Africa. She tells me this is how we do it in Australia. So we combine the two and come together with something. I can't just come out and say oh, women are supposed to be in the kitchen, doing this. I tell her this is what's supposed to be done and she tells me that, and then certify it. We work together. (Manuel)

Most parents reported that they communicated their cultural differences about parenting during the course of the relationship when they had children. They reported that couples need to discuss their cultural differences before they have children:

> For example, we are just deciding now about private and public schools for our son. And we never spoke about that, you don't think to talk about those kinds of thing, what are we going to choose. So I think that you need to talk about that, even before you have kids is a good idea. Communication is the biggest thing. (Naomi)

Two couples reported that they communicated about their parental responsibility and cultural preferences before they got married. As Jeehan and Murielle explained, they discussed their relationship and parenting role well before they got married to prevent any disharmony later:

> I have a lot of friends in intercultural marriages and they have big problems, I think, because they're not, they were never on the same page… that's where we were like from the beginning very clear about these are my standards, this is the way… so that we wouldn't find out five years later that it's not what we are after. A lot of people get married and then work it out whereas, we're quite logical. We're kind of really like kind of negotiators. (Murielle)

> We'd say, "Listen I don't accept this, I don't want that, and well I don't like this, I don't like that. If you do that to me then this marriage is not, you know, what I'm looking for"… so we both like negotiated over long periods of time before we got into the relationship. Okay, this is what we both are looking for. (Jeehan)

John and Rula discussed the importance of discrete communication regarding parenting differences, such as disciplinary practices with respect to the child/children. They emphasised being united as parents and using another language so that the children are not exposed to the discussion:

> We try not to be seen as different in front of the kids… we just had a dialogue in Tongan, to try and not expose the kids to much to what we were talking about. (John)

> Yeah, to stand united, so that the kids can you know "Ok, mum and dad are united" don't try to play us. (Rula)

Two couples described how their communication style about family and personal issues was more effective when they talked about it during evening walks together, and did not engage in heated debates in order to allow the free flow of communication. As Jay and Carol explained:

> We don't yell and carry on. One of the things we do, we always in the evenings go for a walk you know it could be at 6 o'clock or 7 o'clock after dinner, so if there is any issues like that, what needs to be done, we tend to sort it out pretty quickly. (Jay)
>
> We have always done that, we find that is a good time for just the two of us we can go and we can see that V did this or S did that or you did this and we did that or whatever and we just walk for an hour, talk about it and sort it out. (Carol)

Compromise

The willingness to compromise, that is finding a happy medium on certain cultural and personal values, is an important consideration for intercultural parents and their children, in order to sustain a healthy relationship and enrich their own, and particularly their children's lives. For example, Jeehan and his wife Murielle agreed to put aside their personal values and focused on their common religious values as the medium to reach a negotiated compromise. In the conflict resolution process, it appeared that most participants were making decisions in the best interest of their children. As Jeehan and Murielle explained:

> We have problems on some things where she might disagree on and then we'll go into a conversation and say, "Well, why? But why?" And then we'll try to come to a medium for the kid's sake. I'll say: "Well look, you put your defence aside and I'll put my defence aside and we have a common ground here which would be our religious value. What would be the closest thing to what would be permissible for us in this circumstance". And then we negotiate and compromise that way. But most of the times it's mutual on everything. (Jeehan)

> To be honest, if we did not have that, that line of thought as religion being the main rule, I guess the rule maker, then I think we would just clash completely. If I had just my own identity it wouldn't have even worked because I would have just kept arguing. (Murielle)

Tammy echoed similar sentiments about negotiating in the interest of the child:

> I think you have to make compromises at times to be both happy, obviously being from two different places, like you do have to work towards what's best for the children… we have to sometimes compromise on what each other think on something. (Tammy)

In Josh and Ng's case, they were having difficulties with sleep training their child. Ng was keen on her cultural practice of having the child to sleep with them in the same bed so that it was easier to feed and prevent the child from crying. But Josh was not comfortable with that practice and after long talks they came to a compromise:

> If it really gets on my nerves, I will just, we will talk about it and reach a compromise. (Josh)

> I will try it my way and if my way works we will keep doing it and if it doesn't work we go back. (Ng)

Differences in parenting style were also resolved by way of compromise in Jay and Carol's case. Carol thought that her husband Jay was too hard on their son regarding teenage activities, and that he needed to be more positive and allow some grounds for autonomy:

> Sometimes Jay was a bit over the top with what he thought with [son], like getting into those teenage years and it's a hard thing to approach, like how long you let them out for, where you let them go, where are they going. And you know I sort of emphasised how we need to be positive and we need to encourage [son] to talk… and I think together we have had to sort of meet in the middle with that one because sometimes it has been a bit tough. (Carol)

> We talked about it and say that maybe that wasn't the best approach and we will say, "Okay. I need to change how I'm thinking", and then say, "Okay, he can do this but he needs to get home at this time or whatever". (Jay)

Tammy described that, as a woman, she has her opinion and should be considered in decision-making processes to ensure a balanced outcome and a happy relationship. Her husband Manuel agreed with her opinion about compromise in decision-making processes:

> I think in his culture too that is changing with girls are being opinionated. Sometimes that's where we might clash because I always say what I think I don't hold back, obviously with respect in mind. So sometimes it can cause issues but I'm not going to sit and say nothing and then be unhappy. Therefore, I think we need to discuss things and then come to a medium where both parties are happy. Otherwise what sort of relationship or marriage would that be if one is always unhappy all the time and having to give into everything. (Tammy)

> There's no dominance over one another. Everyone puts it in and we're working together to see how we can reach a medium. (Manuel)

Sphere of Influence

Intercultural parenting conflicts can be resolved by recognising and acknowledging one's partner's sphere of influence, in other words, their area of expertise, skills and knowledge in certain domains of parenting and embracing and encouraging them to operate within those parenting domains. For example, Jim believed that his wife's style of parenting was the best and therefore let his wife do the parenting while he focussed on his skills related to external and manual jobs:

> In my culture mothers have the responsibility to raise their kids in the right way, religion, beliefs and values and education. I believe that is the mother's responsibility. And Jim gave me the full control on that aspect. (Michelle)

> My responsibility is the vehicles, the mechanics of the house, something like repairing the house, etc. (Jim)

Malai and Kylie, whilst echoing Jim and Michelle's sphere of influence, also emphasised on mutual respect for each partner's ways of doing things:

> Well, I let Malai do things the way he does. (Kylie)
>
> It's better though… she does a fantastic job. (Malai)

Anya explained that some of her parenting decisions, especially with the children's socialisation, were based on just keeping the children happy but she recognised her husband's sphere of influence in recognising children's risky activities:

> I'll be honest. Sometimes I am thinking more just to make the kids happy. But when I sit down and think about it and I can see his point. (Anya)
>
> Well, agree or disagree… because what happened, the law is very funny here. The kids are running, smoking on the street, kissing and stealing. May be my kid does not want to do that, but it depends on who he is hanging with. (Rajack)

Asymmetric Decision-Making

The asymmetric decision-making process in relationships and parenting is described as a pattern where individuals sacrifice their cultural values in favour of their partners' cultural values. The narratives revealed that in order to prevent conflict, some migrant participants sacrificed their cultural values in favour of their partners' values. In this study, the asymmetric decision-making pattern was manifested mainly in relationships where one partner exercised more power in the relationship due to language, income, personality and gender differences. This was clearly demonstrated in Bill and Azumi's case:

> I always obey his idea. That's the way. He is a boss. (Azumi)
>
> I'm not interested in entertainment and sensational places to go and visit, and have fun, and do slippery slopes… I'm not going to pay

> the money for things I don't want to, so she grudgingly will accept it. I won't do things that we've already done, like I won't repeat a trip in Canberra, which she wants with the kids… I'm a straight person and if I don't like the idea, I'm not movable. I will not change my mind. I'm fixed. (Bill)

Interestingly, differences were also perceived as part of the natural fabric of intercultural relationships, and might not need a resolution:

> Even if there were differences, sometimes differences just are and might not need resolution. That is why we are two different people working together to raise a family. (Daniel)

Cultural Literacy and Embracing Partner's Culture

In order to understand and appreciate each other's culture, it is very important for intercultural parents to learn and embrace their partner's culture. By educating and immersing themselves into their partner's culture, intercultural couples and parents can have firsthand experience of the internal cultural dynamics of the other culture and also to understand why their partners operate and behave in certain ways. As John and his wife Rula explained:

> We try and take the good of the Tongan culture and the good of the Anglo culture and invest that into our children. (John)

> Yeah I think the same thing too. I think to be a good parent you need to understand each other… Dig deep into each other's culture and list in there things that worked in their upbringing that worked for them. (Rula)

John and Rula's experiences were echoed by Kylie:

> We wouldn't have gotten together if we didn't have respect and acceptance for each other's culture. We started off from that position. You have a respect for the other person's culture. (Kylie)

There is much emphasis on the importance of learning some of the migrant partner's language because it helps to break the communication barriers and therefore couples could understand each other's needs and respond more effectively. Misunderstanding and misinterpreting what is said because of language barriers was found to be one of the most serious challenges and cause of conflict among couples in this study.

> We identified lot of issues because of language and misunderstanding language… we need to try and make sure that we're not misunderstanding what each other is doing. It's very important to learn both languages. (Gary)

Having a Plan

Intercultural parents argued their need to have a plan, also interpreted by some as "a constitution", or "a set standard" before they become parents. Couples reported that they need to discuss and agree on how they are going to negotiate and manage their cultural differences in terms of their relationship and parenting approaches and practices. An upfront plan would prevent conflict further down in the relationship because everybody will be clear about their children and their own needs. As Murielle and her husband Jeehan explained:

> I guess have a set standard, you know, that you're starting from rather than guessing along the way and having to go through a whole argument to get to an endpoint say, "Look these are the guidelines" from the beginning… be upfront. (Murielle)

> If you have a constitution in place let's say that red light, if you get that red light and everybody expects those rules, those guidelines are so much more simple. (Jeehan)

Daniel echoed Murielle and her husband Jeehan's plan of having a plan as it helps to prevent conflict during the parenting phase:

> When we knew that he was coming, we had a plan where we would be in agreement on certain things so that we wouldn't have to react to an instance without having some understanding of how we would behave in that instance. (Daniel)

Preparedness for Minority Feeling

Intercultural relationship can sometimes be also a lonely experience for host partners when interacting with the extended family in the migrant partner's homeland and they need to be aware and ready for it. Interactions can be limited due to language barriers and gender socialisation processes:

> Sometimes I guess it felt like I was the foreigner because I was the only Australian in the group… sometimes people weren't willing to talk. No one would try to speak in English, so sometimes I found that difficult you know. I felt a bit lonely at times… There are a lot of ceremonies and things like we did some of the things but we didn't do lots of the Indian things probably a lot of them because I didn't even know about them at the time as well and I guess there was an expectation that we probably should have done more of the things. (Carol)

Carol's husband reported how he needed to protect his wife in his homeland against certain cultural expectations by extended family members as it can be a stressful and unnecessary experience to the partner and the relationship.

> I have to be strong like in the thing as well just to protect you, say if I did everything that was expected of me, how I should be with my kids and all that, it would create a far more stress on our relationship. (Jay)

Child's Sphere

In implementing parenting approaches and practices, intercultural parents reported that their priority was to focus on what is in the best interest of the child. Most couples reported that they refrained from imposing a culture on their children, but rather encouraged multiculturalism, listened and respected their children, were consistent in parenting, and taught children important cultural and societal values.

Children's Culture

Intercultural parents recognised that due to the nature of their children's mixed cultural background, culture should not be imposed on children, but rather discussed with them and given choices otherwise they would be confused and build resistance instead of integration. As Pravin and his wife Naomi explained:

> Don't put too much of your cultural influence on the child because he/she will be confused. I'm not going to tell my son to wear his toga and go to school. I can't tell him that he has to be an Indian. You can talk to them a bit about moral values and respect... He's living in Australia. He should be comfortable here, just like a normal guy. (Pravin)
>
> Not imposing strict regulations that hinder the child's development and growth and really put restrictions, cultural restrictions in a country where we're very liberated, we're very open. There needs to be some learnings, some education about the different culture, but don't smother them or drown them with any culture. (Naomi)

Samuel and his wife Sarah described an example of their friends who spoke Japanese all the time at home and in the process hindered her learning abilities and communication with the children. Samuel and Sarah were against the idea of pushing one's culture on the child, but rather let the child decide for themselves:

> We were talking about our good friends in particular. The difference in languages has caused a huge problem, whether you speak Japanese or other languages, it caused a huge problem in her learning ability I think and the Japanese are super strict. I think that backfired on her in a lot of ways, whereas our kids are finding their own way. We do not push them in any direction that is going on nicely. (Samuel)

> Sometimes you have to let them see for themselves. Don't push your own beliefs, ideas. (Sarah)

Listening and Respecting Children

Participants reported that it is very important to listen, respect and negotiate with their children because they might have different perceptions about things. Couples emphasised that respect is earned and that if parents respect their children, they will respect the parents in return. As Sarah explained:

> Sometimes you have to listen to your children and let them do the asking. Let them ask the question and you can tell them so much stuff and they might not feel or have the same perception of things. (Sarah)

Some participants explained the importance of negotiating issues and outcomes with children instead of being too rigid. This is exemplified in Jeehan and his wife Murielle's case:

> Negotiate with the kids instead of being very rigid, "You do this because I said so. I'm your father." We say respect is earned. You respect the kids, the kids will respect you. Negotiate with them, give them the benefit of the doubt so that they're grown up enough to make decisions and they will respond very positively… and they experiment for themselves. (Jeehan)

> Like when I want my kids to do something, I make sure that they're not doing it just because, like you know, these are the reasons behind why we're saying, you know, this is the better bike to buy, I don't know, or this is the way you cook the rice. It's not just like this is the way we do it and that's it. (Murielle)

Encouraging Multiculturalism

There is a general consensus about the importance of encouraging children to be multicultural in their outlook because it would open their mind about other cultures, enable them to embrace diversity, and benefit them in their life. This is demonstrated in Simla's and her husband Daniel's case:

> It's an opportunity to celebrate that diversity and then you see your child just flourishing within that culture that they live in… I want our son to know that he's from two cultures. He has an African culture and an Australian culture, and to respect both, and to feel comfortable with both. And it's the way we relate with each other and we interact with each other, that he will see and will have no problems with being with both cultures, and be confident in both cultures. (Simla)

> But as it turns out he more clearly identifies with that African side of his background, which is fantastic…and any chance for community engagement is very much encouraged and not only with [wife's] community work, but even just attending childcare and seeing the different cultures there. If you ever wonder if Australia is multicultural, you just see the mix of kids in his particular room in childcare, it covers all nationalities. (Daniel)

Intercultural parents encouraged their children to speak some of their migrant parent's language so that they get the best of both worlds, and are able to communicate with extended family members in their homeland.

> So I think it's very important for them to be able to be both fluent in Mandarin reading and writing as well as fluent in English reading and writing, and to really try to get the best out of both worlds for them… and be able to speak with her grandparents. (Gary)

> It's good that they have Chinese culture in their blood and they know they can use Chinese language, Mandarin. They will have more culture here and also it's good for their future. (Yan)

Consistency with Parenting

There is lot of emphasis on the need for consistency in parenting, especially regarding discipline and to be on the same side and present a united front, otherwise children will manipulate the parents.

Consistency in parenting was viewed as important ingredient to prevent conflict in relationships and importantly, not to confuse the child. The notion of consistency in parenting is well reported by Simla and her husband Daniel:

> One of the things we've said to each other, it's about the parenting of our child in terms of being consistent. If we talk about strategies it is backing each other up on the things that we do… so that he [son] sees that there is, we are both on the same side. Because it's not about playing games with our child and making sure that he knows his parents are his parents, and whatever they say is what we both agree on. It is very important for parents to be on the same side. (Simla)
>
> That's the only change that happened within the family when he first came along. Instead of having two mutually compatible individuals when he came along, it became a family and therefore you make more compromises. You do whatever it takes to keep the family unit protected and working. (Daniel)

Simla's and Daniel's perception and experience of consistency in parenting was validated by all other parents in the study. Manuel and his wife Tammy reported a concrete and successful example of being consistent in parenting

> If we work together, if we want to discipline or do something to the children and say, "Okay we're going to take this away for this time," and we stand by one another and then see that its working it normally does, doesn't it? (Manuel)
>
> Yes, we have children one playing one off against the other, if she comes to me and if he's banned her from something and she comes to me and says can I use it I say, "No, you have to ask dad because dad banned you from using it so you have to ask him". So we stick together in that sense. (Tammy)

There is lot of emphasis also on the importance of not disagreeing or arguing about parenting issues in front of the children, because children are very good at manipulating parents. This is exemplified in Gary's and his wife Yan's case.

> I think that that's important to us as parents. Even if we have a different idea about how something should go down with her we don't discuss it in front of her. As far as she sees, she always sees us as being united in where we're going as parents. My experience is that the children will very quickly divide and conquer if they can see the differences between two parents and start playing you off against each other. I think that would be one of the best things, the consistency in what you're doing and to keep disagreements about stuff behind closed doors. (Gary)

> When we disagree about something we never let other, we never do that in front of her... we just discuss it later. (Yan)

Teaching Children Values

All the parents emphasised the need to teach children good societal, moral and religious values because they believed that the lack of these values is deteriorating families and the society. They want their children to go against that trend and be good citizens:

> A moral value is number one because this will be their most important tool when they have their own family. It is like this is their principle that they have to follow as they get older. They will be good citizens if they have all these values. One of the reasons people, families deteriorate is because there are no values in their family. It has never been emphasised. (Michelle)

Michelle's husband Jim supported her views, and added that it was important for parents to teach children to be responsible, in matters such as having a job.

> I think one of the values is to have a job that they were legally allowed to have. That took a lot of their time in between their study. They had money to buy what they wanted. We do not have the pressure. Working and earning their own money for the children, you get them to realize that you don't get thing for nothing in this world... Also, there are house rules and they have to follow those house rules. If they have work they have a responsibility to do that. (Jim)

Michelle and Jim's views were echoed by Gary, who also emphasised the importance of raising children with spiritual values:

> Our society in a lot of ways seems to be deteriorating, but I'd like my children to go against the trend and they have good values but not just values for values sake, but also the spiritual side of it. (Gary)

Previous studies in the United States and the United Kingdom have documented strategies that intercultural couples used to resolve their conflict over personal and parenting differences (Alibhai-Brown, 2001; Bratawidjaja, 2007; Caballero, Edwards, & Puthussery, 2008; Crippen, 2008; Crippen & Brew, 2013; Falicov, 1995; Ho, 1990; Kenney & Kenney, 2012; Killian, 2013; McDermott & Fukunaga, 1977; Romano, 2001; Root, 1992, 1996; Stoppard, 2006; Thompson, 1990). The strategies ranged from surrendering to the host culture to sustaining cultural differences and developing constructive patterns of cultural adjustments. Studies investigating patterns of cultural adaptation (Bennett & Bennett, 2004; Kim, 2001) revealed that intercultural couples go through three phases of cultural adaptation: culture shock, cultural adjustment and identity change. This process resonates with the experiences of intercultural couples and parents, as couples in intercultural relationships often live in the partner's host country for most of their lives, thus experiencing cultural and identity dissonance.

Ho (1990) found that heterogenous couples made decisions about parenting based on: (1) sphere of influence rule, where each partner takes responsibility for chores that they have an interest in and skill, (2) egalitarian rule, where decisions are made together, and (3) inertia rule, where both parents relinquish their responsibilities over childrearing out of respect to the other's culture. The finding on inertia rule was not apparent in the current study, and the assumption would be that it is a very negative strategy for both the intercultural parents and children. Instead, the findings regarding sphere of influence and egalitarian rules regarding parental role and childrearing were evident in this present study. Most participants respected their partner's areas of interest, experience and skill, such as education and sporting activities, as well as egalitarian rules when tough decisions were made, particularly regarding discipline.

The participants reported that by appreciating and adopting certain positive qualities from each other's culture, they enhanced their relationship and family life.

However, not all decision-making processes were resolved or negotiated in an egalitarian way, particularly in the area of discipline and sleep patterns. Thomson (1990) referred to "rules of power", where sometimes some couples resolved conflicts over parenting by conforming to the cultural values of the host partner or controlling all decisions. These conflict resolution strategies, which are also referred to as asymmetric strategies were manifested in the findings of this present study. The asymmetric/power rule pattern of conflict resolution was evident in Bill and Gary's cases, where in their capacity as the majority host partners, they exercised more power in the relationship due to income, gender and personality differences. The minority immigrant partners resolved the conflict by conceding to the host partner's values. But as they described, the asymmetric, power wielding behaviour left both of the migrant partners feeling "sad" and "unhappy".

Falicov (1995) proposed what she called "mutual acculturation" as an important step to resolve conflicts in intercultural relationships. Mutual acculturation has been described as a bi-directional process of cultural accommodation in intercultural relationships. This process is evident in the findings of this current study. Participants reported that spending time in the minority partner's homeland and trying to learn their language were two important factors that led to increased understanding of the partner's culture and hence better relationships. One couple in particular wanted their child to be bilingual and their capacity to communicate with the child in both languages helped the whole family during their interactions with the extended family and community members overseas and locally.

Bratawidjaja (2007) found that in order to have a successful cross-national marriage, couples displayed essential personal traits such as adventurous spirit, flexibility, curiosity and spontaneity. The findings of the current study support the above, and went further, adding "respect for partner as another person" and "immersion" in their partner's culture as essential attributes that increased the success of intercultural relationships and parenting. For example, couples respected each other as another person, who they are and the way they do things. As one particular participant described, he changed from his country's traditional attitude towards women and respects his wife equally. Immersion related to cultural literacy, where host culture partners particularly, studied their immigrant partner's culture so that they have a greater understanding and appreciation of differences and how to deal with and negotiate the differences in given contexts.

A grounded theory study of intercultural parents in the U.S. (Crippen, 2008; Crippen & Brew, 2013), revealed that in order to negotiate diversity based on cultural differences and degree of mutual acculturation, intercultural parents used diverse strategies of adaptation including *assimilation, cultural tourism, cultural transition, cultural amalgamation and dual biculturalism*. *Assimilation* strategy refers to the context where the immigrant partner assimilated to the dominant culture of the host parent as well as relinquishing their heritage cultural values regarding parenting decisions. *Cultural tourism* refers to a pattern of asymmetrical mutual acculturation, primarily with paternal accommodation. The strategy of cultural tourism includes a degree of enculturation of children "through holiday celebrations, relationships with grandparents, introduction to foods, and short-term tourist visits" (p. 267) to paternal/maternal country of origin. *Cultural transition* refers to a strategy of asymmetrical acculturation with primarily maternal accommodation. In this context, parents "who immigrated from other cultures or raised in traditional immigrant households… identified a tension between their heritage cultures and their culture of residence" (p. 268). *Cultural amalgamation* refers to the process of blending elements in an intercultural relationship. In this context, intercultural parents recognise and acknowledge cultural differences, but view them as complimentary and convergent in significant areas such as religion and core values. *Dual biculturalism* refers to a symmetrical process of acculturation whereby parents encouraged and transmitted both sets of their cultural values, codes, rules, norms and behaviours to their children. The above findings confirm and add to previous studies of strategies of intercultural parenting (Bratawidjaja, 2007; Caballero et al., 2008; Gonzalez & Harris, 2012). The findings of this current study also reflected and supported all the above strategies of cultural adaptation.

An exploratory study of parenting "mixed" children in mixed ethnic, faith and race families (Caballero et al., 2008) and another recent study of intercultural marriage and mixed parenting in Denmark, using an integrative theoretical framework based on a socio-cultural psychological approach (Singla, 2015), have discussed three typical approaches that intercultural parents adopt to understand and negotiate differences, and create belonging in raising their children: single, mixed and individual or cosmopolitan. The current study supported the above findings. Participants were found to use the three approaches when dealing with differences and belonging.

In the "single" approach, the cultural heritage, background and sets of rules, customs and values of only one parent is emphasised. In the current study, the "single" approach was adopted among three couples and they were faith related, including one Christian and two Islamic faith couples. In the Christian example, the migrant wife came from a very religious background and upbringing and brought up the children in the Christian faith. In the Islamic example, the wives became Muslims after marrying their Muslim migrant husbands and brought up their children in the Islamic faith. These three couples emphasised on the importance of bringing up their children in accordance to their faith identity and practice in order to instil a religious set of values in them.

In the "mixed" approach, children's cultural background from both parents is recognised as part of their identity. In the current study, most participants encouraged and involved their children with the dual aspects of their cultural backgrounds. For example, one participant who is married to an Indian man makes it a point to involve and encourage their children to practice both Christian and Indian cultural values in all aspects of their lives.

In the "individual" approach, parents encourage their children to look beyond their cultural identities and to find and feel comfortable with other characteristics of identity. In the current study, participants reported that the "mixedness" in their children is helping them to be global citizens "who are able to fit in and identify with other communities and cultures" (Caballero et al., 2008, p. 23). The participants also reported that when the children become adults and leave home, they have the choice to decide on their own identities and not be necessarily rooted to the ways they were brought up.

The current study supported the above findings. Participants were found to use the three approaches when dealing with differences and belonging. However, this current study drew an important finding about the three approaches used in negotiating differences and belongingness for the children. The single and mixed approaches were not seen regarding dual or mixed-faith practices. The participants in this study raised their children in only one faith. "Mixedness" was only evident regarding race and ethnicity among the participants.

The current study also found that participants used a fourth approach when dealing with differences, referred to here as *personality/individualistic* approach, where parents develop approaches based on their own experience of being parented. Some parents also put aside their cultural or personal differences and focus instead on the best interest and outcome for their children and the family. For the purpose of this study, this parenting style can be termed as "selfless parenting".

This study also challenges the notion that there is a universal way of raising children. Intercultural parents in this study appeared to raise their children within contextual and cultural domains that define their children's identity and belongingness.

An interesting phenomenon in intercultural relationships and family dynamics, referred to as "third culture" (Falicov, 1995; Perel, 2000), and also referred to as "transcultural" (Crippen & Brew, 2013) was apparent in this study. The proposition was that the couples brought two cultures together when they formed a relationship, and eventually developed a third culture, which included sharing and amalgamating their two individual cultures in an effort to recognise, appreciate and sustain their cultural differences and enhance their relationship. In this study, the development of the third culture also became more apparent and critical when the intercultural couples had children, whereupon they had to develop a compromised third culture to raise the children in a consistent and meaningful way. The third culture proposition was exemplified in Daniel and his wife Simla's case. Simla explained that as a couple, she and her husband Daniel brought two cultures together in their relationship. But when their son was born, they developed a compromised third culture which involved other strategies regarding issues about how to raise their son, besides their own cultural strategies. A full investigation of this phenomenon was beyond the scope of this study and further research in that domain would be very useful for intercultural families and relationships.

In order to successfully navigate intercultural relationships and parenting, participants in this study emphasised the need for intercultural couples/parents to actively engage in serious communication about any issues of concern. Communication was the key determinant for their successful relationship and parenting processes. Unfortunately, most of the discussions were carried out during the term of the relationship when they had children. It is therefore important for intercultural couples to discuss childrearing practices before they plan to have children, so that they are clear about their cultural or personal preferences and have a negotiated parenting outcome to prevent cultural dissonance and conflict when the child is born. As some participants said: *"sit down and talk about it" and "have a plan".*

Summary of Strategies for Making Intercultural Parenting Work

This chapter described how intercultural couples/parents used conflict resolution and survival strategies to negotiate their cultural differences with a view to achieve positive parenting and relational outcomes. The strategies were conceptualised into three spheres, including individual sphere, couple's/parents' sphere, and (3) child's sphere. The participants reported that their concerted efforts of developing and adopting coping strategies within the intercultural context greatly enhanced their parenting skills and relationships. The diversity of intercultural relationship and parenting experiences revealed in this present study has positive contributory implications for theory, policy and practice standards and are described in Chapter 6.

References

Alibhai-Brown, Y. (2001). *Mixed feelings: The complex lives of mixed race Britons*. London: Women's Press.

Bennett, J. M., & Bennett, M. J. (2004). Developing intercultural sensitivity: An integrative approach to global and domestic diversity. In D. Landis, J. M. Bennett, & M. J. Bennett (Eds.), *Handbook of intercultural training* (pp. 147–165). Thousand Oaks, CA: Sage.

Bratawidjaja, A. (2007). *The experience of being parents of mixed-heritage children: Phenomenological analysis* (Unpublished doctoral dissertation). Kansas State University, Kansas.

Caballero, C., Edwards, R., & Puthussery, S. (2008). Parenting 'mixed' children: Negotiating difference and belonging in mixed race, ethnicity and faith families. *Joseph Rowntree Foundation*. Retrieved August 15, 2011, from https://www.researchgate.net/profile/Chamion_Caballero/publication/265537866_Parenting_'Mixed'_Children_Difference_and_Belonging_in_Mixed_Race_and_Faith_Families/links/54b911660cf28faced626ac3.pdf.

Crippen, C. (2008). *Cross-cultural parenting: Experiences of intercultural parents and constructions of culturally diverse families* (Unpublished doctoral dissertation). University of New England, Australia.

Crippen, C., & Brew, L. (2013). Strategies of cultural adaptation in intercultural parenting. *The Family Journal: Counselling and Therapy for Couples and Families, 21*(3), 271–263.

Falicov, C. J. (1995). Cross-cultural marriages. In N. S. Jacobson & A. S. Gurman (Eds.), *Clinical handbook of couple therapy* (pp. 231–246). New York: Guildford.

Gonzalez, N. A., & Harris, T. M. (2012). Parenting in intercultural contexts. In N. A. Gonzalez, T. M. Harris, & A. Carlos (Eds.) *Mediating cultures: Parenting in intercultural contexts* (pp. ix–xi). Blue Ridge Summit, PA: Lexington Books.

Ho, M. K. (1990). *Intermarried couples in therapy*. Springfield, IL: Charles Thomas.

Kenney, K., & Kenney, K. (2012). Contemporary multiple heritage couples, individuals and families: Issues, concerns, and counselling implications'. *Counselling Psychology Quarterly, 25*(2), 99–112.

Killian, K. (2013). *Interracial couples, intimacy & therapy: Crossing racial borders*. New York: Columbia University Press.

Kim, Y. Y. (2001). *Becoming intercultural: An integrative theory of communication and cross-cultural adaptation.* Thousand Oaks, CA: Sage.
McDermott, J. F., & Fukunaga, C. (1977). Intercultural family interaction patterns. In W. S. Teng, J. F. McDermott, & T. W. Maretzki (Eds.), *Adjustment in intercultural marriage* (pp. 81–92). Honolulu: University of Hawaii Press.
Perel, E. (2000). A tourist's view of marriage: Cross-cultural couples-challenges, choices, and implications for therapy. In P. Papp (Ed.), *Couples on the fault line: New directions for therapists* (178–204). New York: Guildford.
Romano, D. (2001). *Intercultural marriage: Promises and pitfalls* (3rd ed.). Yarmouth, ME: Intercultural Press.
Root, M. P. P. (Ed.). (1992). *Racially mixed people in America.* Newbury Park, CA: Sage.
Root, M. P. P. (Ed.). (1996). *The multiracial experience: Racial borders as the new frontier.* Thousand Oaks, CA: Sage.
Singla, R. (2015). *Intermarriage and mixed parenting, promoting mental health and wellbeing: Crossover love.* New York: Palgrave Macmillan.
Stoppard, M. (2006). *The Mirror*, 27 January Advice Column.
Thomson, E. (1990). Two in One: Structural models of couple behaviour. In T. W. Draper & A. C. Marcos (Eds.), *Family variables: Conceptualisation, measurement and use*, 129–142. London: Sage.

6

Implications for Theory, Practice and Policy

Implications for Theory and Practice

This study provided much needed findings on the experiences of intercultural parenting in Australia. Although the findings in the Australian context cannot be generalised due to the sample size of the study, it still has the potential of transferability to the experiences of other intercultural parents, given the "thick" description of participants' experiences. Several emergent findings were particular highlights of this current study and add to other perspectives on intercultural parenting and the family system: power dynamics in intercultural parenting; reverse and reciprocal acculturation; family concept of friends and diaspora communities in the host culture; and that intercultural couples/parents also experienced significant benefits and opportunities, besides challenges and constraints.

As mentioned previously, aspects of intercultural parenting can be approached from an individual, couple, parent or child perspective. The latter helped me to understand the couples' experiences from the consistent interactions within and among the parenting domains. The degree of interactions between the factors in each and interacting

D. Bhugun, *Intercultural Parenting and Relationships*,
https://doi.org/10.1007/978-3-030-14060-1_6

domains defined the quality of the parenting experiences. For example, if a factor such as flexibility from the individual domain interacts positively with factors such as openness and acceptance in the couple's domain, it may impact on the outcome of the parenting experience. Equally, if the factors between, for example, the extended family domain interact negatively with the couple's domain, such as rejection and disapproval, then it may impact negatively on the experience of the couple's relationship. It is therefore very important for practitioners in relationship and family counselling to understand the degree of interactions between the different interacting domains and endeavour to obtain rich information about the different domains of client's lives in order to make proper assessments of their experiences.

The next argument is how do practitioners implement the findings of this and previous complementary research to provide effective counselling and therapeutic services to intercultural couples, parents and families? The literature review and findings have revealed both the challenges and benefits that intercultural couples experience and therefore it is imperative that practitioners explore both these dynamics to strengthen their clients. This present study revealed that intercultural parenting was influenced by internal and external contexts. It is therefore important for the practitioner to explore these dynamics from an internal and external context. For example, an internal context related to the perceptions of one's identity from an individual, couple, child, family and religious perspective. It is therefore recommended that practitioners make every effort to understand how couples locate their cultural differences. External context relate to outside factors that impact on the relationship and parenting. For example, some of the external challenges impacting on couples in this study related to the attitude of society, friends and extended family members towards their relationship, children and family and racism and exclusion towards their children at school. It is therefore important for practitioners to explore intercultural parenting dynamics from an internal and external context.

This study revealed that the internal and external domains of family dynamics can often be the source of stressors that impact negatively on couples and parenting. Some of the significant stressors related to: (1) cultural differences among couples, such as language barriers, communication styles, parenting beliefs, values and practices, customs and traditions and socialisation processes; (2) societal attitudes such as racism and disapproval; (3) power relations regarding language, gender, insider/outsider status; and (4) contextual influences such as extended families and the environment. It is therefore crucial for counsellors/therapists to explore and identify those stressors and guide their clients as to how to resolve those differences.

The findings of this current study showed that intercultural couples/parents/children enjoyed many benefits and opportunities other than challenges in the intercultural parenting experience. Of special interest is the fact that intercultural couples and parents can manage and seek help with the challenges as opposed to the benefits and opportunities that are self-acquired, complementary and enriching. Counsellors and therapists can rely on these aspects of benefits and opportunities as sources of strengths in the relationships to encourage and empower their clients.

It is also noteworthy for practitioners to understand that some of the challenges reported by intercultural couples and parents are also experienced by non-intercultural couples and parents, such as concerns for safety, health, education, socialisation processes and power dynamics. The common and unique concerns were comprehensively described in Chapter 3 under the sub-theme "Similarities and Differences in Parenting Practices". Therefore the provision of services and interventions needs to be balanced or measured between cultural needs versus individual contextual needs as opposed to the "intercultural" aspect only. As mentioned above, some intercultural family needs may be other than cultural needs, for example a safe place to live, getting a job and education for the children and parents. Likewise, in the case of couples, the practitioner may need to pay more attention to the contextual situation of the partner rather than focussing on assumed cultural differences because of their "interculturalness".

Based on the findings of this study, the implications for practice mentioned above also align with a set of competencies recently adopted by the American Counselling Association (ACA) (2015) for clinical work with intercultural couples and multiracial families. The purpose of the ACA set of competencies is to serve as a resource and framework for how clinicians can competently provide services to members of the multicultural population. Australian counsellors and the helping professionals working with multicultural population and requiring cultural competencies may find it valuable to draw on the set of competencies of the ACA model.

The findings of this current study can be utilised by counsellors and therapists to increase their understanding of intercultural relationship/parenting, and as a helpful resource when deciding on therapeutic approaches. Some of the popular therapeutic approaches that can be used in intercultural and mixed families' domains are:

- Narrative Therapy (Kim, Prouty, & Roberson, 2012; Molina, Estrada, & Burnett, 2004);
- Cognitive Behavioural Therapy (Beck, Rush, Shaw, & Emery, 1979);
- Solution-Focussed Therapy (de Shazer et al., 1986); and
- Strengths Based Therapy (Bustamante, Nelson, Henriksen, & Monakes, 2011).
- Emotionally Focused Therapy (Greenberg & Johnson, 1988).

According to Molina et al. (2004), narrative therapy is conducive to the needs of intercultural clients. When using the narrative approach, counsellors/therapists help clients to tell a story of their experience, in order to have an understanding of the deeper meaning of their intercultural experiences, and also to make new meaning of the experiences (Molina et al., 2004). When using the Cognitive Behavioural Therapy approach, counsellors/therapists can help clients to identify unrealistic beliefs and expectations, negative perceptions and subconscious negative thoughts about themselves and others in their environment (Beck et al., 1979). Therapists and counsellors can use this approach to guide intercultural couples/parents to build positive attributes about their intercultural perceptions and experiences.

The Solution-Focussed Therapy, also known as Solution-Focussed Brief Therapy, is an effective tool that counsellors/therapists can use to empower intercultural clients. De Shazer et al. (1986) described this approach as "utilising what clients bring with them to help them meet their needs in such a way that they can make satisfactory lives for themselves" (p. 207). Solution-Focussed therapy falls under the social constructionism metatheory given that it's philosophy and belief reinforces the fact that language is used to construct the reality of clients (Franklin, 1998). This approach has been used in previous studies of couples therapy, multiracial families and immigrants (Cheung, 2005; Choi & Akdeniz, 2014; Fong & Urban, 2014). This current study revealed that intercultural couples/parents enjoyed many benefits and opportunities in their intercultural parenting experience such as richness and best of both world for couples, parents and children; cultural competency, holistic family life; other models of parenting; job opportunities for children; extended family supports; adaptability, tolerance/acceptance and open-mindedness; and rich food culture, traditions and customs. As such, counsellors and therapists can rely on these aspects of benefits and opportunities as sources of strengths in the relationships to encourage and empower their clients and help them to change any negative thoughts about their experience (Bratawidjaja, 2007; Bustamante et al., 2011; Hsu, 2001). Bratawidjaja's study (2007) showed evidence that cross-national couples could strive and survive in their relationship which can be used as useful information to encourage and empower clients.

Therapists using the Strengths Based approach can guide and encourage their clients to reflect on successful coping strategies they have used that helped their differences, thus offering them a sense of hope that their problems can be resolved. This current research showed that intercultural couples/parents used several approaches to cope with their relationship and parenting differences, such as, communication, flexibility and openness to their partner's culture, respect and support for each other, and sometimes cultural deference where one partner defers to the other partner's culture. The strengths based approach can be used to help intercultural couples/parents deal with challenges in a positive way.

Emotionally Focused Therapy (EFT) is a short-term form of therapy that focuses on adult relationships and attachment/bonding. The therapist and clients look at patterns in the relationship, encourages couples to look at their current emotional issues and then help them discover feelings and emotions that they may not realise they have. EFT focuses on the present time to makes changes in the here and now. There are three steps of EFT: (1) the therapist helps to de-escalate the couple's or family member's negative cycle of interactions, and help them see and understand what is happening in their relationship; (2) restructure interactions, wherein the therapist helps couples discuss their fears in the relationship. Clients learn to turn toward each other and discuss their needs and they become more open and responsive to each other; (3) consolidation, wherein the therapist helps clients see how they got into negative patterns and points out how they were able to change those patterns and can continue these types of conversations in the future (Greenberg & Goldman, 2008; Greenberg & Johnson, 1988).

Finally, counsellors and therapists would enrich and enhance their therapeutic approaches and provide more effective services to their clients by exercising reflexivity, that is setting aside their own bias and prior assumptions (Alvesson & Skoldberg, 2000; Patton, 2002) about intercultural relationship and mixed families; promoting notions of adaptability, flexibility, tolerance, appreciation, acceptance and open-mindedness; encouraging cultural literacy in the form of psycho-social-education; emphasising on the positives, benefits and strengths of "interculturalness"; and addressing intercultural clients issues within an integrated systemic, ecological and contextual framework.

Implications for Policy

This study showed that some intercultural couples/parents were quite confused in explaining the "mixedness" of their relationship and that of their children in social contexts and official documents. Although the couples were relating their mixed-ness to their ethnic background, they explained that their children were quite confused about which parent's ethnic group they belong to, even though they are born in Australian and Australian as such. Caballero, Edwards, & Puthussery (2008) found that in the UK, the "mixedness" issue was successfully resolved by including the "mixed" category in the 2001 UK census ethnic group question. The inclusion was widely accepted and influential in shaping other ethnic minority forms, and the visibility of people who are labelled “mixed”. Generally, this administrative category is considered as socially significant and defines an image of the composition of the society. Although the notion of being “mixed” is not unproblematic, Caballero et al. argues that the “restrictive nature of the standardised census categories cannot fully reflect the subtlety and complexity of the experience and patterns common to mixed families and people from mixed backgrounds” (p. 55). It is therefore important to include the “mixed” category in the Australian census to help researchers and policy-makers access data that can be used to identify issues and develop programmes that can successfully address mixed family issues. Other multicultural countries such as Canada, USA and Germany may also consider inclusion of the “mixed” in their census.

Australia, like the United States and Canada, is becoming an increasingly multicultural and pluralistic society. The increase in intercultural marriages and relationships, and parenting requires culturally appropriate service delivery. Based on the findings of this current study, several recommendations are noteworthy to provide effective service delivery to intercultural couples, parents and families. First, there is a need for all educational institutions that provide marriage and relationship counselling courses, to introduce particular cultural literacy modules that focus on intercultural relationships and families. Second, professional helping organisations need to be fully conversant with the cultural implications and needs of this specific intercultural phenomenon and population and provide education, information and support services that is exclusive and appropriate to the needs of intercultural families. Third, public and private organisations that provide services to this specific group of intercultural couples and parents seem to be too focused on cross-cultural competency as an organisational policy and standards of service. Due to the extent of global cultural values, beliefs and traditions, cross-cultural competency is not an easy approach to deliver the best results. This study has revealed that cultural awareness and sensitivity are important approaches that need to be considered and implemented when dealing with intercultural couples and parents.

The findings of this study in relation to intercultural parenting have significant mental health implications for immigrant families regarding parenting. State regulations regarding the welfare of children, particularly regarding disciplinary practices of parents, ignore immigrants' and refugees' cultural concepts of parenting, particularly for those from Africa, the Middle East and Asia. Immigrant and refugee parents do not understand the state legislated western influenced laws and policies regarding child protection and safety, and are very confused and stressed when their children are removed from the family (Papps, Walker, Trimboli, & Trimboli, 1995; Renzaho, 2011; Renzaho, McCabe, & Sainsbury, 2011; Sims & Omaji, 1999). In the State of Queensland, the Child Protection Act 1999, Section 5C incorporates additional principles for Aboriginal or Torres Strait Islander children: (a) the child should be allowed to develop and maintain a connection with the child's family, culture, traditions, language and community; (b) the long-term effect of a decision on the child's identity and connection with their family and community should be taken into account.

Unfortunately, although nearly 28% of the population of Australia are immigrants with different cultural beliefs and values about parenting, there are no additional principles in the Child Protection Act regarding children and parenting for immigrants and refugees. It is therefore very important that the national and state-based child protection services implement additional policies specific to immigrant and refugee parents and children regarding child safety. Child safety workers need to understand the cultural concepts of parenting and familiarise themselves with the needs and counselling issues of intercultural couples, parents and families, especially the implications and needs of immigrants and refugee parents in Australia. All government and non-government organisations need to develop and implement policies with regard to educating professionals, students, supervisees and service users about intercultural, interethnic and interracial issues. Finally, given the adverse impact on the mental health of this specific group of the population, it is important for immigrants, refugee parents and intercultural parents and families to be considered for Focussed Psychological Strategies health care plans under the Medicare Benefits Scheme.

Strengths and Limitations of the Study

This section discusses the strengths and limitations of the study, particularly reflecting on the study's methodological approach. The study was conducted within the context of a growing multicultural Australian society, and therefore required an exploration of both the deficit and strength perspectives of intercultural relationship and parenting. It involved a broader diversity of cultures which helped to generate valid and broader perspectives about the issues of intercultural couples and parents compared to studies with singular or restricted cultural representations, such as in the case of an African or Asian person married to a white Anglo-Australian. As a result, this study generated insights into issues besides culture that impacted on intercultural couples/parents, such as gender, religion, socio-economic status, extended family and the environment. The results of this broader intercultural study can also be compared with other research involving intercultural couples from only two different cultures, such as Samoan with New Zealand Europeans (Hubber, 1998), to examine whether the universal issues are consonant with issues in singular intercultural relationship and parenting.

Intercultural parents from different socio-economic status, ranging from labourers, drivers, tradesmen, housewives, teachers, business managers, office workers and professionals shared their experiences of intercultural parenting. The educational levels of the participants ranged from trade qualifications, secondary, college, tertiary, university graduates and post graduate education. The broad level of socio-economic status among the participants generated different experiences and perspectives about intercultural parenting. Most of the previous studies on this phenomenon included participants who were middle-class to higher economic status (Bratawidjaja, 2007; Crippen, 2008; Edwards, Caballero, & Puthussery, 2010; Nabeshima, 2005), and therefore the likelihood of generating different experiences of intercultural parenting is probably higher as compared to those from low socio-economic status.

Most overseas studies (Bratawidjaja, 2007; Crippen, 2008; Edwards et al., 2010; Hubber, 1998) included parents with children aged between 0 and 18 years approximately. In this study, the inclusion of parents with children aged 0–23 years helped to reflect on their extended parenting experiences within all the developmental stages of the children, especially teenagers and young adults who negotiate their own identities and divert from their parents' expectations and goals and values for children. This proposition is substantiated by Kich (1992), latter suggesting that one's identity formation is achieved through age-appropriate progression. In this study, participants from the minority ethnic culture were born and grew up in their heritage country. The fact that they were not fully acculturated in the host country made their cultural experiences more conspicuous.

My role as the researcher and my insider status in relation to the phenomenon from being an intercultural parent and a relationship counsellor was discussed, including my obligations to observe reflexivity in the research process. It was made clear to the participants that I was also an intercultural parent in a mixed marriage. This knowledge seemed to have a positive impact on the participants because they all expressed a sense of commonness, comfort and the feeling of being understood when describing their experiences. This view was also supported by Bratawidjaja (2007) and Nabeshima (2005) in view of their research on the experience of being parents of mixed-heritage children.

This study also had its limitations. It was limited to one state in Australia. Although the demographical status, described in the introduction section and Chapter 2, reflected the broader societal composition of Australia, I acknowledge that there would be some variables pertinent to other states that were not revealed in this study. This study also did not include intercultural couples/parents from the Australian Indigenous and Anglo-Australian backgrounds. I was personally interested in adding this group to the research, but unfortunately this was not possible for two reasons. Firstly, the focus was on those with a migration experience. Secondly, no intercultural couples/parents from this group responded to my recruitment efforts. This is understood in the Australian context given the history of oppression against the Aboriginal community, power differentials, the legacy of the Stolen

Generation and the recent forced removal of children from Aboriginal families by the Liberal Party government. Racial identification between white Australians and Aboriginal people continues to prevail in Australia despite its multicultural composition. Given the explosive climate around the sensitive topic of parenting in Aboriginal families, the non-participation of this group/category in this study is understood and plausible.

Finally, this study did not include intercultural separated parents, single mothers and fathers, non-resident parents, adoptive parents, blended families and same sex couples. The inclusion of participants from these groups of intercultural parents and families could have added another dimension and perspective to the phenomenon. Further studies into these particular groups of parents are necessary to generate broader knowledge about their experiences of intercultural parenting.

Only intercultural couples were interviewed. Children and members of extended families were not included as it would have moved the focus away from the main units of analysis, that is, the intercultural couple and parenting. This study revealed the important role of the extended family, especially grandparents, in children's lives and overall help for the family. The inclusion of the grandparents in this study could have shed more light on their own experiences of parenting and being part of the intercultural family. The focus on culture also limits insights into other issues such as gender, age, religion and socio-economic status. Fortunately, some of these factors, particularly the influence of religion on intercultural parenting and couples were precipitated by the participants themselves, which extended the findings of this study.

Only in-depth interviews with intercultural parents were conducted. Observation techniques of participants, their interpersonal relationship, and how they interact with their children and the environment would have added another analytical dimension to the relatedness and corroboration between the narratives of the participants and what was observed in their natural setting. Unfortunately, observational technique of participants and their environment was limited because of time constraints and the scope of this study.

Another limitation was the intention of the study to interview each couple together. If only one partner agreed to participate in the study, he/she was not included. This approach allowed the researcher the opportunity to study how couples communicate and negotiate issues, co-construct meaning of their experience together and interact in a family situation. However, this approach had potential limitations, such as the suppression of data from one partner due to the presence of the other, being overpowered by one partner talking more than the other, and fear of reprisals (Horowitz, 1999). Separate interviews could facilitate couples who chose to be interviewed separately for personal, cultural reasons and concerns about confidentiality. Participants might have also talked about gender and power experiences differently if they were interviewed separately.

Although the results of this study cannot be generalised because of the sample size and qualitative approach, the rich information generated can be transferable and useful to other similar contexts and phenomenon (Kvale & Brinkmann, 2009; Lincoln & Guba, 1985). The diversity of intercultural relationships and parenting experience revealed in this study has positive contributory implication for theory, practice standard and policy.

Future Research Opportunities

This study demonstrated the importance of further research into the experiences of intercultural parenting in Australia especially because of Australia's growing multicultural and pluralistic society. Intercultural parenting is becoming an important issue in the Australian society and therefore an expansion of literature and knowledge in this domain would benefit helping professionals such as counsellors and therapists and general services. The findings of this broader intercultural research could also be compared with other studies involving singular intercultural couples.

This research has shown that minority immigrant partners, particularly Asian, African, Indian and Muslim/Islamic partners practise reverse acculturation, that is, they introduce their heritage culture into their relationship and parenting practices, beliefs and values. Also, several host culture partners showed preferences for their immigrant ethnic partner's cultural and parenting values and engaged into reciprocal acculturation processes, especially in the parenting and extended family domains. At the time of this research, attempts to locate any research on reverse acculturation and reciprocal acculturation in Australia were unsuccessful. It is therefore important for further studies to be carried out to define and locate reverse and reciprocal acculturation concurrent to the cosmopolitan, multicultural and pluralistic global culture.

This study showed that friends and diaspora communities became the "new family" for several minority ethnic immigrant partners in the host country, because they lived so far away from their own families, and felt isolated. There is a need for further studies of this "new family" development in the Australian and global context. The study also revealed the important role of the extended family, especially grandparents, sisters and aunties in children's lives and overall support for the family, which according to the participants is almost inexistent in the Australian context. The experiences of extended family members, particularly grandparents would be a substantial contribution to future studies of intercultural parenting.

This study revealed that many intercultural parents could not confidently identify the cultural identity of their children because the children perceived their identity differently to their parents' perception. Those who tried to influence the children towards the minority culture and associated values, such as the use of a particular language, were often disappointed because the children were not always keen on the language aspect. Likewise when parents asked their children to qualify their cultural identity, the children were most of the time confused. Most of the children, according to the participants, related their identity to their physical features, such as looks. For example, if they looked African, they would describe themselves as African and associate more easily with people and communities that look like them. Further studies about the perception and experience of children in intercultural families, relevant to the cultures and context of Australia, are required as they will help to understand this conflicting intercultural family dynamic.

Finally, a comprehensive separate research on this topic of intercultural parenting between Anglo-Australians and Aboriginal couples would be a great addition to the current study when the climate is right to do so, because it will presumably reveal a different perspective to the results of this current study.

Conclusion

Intercultural relationships and parenting is a growing phenomenon in Australia in the face of the globalised, multicultural and cosmopolitan demography of our society. Unfortunately, there are some prevailing negative stereotypes and assumptions in society about intercultural relationships and mixed-children, based on cultural differences. As such, it was my academic aim and objective as a psychosocial clinician to conduct this study to address the stereotypes and stigmatisation of intercultural parenting and relationship. The experiences of intercultural parents themselves were explored to broaden our knowledge about their relationship and particularly their parenting practices and relational experiences.

This study generated rich descriptions of how intercultural couples managed and survived their cultural differences. Although the findings cannot be generalised, they have the potential of transferability to similar contexts in other countries, societies and multicultural settings. There is no doubt that intercultural couples experience similar parenting challenges as mono-cultural couples, but their challenges are exacerbated because of the cultural differences. As mentioned before, intercultural parents and couples are keen to make their experiences positive by acknowledging differences in their internal and interpersonal domains, and negotiating, compromising, respecting and accommodating each other's parenting styles, practices and relational dynamics.

Whilst parents/couples endeavour to harmonise their parenting and relationship experiences from an internal perspective, their experiences are also influenced by other external, contextual, ecological and systemic factors such as the environment, gender, socio-economic status, extended family, friends, diasporic communities, religion and individual/personality traits. The external influences, which are usually based on stereotypes and lack of cultural literacy, are beyond their control. It is therefore imperative that intercultural parents are flexible, compromise, communicate and develop strategies that produce the best outcome for the family as a whole. Cultural literacy for the children is also a necessity to boost their identity development.

This current study revealed some important new findings within the Australian context such as reverse acculturation, reciprocal acculturation, shift towards authoritative parenting styles, selfless parenting style, power relations in parenting practices and relational dynamics, gender power as an attribute of religious values, minority status experienced by majority ethnic host partners, racism manifested from ethnic minority cultural groups, and flexibility from collectivist partners regarding gender roles in intercultural relationships and parenting as an adaptive process to reduce conflict. Other new findings included a significant and consistent disparity about the level of support and involvement intercultural couples received from ethnic extended families, compared to their white Australian counterparts; friends became family members for immigrant partners because of the distance from their own family of origin; and finally, most studies emphasise challenges of intercultural parenting and relationships. This study, in contrast, reveals that intercultural parents and couples also derive significant positive experiences of intercultural parenting and relationship.

Three interpretations can be drawn from the findings of this present study. First, the findings on the experience of intercultural parenting in Australia concur with much of the literature as discussed in the introduction. Second, this study included a greater diversity of cultures than has been typically the case in prior studies. The diversity of intercultural relationship and parenting experiences added new insights into parenting and relational dynamics and would have positive contributory implications for theory, policy and practice standards. Thirdly, this study, in contrast to several previous studies, reveals that intercultural parents and couples also derive significant positive experiences of intercultural parenting and relationship. Counsellors and therapists would benefit from exploring and focussing on the positive experiences as sources of strengths for their clients. The helping professions also need to show cultural sensitivity, other than cultural awareness and respect when dealing with intercultural couples and families. A number of organisational policy and recommendations for future research have been suggested, although more policies and psychosocial services need to be explored to enhance the well-being of intercultural parents and couples.

Finally, this study serves as a useful platform for further studies into the experiences of intercultural parents in Australia, in order to help current and future intercultural parents, couples and practitioners in the family domain. I hope that the voices of the intercultural parents and couples about their inner experiences of intercultural parenting and relationship served the aim and objective of this book in highlighting both the challenges and transformative opportunities of intercultural parenting and relationships.

References

ACA. (2015). *Competencies for counseling the multiracial population: Multiracial/ethnic counseling concerns (MRECC) interest network of the American Counseling Association taskforce.* Alexandria, VA: American Counseling Association.

Alvesson, M., & Skoldberg, K. (2000). *Reflexive methodology: New vista for qualitative research.* London: Sage.

Beck, A. T., Rush, A. J., Shaw, B. F., & Emery, G. (1979). *Cognitive therapy of depression.* New York: Guilford Press.

Bratawidjaja, A. (2007). *The experience of being parents of mixed-heritage children: Phenomenological analysis* (Unpublished doctoral dissertation). Kansas State University, Kansas.

Bustamante, R. M., Nelson, J. A., Henriksen, R. C., Jr., & Monakes, S. (2011). Intercultural couples: Coping with culture-related stressors. *The Family Journal: Counselling and Therapy for Couples and Families, 19*(2), 154–164. https://doi.org/10.1177/1066480711399723.

Caballero, C., Edwards, R., & Puthussery, S. (2008). Parenting 'mixed' children: Negotiating difference and belonging in mixed race, ethnicity and faith families. *Joseph Rowntree Foundation.* Retrieved August 15, 2011, from https://www.researchgate.net/profile/Chamion_Caballero/publication/265537866_Parenting_'Mixed'_Children_Difference_and_Belonging_in_Mixed_Race_and_Faith_Families/links/54b911660cf28faced626ac3.pdf.

Cheung, S. (2005). Strategic and solution-focussed couples therapy. In M. Harway (Ed.), *Handbook of couples therapy* (pp. 194–210). New York: Wiley.

Choi, J. J., & Akdeniz, R. (2014). Solution-focussed approach with multicultural families. In J. S. Kim (Ed.), *Solution-focussed brief therapy:*

A multicultural Approach (pp. 133–149). Los Angeles and Denver: Sage and University of Denver.

Crippen, C. (2008). *Cross-cultural parenting: Experiences of intercultural parents and constructions of culturally diverse families* (Unpublished doctoral dissertation). University of New England, Australia.

de Shazer, S., Berg, I. K., Lipchik, E. V. E., Nunnally, E., Molnar, A., Gingerich, W., & Weiner-Davis, M. I. (1986). Brief therapy: Focused solution development. *Family Process, 25*(2), 207–221.

Edwards, R., Caballero, C., & Puthussery, S. (2010). Parenting children from 'mixed' racial, ethnic and faith backgrounds: typifications of difference and belonging. *Ethnic and Racial Studies, 33*(6), 949–967.

Fong, R., & Urban, B. (2014). Solution-focussed approach with Asian immigrants. In J. S. Kim (Ed.), *Solution-focussed brief therapy: A multicultural approach* (pp. 122–132). University of Denver, LA: Sage Publications.

Franklin, C., & Jordan, C. (1998). *Family practice: Brief systems methods for social work*. Pacific Cove, CA: Brooks/Cole.

Greenberg, L. S., & Goldman, R. N. (2008). *Emotion-focused couples therapy: The dynamics of emotion, love, and power*. Washington, DC: American Psychological Association.

Greenberg, L. S., & Johnson, S. M. (1988). *Emotionally focused therapy for couples*. New York: Guilford Press.

Horowitz, J. A. (1999). Negotiating couplehood: The process of resolving the December dilemma among interfaith couples. *Family Process, 39*(3), 303–323. https://doi.org/10.1111/j.1545-5300.1999.00303.x.

Hsu, J. (2001). Marital therapy for intercultural couples. In W. S. Tseng & J. Streltzer (Eds.), *Culture and psychology: A guide to clinical practice* (pp. 225–242). Washington, DC: American Psychiatric Publishing.

Hubber, T. (1998). *An exploration of intercultural parenting: The experience of Samoan & New Zealand-European couples* (Unpublished dissertation). University of Auckland, New Zealand.

Kich, G. K. (1992). The developmental process of asserting a biracial, bicultural identity. In M. P. Root (Ed.), *Racially mixed people in America* (pp. 304–317). Newbury Park, CA: Sage.

Kim, H., Prouty, A. M., & Roberson, P. N. E. (2012). Narrative therapy with intercultural couples: A case study. *Journal of Family Psychotherapy, 23*(4), 273–286.

Kvale, S., & Brinkmann, S. (2009). *Interviews: Learning the craft of qualitative research* interviewing. New Delhi: Sage.

Lincoln, Y., & Guba, E. (1985). *Naturalistic inquiry*. Newbury Park, CA: Sage.

Molina, B., Estrada, D., & Burnett, J. A. (2004). Cultural communities: Challenges and opportunities in the creation of "Happily Ever After" stories of intercultural couplehood. *The Family Journal: Counselling and Therapy for Couples and Families, 12*(2), 139–147.

Nabeshima, N. (2005). *Intercultural marriage and early parenting: A qualitative study of American and Japanese couples in the U.S.* (Doctoral dissertation). Wright Institute. Retrieved January 15, 2016, from http://www.worldcat.org/title/intercultural-marriage-and-early-parenting-a-qualitative-study-of-american-and-japanese-couples-in-the-us/oclc/711907443.

Papps, F., Walker, M., Trimboli, A., & Trimboli, C. (1995). Parental discipline in Anglo, Greek, Lebanese, and Vietnamese cultures. *Journal of Cross-Cultural Psychology, 26*(1), 49–64.

Patton, M. Q. (2002). *Qualitative research and evaluation methods*. Thousand Oaks, CA: Sage.

Renzaho, A. M. N. (2011). *Parenting in a new culture: A challenge for African migrant families*. Retrieved September 14, 2011, from http://www.deakin.edu.au/news/2011/260711africanmigrants.php.

Renzaho, A. M. N., McCabe, M., & Sainsbury, W. J. (2011). Parenting, role reversals and the preservation of cultural values among Arabic speaking migrant families in Melbourne, Australia. *International Journal of Intercultural Relations, 35*(4), 416–424. https://doi.org/10.1016/j.ijintrel.2010.09.001document.

Sims, M. R., & Omaji, A. K. (1999). Migration and parenting: A pilot study. *Journal of Family Studies, 5*(1), 84–96.

References

ACA. (2015). *Competencies for counseling the multiracial population: Multi-racial/ethnic counseling concerns (MRECC) interest network of the American Counseling Association taskforce*. Alexandria, VA: American Counseling Association.

Adams, J. (2004). "This is not where I belong": The emotional, ongoing, and collective aspects of couples' decision making about where to live. *Journal of Comparative Family Studies, 35*(3), 459–485.

Alibhai-Brown, Y. (2001). *Mixed feelings: The complex lives of mixed race Britons*. London: Women's Press.

Alvesson, M., & Skoldberg, K. (2000). *Reflexive methodology: New vista for qualitative research*. London: Sage.

Andreoni, H., & Fujimori, K. (1998). Shitsuke: Child-rearing values and practices in a Japanese community in Sydney. *Journal of Intercultural Studies, 19*(1), 69–83.

Arendell, T. (1997). A social constructionist approach to parenting. In T. Arendell (Ed.), *Contemporary parenting: Challenges and issues* (pp. 1–44). Thousand Oaks, CA: Sage.

Australian Bureau of Statistics. (2014). *Australian social trends 2014: ABS 4102.0*. Canberra: Australian Bureau of Statistics.

Australian Bureau of Statistics. (2017, March). *Australian Demographics Statistics*. Canberra: Australian Bureau of Statistics.

D. Bhugun, *Intercultural Parenting and Relationships*,
https://doi.org/10.1007/978-3-030-14060-1

Baumrind, D. (1967). Socialisation processes associated with dimensions of competence in preschool boys and girls. *Child Development, 38*(20), 291–327.

Baumrind, D. (1971). Current patterns of parental authority. *Developmental Psychology Monograph, 4*(1, Pt. 2), 1–103. https://doi.org/10.1037/h0030372.

Baumrind, D. (1989). Rearing competent children. In W. Damon (Ed.), *Child development today and tomorrow* (pp. 349–378). San Francisco: Jossey-Bass.

Barrett, S., Chin, J. L., Diaz, L. C., Espin, O., Greene, B., & McGoldrick, M. (2005). Multicultural feminist therapy: Theory in context. *Women & Therapy, 28*(3/4), 27–61. https://doi.org/10.4324/9780203047125.

Beck, A. T. (1988). *Love is never enough: How can couples overcome misunderstandings, resolve conflicts, and solve relationship problems through cognitive therapy*. New York: HarperCollins.

Beck, A. T., Rush, A. J., Shaw, B. F., & Emery, G. (1979). *Cognitive therapy of depression*. New York: Guilford Press.

Beech, H. (2013, August 19). I am Australian. So Am I. *Time Magazine, 182*(8).

Belsky, J. (1984). The determinants of parenting: A process model. *Child Development, 55*(1), 83–96. https://doi.org/10.2307/1129836.

Bennett, J. M., & Bennett, M. J. (2004). Developing intercultural sensitivity: An integrative approach to global and domestic diversity. In D. Landis, J. M. Bennett, & M. J. Bennett (Eds.), *Handbook of intercultural training* (pp. 147–165). Thousand Oaks, CA: Sage.

Berg-Cross, L. (2001). *Couples therapy* (2nd ed.). New York: Hawthorne.

Berger, P., & Luckmann, T. (1996). *The social construction of reality: A treatise in the sociology of knowledge*. Garden City: Anchor.

Berry, J. W. (1990). Psychology of acculturation: Understanding individuals moving between cultures. In R. W. Brislin (Ed.), *Applied cross-cultural psychology* (pp. 232–253). Thousand Oaks, CA: Sage.

Berry, J. W. (1997). Immigration, acculturation, and adaptation. *Applied Psychology: An International Review, 46*(1), 5–34.

Bhatia, S., & Ram, A. (2009). Theorizing identity in transnational and diaspora cultures: A critical approach to acculturation. *International Journal of Intercultural Relations, 33*(2), 140–149. https://doi.org/10.1016/j.ijintrel.2008.12.009.

Bhugra, D., & De Silva, P. (2000). Couple therapy across culture. *Sexual and Relationship Therapy, 15*(2), 184–192.

Bhugun, C. D. (2016). *The experiences of intercultural parenting in Australia* (PhD thesis). Southern Cross University, Australia.

Bhugun, D. (2017a). Intercultural parenting in Australia: Managing cultural differences. *The Family Journal: Counselling and Therapy for Couples and Families, 25*(2), 187–195.

Bhugun, D. (2017b). Parenting advice for intercultural couples: A systemic perspective. *Journal of Family Therapy, 33*(3), 454–477.

Biever, J. L., Bobele, M., & North, M. W. (1998). Therapy with intercultural couples: A post-modern approach. *Counselling Psychology Quarterly, 11*(2), 181–188. https://doi.org/10.1080/09515079808254053.

Bikel & Mandarano LLP. (2012). When intercultural relationships fail: What happens to the children? In Bikel & Mandarano LLP (Ed.), *Offers guidelines for American Judicial System.* New York: Globe Newswire.

Bornstein, M. H. (Ed.). (1991). *Cultural approaches in parenting.* Hillsdale, NJ: Lawrence Erlbaum.

Bornstein, M. H. (2012). Cultural approaches to parenting. *Parenting Science Practice, 12*(2/3), 212–221.

Bornstein, M. H., & Cote, L. R. (2003). Cultural and parenting cognitions in acculturating cultures. *Journal of Cross-Cultural Psychology, 34*(3), 323–340. https://doi.org/10.1177/0022022103034003007.

Bratawidjaja, A. (2007). *The experience of being parents of mixed-heritage children: Phenomenological analysis* (Unpublished doctoral dissertation). Kansas State University, Kansas.

Braun, V., & Clarke, V. (2006). Using thematic analysis in psychology. *Qualitative Research in Psychology, 3*(2), 77–101.

Bronfenbrenner, U. (1979). *The ecology of human development.* Cambridge, MA: Harvard University Press.

Burgess, R. G. (1984). *In the field: An introduction to field research.* London: Routledge.

Bustamante, R. M., Nelson, J. A., Henriksen, R. C., Jr., & Monakes, S. (2011). Intercultural couples: Coping with culture-related stressors. *The Family Journal: Counselling and Therapy for Couples and Families, 19*(2), 154–164. https://doi.org/10.1177/1066480711399723.

Bystydzienski, J. (2011). *Intercultural couples: Crossing boundaries, negotiating differences.* New York and London: New York University Press.

Caballero, C., Edwards, R., & Puthussery, S. (2008). Parenting 'mixed' children: Negotiating difference and belonging in mixed race, ethnicity and faith families. *Joseph Rowntree Foundation.* Retrieved August 15, 2011, from https://www.researchgate.net/profile/Chamion_Caballero/publication/265537866_Parenting_'Mixed'_Children_Difference_and_Belonging_in_Mixed_Race_and_Faith_Families/links/54b911660cf28faced626ac3.pdf.

Cerroni-Long, E. L. (1985). Marrying out: Socio-cultural and psychological implications of intermarriage. *Journal of Comparative Family Studies, 16*(1), 25–46.

Chan, A. Y., & Smith, K. R. (1995). Perceptions of marital stability in black-white marriages. In C. K. Jacobson (Ed.), *American families: Issues in race and ethnicity* (pp. 369–386). New York: Guildford.

Chan, L. L. (2013). *Reverse acculturation: A global rebalancing phenomenon or driven by globalised diaspora* (Unpublished doctoral dissertation). Gordon Institute of Business Science, University of Pretoria, South Africa.

Chao, R. K. (1994). Beyond parental control and authoritarian parenting style: Understanding Chinese parenting through the cultural notion of training. *Child Development, 65*(4), 1111–1120. https://doi.org/10.2307/1131308.

Chao, R. K. (2000). The parenting of immigrant Chinese and European American mothers: Relations between parenting styles, socialization goals, and parental practices. *Journal of Applied Developmental Psychology, 21*, 233–248. https://doi.org/10.1016/so193-3973(99)00037-4.

Chatters, L. M., Taylor, R. J., & Jayakody, R. (1994). Fictive kinship relationships in black extended families. *Journal of Comparative Family Studies, 25*(3), 297–312.

Cheah, C. S. L., Leung, C. Y., Tahseen, M., & Schultz, D. (2009). Authoritative parenting among immigrant Chinese mothers of pre-schoolers. *Journal of Family Psychology, 23*(30), 311–320. https://doi.org/10.1037/a0015076.

Cheung, S. (2005). Strategic and solution-focussed couples therapy. In M. Harway (Ed.), *Handbook of couples therapy* (pp. 194–210). New York: Wiley.

Choi, J. J., & Akdeniz, R. (2014). Solution-focussed approach with multicultural families. In J. S. Kim (Ed.), *Solution-focussed brief therapy: A multicultural approach* (pp. 133–149). Los Angeles and Denver: Sage and University of Denver.

Cleveland, M., & Laroche, M. (2007). Acculturation to the global consumer culture: Scale development and research paradigm. *Journal of Business Research, 60*(3), 249–259. https://doi.org/10.1016/j.ijintrel.2008.12.008.

Cohen, N. (1982). Same or different? A problem of identity in cross-cultural marriages. *Journal of Family Therapy, 4*(2), 177–199.

Cottrell, A. (1990). Cross-national marriages: A review of the literature. *Journal of Comparative Family Studies, 21*(2), 151–169.

Creswell, J. W. (1998). *Qualitative inquiry and research design: Choosing among five traditions*. Thousand Oaks, CA: Sage.

Creswell, J. W. (2003). *Research design: Qualitative, quantitative and mixed-methods approaches* (2nd ed.). Thousand Oaks, CA: Sage.

Crippen, C. (2008). *Cross-cultural parenting: Experiences of intercultural parents and constructions of culturally diverse families* (Unpublished doctoral dissertation). University of New England, Australia.

Crippen, C. (2011). *Working with intercultural couples and families: Exploring cultural dissonance to identify transformative opportunities*. Retrieved June 20, 2012, from https://www.counseling.org/resources/library/vistas/2011-V-Online/Article_21.pdf.

Crippen, C., & Brew, L. (2007). Intercultural parenting and transcultural family: A literature review. *The Family Journal: Counselling and Therapy for Couples and Families, 15*(2), 107–115. https://doi.org/10.1177/1066480706297783Document.

Crippen, C., & Brew, L. (2013). Strategies of cultural adaptation in intercultural parenting. *The Family Journal: Counselling and Therapy for Couples and Families, 21*(3), 271–263.

Crohn, J. (1995). *Mixed matches: How to create successful interracial, interethnic, and interfaith relationships*. New York: Random House.

Crohn, J. (1998). Intercultural couples. In M. McGoldrick (Ed.), *Revisioning family therapy: Race, culture, and gender in clinical practice* (pp. 295–308). New York: Guildford.

de la Peña, M. (2009). *We were here*. New York: Delacorte Press.

Denzin, N. K., & Lincoln, Y. S. (2000). *The Sage handbook of qualitative research*. Thousand Oaks, London, and New Delhi: Sage.

de Shazer, S., Berg, I. K., Lipchik, E. V. E., Nunnally, E., Molnar, A., Gingerich, W., & Weiner-Davis, M. I. (1986). Brief therapy: Focused solution development. *Family Process, 25*(2), 207–221.

Driscoll, A., & Nagel, N. G. (2008). *Early childhood education, birth–8: The world of children, families, and educators*. Boston, MA: Allyn & Bacon.

Durodoye, B. (1994). Intermarriage and marital satisfaction. *Texas Counseling Association Journal, 22*(1), 3–9.

Ebbeck, M. A., & Cerna, C. H. D. (2007). A study of child rearing practices among selected Sudanese families in South Australia: Implications for child care service selection. *Early Childhood Education Journal, 34*(5), 307–314. https://doi.org/10.1007/s10643-006-0129-4.

Edwards, R., Caballero, C., & Puthussery, S. (2010). Parenting children from 'mixed' racial, ethnic and faith backgrounds: Typifications of difference and belonging. *Ethnic and Racial Studies, 33*(6), 949–967.

Falicov, C. J. (1995a). Cross-cultural marriages. In N. S. Jacobson & A. S. Gurman (Eds.), *Clinical handbook of couple therapy* (pp. 231–246). New York: Guildford.

Falicov, C. J. (1995b). Training to think culturally: A multidimensional comparative framework. *Family Process, 34*, 389–399.

Falicov, C. J. (2014). *Latino families in therapy* (2nd ed.). New York: Guilford Press.

Falicov, C. J. (2016). *Intercultural couples.* Plenary Presentation. European Family Therapy.

Fong, R., & Urban, B. (2014). Solution-focussed approach with Asian immigrants. In J. S. Kim (Ed.), *Solution-focussed brief therapy: A multicultural approach* (pp. 122–132). University of Denver, LA: Sage Publications.

Fontana, A., & Frey, J. H. (2003). The interview: From structured questions to negotiated text. In N. K. Denzin & Y. S. Lincoln (Eds.), *Collecting and interpreting qualitative materials* (2nd ed., pp. 61–106). New York: Sage.

Forehand, R., & Kotchick, B. A. (1996). Cultural diversity: A wake-up call for parent training. *Behavior Therapy, 27*, 187–206.

Frame, M. W. (2004). The challenges of intercultural marriage: Strategies for pastoral care. *Pastoral Psychology, 52*(3), 219–232.

Franklin, C., & Jordan, C. (1998). *Family practice: Brief systems methods for social work.* Pacific Cove, CA: Brooks/Cole.

Fu, X., Tora, J., & Kendall, H. (2001). Marital happiness and interracial marriage: A study in a multi-ethnic community in Hawaii. *Journal of Comparative Studies, 32*(1), 47–64.

Gaines, S. O., Jr., & Agnew, C. R. (2003). Relationship maintenance in intercultural couples: An interdependence analysis. In D. J. Canary & M. Dainton (Eds.), *Maintaining relationships through communication: Rational, contextual, and cultural variations* (pp. 231–253). Mahwah, NJ: Lawrence Erlbaum.

Gaines, S. O., & Brennan, K. A. (2001). Establishing and maintaining satisfaction in multicultural relationships. In J. Harvey & A. Wenzel (Eds.), *Close romantic relationships: Maintenance and enhancement* (pp. 237–253). Mahwah, NJ: Lawrence Erlbaum.

Garcia, D. R. (2006). Mixed marriages and transnational families in the intercultural context: A case study of African-Spanish couples in Catalonia.

Journal of Ethnic and Migration Studies, 32(3), 403–433. https://doi.org/10.1080/13691830600555186.

Gergen, K. J. (1985). The social constructionist movement in modern psychology. *American Psychologist, 40*(3), 266–275.

Gergen, K. J. (2009). *Relational being: Beyond self & community*. New York: Oxford University Press.

Giallo, R., Treyvaud, K., Cooklin, A., & Wade, C. (2013). Mothers' and fathers' involvement in home activities with their children: Psychosocial factors and the role of parental self-efficacy. *Early Child Development and Care, 183*(3–4), 343–359. https://doi.org/10.1080/03004430.2012.711587.

Glesne, C., & Peshkin, A. (1992). *Becoming qualitative researchers: An introduction*. White Plains: Longman.

Globe Newswire. (2012, June 12). *When intercultural relations fail—What happens to the children? Bikel & Mandarano, LLP offers guidelines for American judicial system*. Retrieved January 6, 2016, from http://globenewswire.com/news-release/2012/06/12/479231/259017/en/When-Intercultural-Relations-Fail-What-Happens-to-the-Children.html.

Goldstein, A. E., Safarik, L., Reibolt, W., Albright, L., & Kellett, C. (1996). An ethnographic approach to understanding service use among ethnically diverse low income families. *Marriage and Family Review, 24*(3–4), 297–321. https://doi.org/10.1300/J002v24n03_04.

Gonzales, N. A., Cauce, A. M., Friedman, R. J., & Mason, C. A. (1996). Family, peer, and neighbourhood influences on academic achievement among African American adolescents: One year prospective effect. *American Journal of Community Psychology, 24*(3), 365–387.

Gonzalez, N. A., & Harris, T. M. (2012). Parenting in intercultural contexts. In N. A. Gonzalez, T. M. Harris, & A. Carlos (Eds.), *Mediating cultures: Parenting in intercultural contexts* (pp. ix–xi). Blue Ridge Summit, PA: Lexington Books.

Goodnow, J. J., Cashmore, L., Cotton, S., & Knight, R. (1984). Mother's developmental time tables in two cultural groups. *International Journal of Psychology, 19*(1–4), 193–205.

Greenbank, P. (2003). The role of values in educational research: The case for reflexivity. *British Educational Research Journal, 29*(6), 791–801.

Greenberg, L. S., & Goldman, R. N. (2008). *Emotion-focused couples therapy: The dynamics of emotion, love, and power*. Washington, DC: American Psychological Association.

Greenberg, L. S., & Johnson, S. M. (1988). *Emotionally focused therapy for couples*. New York: Guilford Press.

Gupta, L. (2008). A comparison of parenting behaviour between European American and Asian Indian parents. In *ProQuest Dissertations and Theses*. Fayetteville, AR: University of Arkansas.

Hall, E. T. (1976). *Beyond culture*. New York: Doubleday.

Hammami, M. M., Al-Jawarneh, Y., Hammami, M. B., & Al Qadire, M. (2014). Information disclosure in clinical informed consent: "Reasonable" patient's perception of norm in high-context communication culture. *BMC Medical Ethics, 15*(1), 3.

Harkness, S., & Super, C. M. (1995). Culture and parenting. In M. H. Bornstein (Ed.), *Handbook of parenting: Biology and ecology of parenting* (Vol. 2, pp. 211–234). Mahwah, NJ: Lawrence Erlbaum Associates.

Heller, P. E., & Wood, B. (2000). The influence of religious and ethnic differences on marital intimacy: Intermarriage versus intra-marriage. *Journal of Marital and Family Therapy, 26*(2), 241–252. https://doi.org/10.1111/j.1752-0606.2000.tb00293.x.

Hiew, D. N., Halford, W. K., Van de Vijver, F. J. R., & Liu, S. (2015). Relationship standards and satisfaction in Chinese, Western, and intercultural Chinese-Western couples in Australia. *Journal of Cross-Cultural Psychology, 46*(5), 684–701.

Ho, M. K. (1990). *Intermarried couples in therapy*. Springfield, IL: Charles Thomas.

Hoff, E., Laursen, B., & Tardif, T. (2002). Socioeconomic status and parenting. In H. Bornstein (Ed.), *Biology and ecology of parenting* (pp. 231–252). Mahwah, NJ: Erlbaum.

Hofstede, G. (1980). *Culture's consequences: International differences in work-related values*. Beverly Hills, CA: Sage.

Hornsten, A., Sandstrom, H., & Lundman, B. (2004). Personal understandings of illness among people with type 2 diabetes. *Journal of Advanced Nursing, 47*(2), 174–182.

Horowitz, J. A. (1999). Negotiating couplehood: The process of resolving the December dilemma among interfaith couples. *Family Process, 39*(3), 303–323. https://doi.org/10.1111/j.1545-5300.1999.00303.x.

Hsu, J. (2001). Marital therapy for intercultural couples. In W. S. Tseng & J. Streltzer (Eds.), *Culture and psychology: A guide to clinical practice* (pp. 225–242). Washington, DC: American Psychiatric Publishing.

Hubber, T. (1998). *An exploration of intercultural parenting: The experience of Samoan & New Zealand-European couples* (Unpublished dissertation). University of Auckland, New Zealand.

Imamura, A. E. (1990). Strangers in a strange land: Coping with marginality in international marriage. *Journal of Comparative Family Studies, 21*(2), 171–191.

Irastorza, N., & Devoretz, D. (2009). *Factors affecting international marriage survival: A theoretical approach.* Retrieved January 15, 2016, from http://www.sfu.ca/~devoretz/lecturenotes/sem9.pdf.

Jamrozik, A., & Sweeney, T. (1996). *Children and society: The family, the state and social parenthood.* South Melbourne: Macmillan Education Australia.

Johnson, N. C. (2012). Global journeys: From transnationalism to diaspora. *Journal of International and Global Studies, 4*(1), 41–58.

Joshi, M. S., & Krishna, M. (1998). English and North American daughters-in-law in the Hindu joint family. In R. Breger & R. Hill (Eds.), *Cross-cultural marriage: Identity and choice* (pp. 171–191). New York: Oxford International.

Keller, H. (2009). Gender perspectives in cross-cultural couples. *Clinical Social Work Journal, 37*(3), 224–229.

Keller, H., Lohaus, A., Kuensemueller, P., Abels, M., Yosvi, R., Voelker, S., & Mohite, P. (2004). The bio-culture of parenting: Evidence from five cultural communities. *Parenting: Science and Practice, 4*(1), 25–50.

Kellner, J. (2009). Gender perspective in cross-cultural couples. *Clinical Social Work Journal, 37*(3), 224–229. https://doi.org/10.1007/s10615-009-0214-4.

Kenney, K., & Kenney, K. (2012). Contemporary multiple heritage couples, individuals and families: Issues, concerns, and counselling implications'. *Counselling Psychology Quarterly, 25*(2), 99–112.

Khatib-Chahidi, J., Hill, R., & Paton, R. (1998). Chance, choice and circumstance: A study of women in cross-cultural marriages. In R. Breger & R. Hill (Eds.), *Cross-cultural marriage: Identity and choice* (pp. 49–66). Oxford: Berg.

Kich, G. K. (1992). The developmental process of asserting a biracial, bicultural identity. In M. P. Root (Ed.), *Racially mixed people in America* (pp. 304–317). Newbury Park, CA: Sage.

Killian, K. D. (2001). Reconstituting racial histories and identities. *Journal of Marital and Family Therapy, 27*(1), 27–42. https://doi.org/10.1111/j.1752-0606.2001.tb01137.x.

Killian, K. D. (2013). *Interracial couples, intimacy and therapy: Crossing racial borders.* New York: Columbia University Press.

Kim, H., Prouty, A. M., & Roberson, P. N. E. (2012). Narrative therapy with intercultural couples: A case study. *Journal of Family Psychotherapy, 23*(4), 273–286.

Kim, Y., & Park, S. (2009). Reverse acculturation: A new cultural phenomenon examined through an emerging wedding practice of Korean Americans in the United States. *Family and Consumer Sciences Research Journal, 37*(3), 359–375. https://doi.org/10.1177/1077727X08330758.

Kim, Y. Y. (2001). *Becoming intercultural: An integrative theory of communication and cross-cultural adaptation*. Thousand Oaks, CA: Sage.

Kolar, V., & Soriano, G. (2000). *Parenting in Australian families: A comparative study of Anglo, Torres Strait Islander, and Vietnamese communities.* Melbourne: Australian Institute of Family Studies.

Kotchick, B. A., & Forehand, R. (2002). Putting parenting in perspective: A discussion of the contextual factors that shape parenting practices. *Journal of Child and Family Studies, 11*(3), 255–269. https://doi.org/10.1023/A:1016863921662.

Kvale, S., & Brinkmann, S. (2009). *Interviews: Learning the craft of qualitative research interviewing*. New Delhi: Sage.

Lamb, M. E., & Lewis, C. (2010). The development and significance of father-child relationships in two-parent families. In M. E. Lamb (Ed.), *The role of the father in child development* (5th ed., pp. 94–153). Hoboken, NJ: John Wiley & Sons.

Laszloffy, T., & Hardy, K. (2000). Uncommon strategies for a common problem: Addressing racism in family therapy. *Family Process, 39*(1), 35–50. https://doi.org/10.1111/j.1545-5300.2000.39106.x.

Lee, C. (2013). *Fictive kinship: Family reunification and the meaning of race and nation in American immigration*. New York: Russell Sage Foundation.

Leeds-Hurwitz, W. (2002). *Communicating cultural identities through ritual.* Mahwah, NJ: Lawrence Erlbaum.

Leeds-Hurwitz, W. (2009). Social construction of reality. In S. Littlejohn & K. Foss (Eds.), *Encyclopedia of communication theory* (pp. 892–895). Thousand Oaks, CA: Sage.

LeVine, R. A. (1988). Human parental care: Universal goals, cultural strategies, individual behaviour. In R. A. LeVine, P. M. Miller, & M. Maxwell West (Eds.), *Parental behaviour in diverse societies* (pp. 3–12). San Francisco: Jossey-Bass.

Lewis, M. B. (2010). Why are mixed-race people perceived as more attractive? *Perception, 39*(1), 136–138. https://doi.org/10.1068/p6626.

Leyendecker, B., Harwood, R. L., Comparini, L., & Yalcinkaya, A. (2005). Socioeconomic status, ethnicity, and parenting. In T. Luster & L. Okagaki (Eds.), *Parenting: An ecological perspective* (pp. 319–341). Hillsdale, NJ: Lawrence Erlbaum.

Lincoln, Y., & Guba, E. (1985). *Naturalistic inquiry*. Newbury Park, CA: Sage.

Lindahl, K. M., & Malik, N. M. (1999). Observations of marital conflict and power: Relations with parenting in the triad. *Journal of Marriage and the Family, 61*(2), 320–330. https://doi.org/10.2307/353751.

Luke, C., & Carrington, V. (2000). Race matters. *Journal of Intercultural Studies, 21*(1), 5–24.

Luke, C., & Luke, A. (1998). Interracial families: Difference within difference. *Ethnic and Racial Studies, 21*(4), 728–753. https://doi.org/10.1080/014198798329847.

Maccoby, E., & Martin, J. A. (1983). Socialization in the context of the family: Parent–child interaction. In P. Mussen & E. M. Hetherington (Eds.), *Handbook of child psychology* (Vol. 4, pp. 1–101). New York: Wiley.

Mackey, R. A., & O'Brien, B. A. (1998). Marital conflict management: Gender and ethnic differences. *Social Work, 43*(2), 128–141. https://doi.org/10.1093/sw/43.2.128.

Mann, E., & Waldron, J. A. (1977). Intercultural marriage and child rearing. In W. S. Teng, J. F. McDermott, & T. W. Maretzki (Eds.), *Adjustment in intercultural marriage* (pp. 62–80). Honolulu: University of Hawaii Press.

Maxwell, A. (1998). Not all issues are black or white: Some voices from the offspring of cross-cultural marriage. In R. Bregger & R. Hill (Eds.), *Cross-cultural marriage: Identity and choice* (pp. 129–152). New York: Berg.

McDermott, J. F., & Fukunaga, C. (1977). Intercultural family interaction patterns. In W. S. Teng, J. F. McDermott, & T. W. Maretzki (Eds.), *Adjustment in intercultural marriage* (pp. 81–92). Honolulu: University of Hawaii Press.

McFadden, J., & Moore, J. L. (2001). Intercultural marriage and intimacy: Beyond the continental divide. *International Journal for the Advancement of Counselling, 23*(4), 261–268. https://doi.org/10.1023/a:1014420107362.

McNeil, T., Nicholas, D., Beaton, J., Montgomery, G., MacCulloch, R., Gearing, R., & Selkirk, E. (2014). The coconstruction of couples' roles in parenting children with a chronic health condition. *Qualitative Health Research, 24*(8), 1114–1125.

Miller, M. J. (2010). Testing a bilinear domain-specific model of acculturation and enculturation across generational status. *Journal of Counselling Psychology, 57*(2), 179–185.

Minichiello, V., Sullivan, G., Greenwood, K., & Axford, R. (Eds.). (2004). *Research methods for nursing and health sciences* (2nd ed.). Sydney: Pearson Education Australia.

Moffitt, K. R. (2012). Intercultural parenting in the White House: The transcultural strategies of the Obamas. In A. Gonzalez & T. M. Harris (Eds.), *Mediating cultures: Parenting in intercultural contexts* (p. 62). Blue Ridge Summit, PA: Lexington Books.

Mogra, I. (2014). Anchoring identity in faith: Narrative of an Anglo-Asian Muslimah in Britain. *The Qualitative Report, 19*(3), 1–22.

Molina, B., Estrada, D., & Burnett, J. A. (2004). Cultural communities: Challenges and opportunities in the creation of "Happily Ever After" stories of intercultural couplehood. *The Family Journal: Counselling and Therapy for Couples and Families, 12*(2), 139–147.

Monahan, T. (1970). Are intermarriages less stable? *Social Forces, 48*(4), 461–473.

Nabeshima, N. (2005). *Intercultural marriage and early parenting: A qualitative study of American and Japanese couples in the U.S.* (Doctoral dissertation), Wright Institute. Retrieved January 15, 2016, from http://www.worldcat.org/title/intercultural-marriage-and-early-parenting-a-qualitative-study-of-american-and-japanese-couples-in-the-us/oclc/711907443.

Nakazawa, D. J. (2003). *Does anybody else look like me? A parent's guide to raising multicultural children*. Cambridge, MA: Perseus.

Negy, C., & Snyder, D. K. (2000). Relationship satisfaction of Mexican American and non-Hispanic White American interethnic couples: Issues of acculturation and clinical intervention. *Journal of Marital and Family Therapy, 26*(3), 293–304.

Ogbu, J. U. (1999). Cultural context of children's development. In H. E. Fitzgerald, B. M. Lester, & B. S. Zuckerman (Eds.), *Children of colour: Research, health and policy issues* (pp. 73–92). New York: Garland Press.

Okitikpi, T. (2009). *Understanding Interracial Relationships*. Dorset, UK: Russell House Publishing.

Olofsson, E. (2004). Review of cross-cultural marriage: Identity and choice. *Transcultural Psychiatry, 41*(2), 300–301.

Owen, J. D. (2002). *Mixed matches: Interracial marriage in Australia*. Sydney: University of New South Wales Press.

Papps, F., Walker, M., Trimboli, A., & Trimboli, C. (1995). Parental discipline in Anglo, Greek, Lebanese, and Vietnamese cultures. *Journal of Cross-Cultural Psychology, 26*(1), 49–64.

Pare, D. A. (1996). Culture and meaning: Expanding the metaphorical repertoire of family therapy. *Family Process, 35*(1), 21–42.

Parsons, T., & Bales, R. F. (1955). *Family socialisation and interaction process.* New York: Free Press of Glencoe.

Patcher, L. M., & Dumont-Mathieu, T. (2004). Parenting in culturally divergent settings. In M. Hoghugi & N. Long (Eds.), *Handbook of parenting: Theory and research for practice* (pp. 88–97). London: Sage.

Patton, M. Q. (2002). *Qualitative research and evaluation methods.* Thousand Oaks, CA: Sage.

Perel, E. (2000). A tourist's view of marriage: Cross-cultural couples-challenges, choices, and implications for therapy. In P. Papp (Ed.), *Couples on the fault line: New directions for therapists* (pp. 178–204). New York: Guildford.

Qian, Z., & Lichter, D. T. (2007). Social boundaries and marital assimilation: Interpreting trends in racial and ethnic intermarriage. *American Sociological Review, 72*(1), 68–94. https://doi.org/10.1177/000312240707200104.

Rankin, R., & Maneker, J. (1987). Correlates of marital duration and black-white intermarriage in California. *Journal of Divorce, 11*(2), 51–57. https://doi.org/10.1300/J279v11n02_04.

Rastogi, M., & Thomas, V. K. (Eds.). (2009). *Multicultural couple therapy.* New Delhi: Sage.

Reiter, M. J., & Gee, C. B. (2008). Open communication and partner support in intercultural and interfaith romantic relationships: A relational maintenance approach. *Journal of Social and Personal Relationships, 25*(4), 539–559. https://doi.org/10.1177/0265407508090872.

Renzaho, A. M. N. (2011). *Parenting in a new culture: A challenge for African migrant families.* Retrieved September 14, 2011, from http://www.deakin.edu.au/news/2011/260711africanmigrants.php.

Renzaho, A. M. N., McCabe, M., & Sainsbury, W. J. (2011). Parenting, role reversals and the preservation of cultural values among Arabic speaking migrant families in Melbourne, Australia. *International Journal of Intercultural Relations, 35*(4), 416–424. https://doi.org/10.1016/j.ijintrel.2010.09.001Document.

Rivers, J., Mullis, A. K., Fortner, L. A., & Mullis, R. L. (2012). Relationships between parenting styles and the academic performance of adolescents. *Journal of Family Social Work, 15*(3), 202–216.

Rockquemore, K. A., & Brunsma, D. L. (2004). Negotiating racial identity: Biracial women and interactional validation. In A. R. Gillem & C. A. Thompson (Eds.), *Biracial women in therapy: Between the rock of gender and the hard place of race* (pp. 85–102). New York: Haworth Press.

Rockquemore, K. A., & Laszloffy, T. (2005). *Raising biracial children*. Landham, MD: Alta Mira Press.

Romano, D. (1998). *Inter-cultural marriage*. Yarmouth, ME: Intercultural Press.

Romano, D. (2001). *Intercultural marriage: Promises and pitfalls* (3rd ed.). Yarmouth, ME: Intercultural Press.

Romano, D. (2008). *Intercultural marriage: Promises and pitfalls* (3rd ed.). Yarmouth, ME: Intercultural Press.

Root, M. P. P. (Ed.). (1992). *Racially mixed people in America*. Newbury Park, CA: Sage.

Root, M. P. P. (Ed.). (1996). *The multiracial experience: Racial borders as the new frontier*. Thousand Oaks, CA: Sage.

Rosenblatt, P. C., Karis, T. A., & Powell, R. D. (1995). *Multiracial couples-black & white voices*. Thousand Oaks, CA: Sage.

Rubalcava, L. A., & Waldman, K. M. (2004). Working with intercultural couples: An intersubjective-constructivist perspective. In W. J. Coburn (Ed.), *Transformations in self psychology: Progress in self-psychology* (pp. 127–149). Hillsdale, NJ: Analytic Press.

Rubin, H. J., & Rubin, I. S. (1995). *Qualitative interviewing: The art of hearing data*. Thousand Oaks, CA: Sage.

Ruebelt, S. G., Singaravelu, H., Daneshpour, M., & Brown, C. M. (2015). Exploration of cross-cultural couples' marital adjustment: Iranian American women married to European American man. *Current Psychology, 35*, 437–449.

Santrock, J. W. (2007). *A topical approach to life-span development* (3rd ed.). New York: McGraw-Hill.

Schwandt, T. A. (2003). Three epistomological stances for qualitative inquiry: Interpretivism, hermeneutics, and social constructionism. In N. Denzin & Y. Lincoln (Eds.), *The landscape of qualitative research: Theories and issues* (pp. 292–331). Thousand Oaks, CA: Sage.

Seshadri, G., & Knudson-Martin, C. (2013). How couples manage interracial and intercultural differences: Implications for clinical practice. *Journal of Marital and family Therapy, 30*(1), 43–58. https://doi.org/10.1111/j.1752-0606.2011.00262.x.

Seto, A. C., & Cavallaro, M. (2007). Cross-national couples in the Mainland United States. *The Family Journal, 15*(3), 258–264. https://doi.org/10.1177/1066480707301315.

Sims, M. R., & Omaji, A. K. (1999). Migration and parenting: A pilot study. *Journal of Family Studies, 5*(1), 84–96.

Singla, R. (2015). *Intermarriage and mixed parenting, promoting mental health and wellbeing: Crossover love*. New York: Palgrave Macmillan.
Skowronski, D., Othman, A. B., Wong, J. Y., Tan, W. S. D., Lum, W. H. G., & Waszynska, K. (2014). The outline of selected marital satisfaction factors in intercultural couples based on the Westerner and non-Westerner relationships. *Polish Psychological Bulletin, 45*(3), 345–356.
Smith, J., & Dunworth, F. (2003). Qualitative methodology. In J. Valsiner & J. K. J. Connolly (Eds.), *The handbook of developmental psychology*. London: Sage.
Sodowsky, G. R., Lai, E. W. M., & Plake, B. S. (1991). Moderating effects of sociocultural variables on acculturation variables of Hispanics and Asian Americans. *Journal of Counselling and Development, 70*(1), 194–204.
Stoppard, M. (2006). *The Mirror*, 27 January Advice Column.
Streubert, H. J., & Carpenter, D. R. (1999). *Qualitative research in nursing: Advancing the humanistic imperative* (2nd ed.). Philadelphia, PA: Williams & Wilkins.
Sue, D. W., & Sue, D. (1990). *Counselling the culturally different: Theory and practice* (2nd ed.). New York: Wiley.
Suizzo, M. A. (2007). Parents' goals and values for children: Dimensions of independence and interdependence across four U.S. ethnic groups. *Journal of Cross-Cultural Psychology, 38*(4), 506–530.
Sullivan, C., & Cottone, R. R. (2006). Culture based couple therapy and intercultural relationships: A review of the literature. *The Family Journal, 14*(3), 221–225.
Tanaka, M., Kitamura, T., Chen, Z., Murakami, M., & Goto, Y. (2009). Do parents rear their children as they were reared themselves? Intergenerational transmission of parental styles (warmth and control) and possible mediation of personality traits. *The Open Family Studies Journal*, 2, 82–90.
Thomas, V., Karis, T. A., & Wetchler, J. L. (2003). *Clinical issues with interracial couples: Theories and research*. New York: Hawthorne Press.
Thomson, E. (1990). Two in one: Structural models of couple behaviour. In T. W. Draper & A. C. Marcos (Eds.), *Family variables: Conceptualisation, measurement and use* (pp. 129–142). London: Sage.
Till, T. R., & Barker, G. G. (2015). Communication in intercultural marriages: Managing cultural differences and conflicts. *Southern Communication Journal, 80*(3), 189–210.
Ting-Toomey, S. (1999). *Communicating across cultures*. New York: Guilford.
Tizard, B., & Phoenix, A. (1993). *Black, white or mixed race? Race and racism in the lives of young people of mixed parentage*. London: Routledge.

Triandis, H. C. (1994). *Culture and social behaviour*. New York: McGraw-Hill.
Tseng, W. S. (1977). Adjustment in intercultural marriage. In W. S. Teng, J. F. McDermott, & T. W. Maretzki (Eds.), *Adjustment in intercultural marriage* (pp. 93–103). Honolulu: University of Hawaii Press.
Tseng, W. S., & Hsu, J. (1991). *Culture and family: Problems and therapy*. New York: Haworth.
Voas, D. (2008). Intermarriage and the demography of secularization. *The British Journal of Sociology, 59*(1), 83–108.
Voorpostel, M. (2013). Just like family: Fictive kin relationships in the Netherlands. *The Journal of Gerontology, 68*(5), 816–824.
Waldman, K., & Rubalcava, L. (2005). Psychotherapy with intercultural couples: A contemporary psychodynamic approach. *American Journal of Psychotherapy, 59*(3), 227–245.
Wu, R. (2011, June 7–8). *A narrative inquiry into the lived experiences of Chinese-White heterosexual couples within a Canadian context.* Paper presented in Metissage, Mestizaje, Mixed 'Race' and beyond, 6th Critical Multicultural Counselling & Psychotherapy Conference, Ontario Institute for Studies and Education (OISE).
Yancey, G., & Lewis, R. (2009). *Interracial families: Current concepts and controversies*. New York: Routledge.
Yodanis, C., Lauer, S., & Ota, R. (2012). Interethnic romantic relationships: Enacting affiliative ethnic identities. *Journal of Marriage and Family, 74*(5), 1021–1037.
Young, R. A., & Colin, A. (2004). Introduction: Constructivism and social constructionism in the career field. *Journal of Vocational Behaviour, 64*(3), 373–388.
Zebroski, S. A. (1999). Black-White intermarriages: The racial and gender dynamics of support and oppositions. *Journal of Black Studies, 30*(1), 123–132.
Ziv, A. (2006). *Breeding between the lines: Why interracial people are healthier and more attractive*. Fort lee, NJ: Barricade Books.

Author Index

D. Bhugun, *Intercultural Parenting and Relationships*,
https://doi.org/10.1007/978-3-030-14060-1

Subject Index

D. Bhugun, *Intercultural Parenting and Relationships*,
https://doi.org/10.1007/978-3-030-14060-1

Kolibri 360 GmbH
Ferdinand-Jühlke-Straße 7
99095 Erfurt, Deutschland
produktsicherheit@kolibri360.de